JESUS'S BELOVED DISCIPLE CALLING

SEIZE LIFE NOW!

JESUS'S BELOVED DISCIPLE CALLING

SEIZE LIFE NOW!

LOU & NICOLE MERTES

The Impact Organization, Inc.
BELLEVUE, WASHINGTON

Published in 2016 by
The Impact Organization, Inc.
500 106ᵗʰ Ave NE, Suite 1801
Bellevue WA 98004

All Bible quotations in this publication are taken from the Revised Standard Version of the Bible (RSV), copyright 1952 (2nd edition, 1971) by the Division of Christian Education of the National Council of the Churches of Christ in the United States of America. Used by permission. All rights reserved. All emphasis in Scripture quotations has been added by the authors.

ISBN 978-0-9832421-2-3 (soft-cover)

Library of Congress Control Number: 2016954828

Cover & Interior Design by Scribe Freelance Book Design Company

PUBLISHER CATALOGING IN PUBLICATION INFO

———————————

Mertes, Lou & Mertes, Nicole
Jesus's Beloved Disciple Calling Seize Life Now!/ Lou Mertes & Nicole Mertes

1.   Bible. N.T.   John—Criticism, interpretation, etc. I Title. II. Volume

2.   Christian life—Biblical teaching   I Title. II. Volume

BS2615   2016

Acknowledgments

We wish to recognize the following scholars whose writings enabled us to build on their enlightened and foundational insights; for without these fortuitous encounters, this book may never have come to life.

Richard G. Moulton, professor emeritus of Literature in English, University of Chicago, who is considered the father of literary analysis of the Bible, *Author of the Modern Reader's Bible A series of Works from the Sacred Scriptures Presented in Modern Literary Form*, 1897.

Raymond E. Brown, S.S., the twentieth-century Johannine scholar par excellence whose contribution was to gather the work of scholars to synthesize their divergent approaches to the Gospel and Epistles of John through his three-volume introduction, notes, and commentary on John, *The Anchor Bible, The Gospel According to John (I–XII and XII–XXI)* and *The Epistles of John*.

Peter F. Ellis, professor emeritus of New Testament, Fordham University, as author of *The Genius of John* effectively demonstrated the existence of structural parallelism in John's writings and its crucial contribution to accurately comprehend scriptural text.

Fr. John Breck, professor of patristic exegesis and bioethics, St. Sergius Orthodox Theological Institute, Paris, France. As author of *The Shape of Biblical Language: Chiasmus in Scriptures and Beyond*, he noted the spiraling motion found in certain parallel structures that led to our development of an aural version of John's writings that we call RSAV (Revised Standard Aural Version).

David A. Dorsey, author of *The Literary Structure of the Old Testament, A Commentary on Genesis–Malachi*.

We thank our preview readers and others— too many to name—who have helped us with this project.

About the Authors

Lou and Nicole Mertes

Lou and Nicole have served on the Seattle Pacific Seminary Advisory Council and are directors of the Bible Reading Breakthrough™ Project, a ministry dedicated to bringing enthusiasm back to Bible study. Their work enables today's readers:

- to comprehend God's word as the original audiences would have heard and understood it,
- to provide more clarity and accuracy of interpretation, and
- to more fully engage in Bible study.

When they are not writing, they compete in tall-building-stair-climbing fundraising events.

About Lou

Lou brings the same innovative spirit to Bible study that he was recognized for throughout his career as a chief information executive. He was recognized in *Time* magazine's 1983 "computer of the year issue" for spearheading the largest implementation of e-mail and office automation to that date. He authored a *Harvard Business Review* article on that topic that was one of the most requested reprints. He was invited to speak worldwide and to contribute to the book *Communications in the Twenty-first Century*.

While completing his degree in theology in 2006, Lou saw how to develop an easier and more understandable way for today's Bible readers to comprehend John the Evangelist's writings as his first-century listeners did. Lou has been researching and writing about it ever since.

About Nicole

Nicole saw the potential for teaching managers how to realize their capacity to be catalysts for positive change. She founded a company to offer instructional and software products for ongoing improvement initiatives. During the company's twenty-eight years, thousands of clients received raises, bonuses, and promotions by putting the techniques she developed into practice. She taught at the University of Wisconsin's summer program for seven years. Her company's vanguard software was endorsed by the American Bankers Association and featured on the cover of *Quality Digest*.

Nicole is the designer of eight instructional products, one receiving the highest award for instructional excellence from the International Society for Performance and Instruction. Today, she relishes collaborating with Lou by writing about his research so people may realize the inspiring power of the Bible.

Contents

1

Introduction

Introduction

Introduction

Why Read This Book?

JOHN WILL OPEN YOUR HEART

If your goals are to be closer to God, to find support for your faith journey, and to find hope and encouragement, then reading what John says about God's plan is the perfect place to begin. Why? There are three overarching reasons:

- John writes from the unique perspective of being an eyewitness to all that he writes about.
- John's writings are of unique importance because he not only introduces you to Jesus as he personally knew him but also includes theological and Christological information that formulate the roots of Christianity, much of which is contained in *no* other gospel.
- The depiction of John's gospel and letters in this book bring the very breakthrough in clarity that scholars have sought for centuries.

The reason for this book's existence is to share the words of John in a new and easy-to-understand format that will be like taking a sunshine break. Clouds of confusion and misunderstanding will disappear in light of the newly visible inspirations of John.

JOHN'S UNIQUE POSITION AS A GOSPEL WRITER

Only two gospel writers, John and Matthew, physically received the Holy Spirit (the Spirit of truth) that the resurrected and glorified Jesus breathed into the disciples after he returned to them. This means that you will be reading what John, who stood before the Divine Jesus face-to-face, wrote! And as Jesus's beloved disciple, John's words powerfully transmit his supreme love of Jesus, his Lord and Teacher.

John's position as an eyewitness is unique in that he was truly there from the beginning. When he heard John the Baptist, his former teacher, declare that Jesus was the Lamb of God, John immediately followed Jesus. John was the only disciple who was at the cross, and it was there that Jesus entrusted his mother's care to him.

John was with Jesus after he resurrected and returned to the disciples to grant them eternal life and send them to continue his mission. When you read John, you will read his proclamations in faithful fulfillment of his commission. He will explicitly tell you how to grow so close to the Son and the Father that those who do what he says will receive eternal life.

John backs this up not only by his own testimony but also by identifying second-generation disciples in his own community who succeeded in overcoming evil to receive eternal life. Indeed, John's urging his audience to seize life now will bring true hope and encouragement that will contribute greatly to your faith journey.

THE POWER OF JOHN'S WORDS

As Jesus's beloved disciple, John's words powerfully transmit his supreme love of God and Jesus, his Son. According to the American Bible Society, one of the most memorable biblical passages for Americans is from John's statement of God's sovereign love of the world. Indeed, John does leave a mark on one's soul.[1]

> *For God so loved the world that he gave his only Son, that whoever*
> *believes in him should not perish but have eternal life* (Jn 3:16 RSV).

John not only defines God as love, but he writes this passage to state that love is the basis of God's plan for reunification with humanity. God's motivation can only be love because he is love!

John will describe God's incarnate Son, Jesus, as having the same motivation when Jesus fulfills God's will by all he does on earth. Judgment, sin, and wrath will not open one's heart; only love will. You will be blessed by what the beloved disciple has to say.

JOHN'S CORE MESSAGE

John's core message begins with the world's problem. He uses the word *world* to refer to the place where evil reigns and people turn away from God as Adam and Eve did. God banished them from the Garden of Eden, symbolizing humanity's inability to abide in God's eternal and loving presence. God sent Jesus to turn this situation around, and he did.

---

[1] The American Bible Society, "The State of the Bible 2014," commissioned by ABS (New York, NY), conducted by Barna Group (Ventura, CA), ccopyright 2014.

God sent the Son, not to condemn the world, but that the world
might be saved through him (Jn 3:17 RSV).

Jesus brought liberation from evil's stronghold when he proved that love of God overpowers evil.

John writes his gospel and letters to describe who Jesus is, what he did, and how everyone can become the beneficiary of his gift of eternal life. Freewill is always in play, and God honors it, so John writes to encourage people to use their power of choice to believe in Jesus and turn to love as the basis of their life.

- In his gospel, John introduces you to Jesus as he knew him as both human and Divine so that you can believe and have faith in him.
- In his epistles, John explains what to do to be able to abide with God eternally.

MEET JESUS THROUGH JOHN'S EYES

While the other gospels focus on Jesus as the human, the Son of man, John's is the only gospel that states Jesus is the incarnate Word of God who was preexistent with God. John describes Jesus as both human and Divine. He is simultaneously personal and universal. This twofold role is the unique and crucial element of Christianity. Jesus is eternally available to help people succeed in their quest to be with God, and he has exclusive power to grant its fulfillment.

JOHN ENCAPSULATES THE ENTIRE CHRISTIAN STORY IN HIS NARRATIVE

As in the other gospels, John recounts key events related to Jesus; however, only John comprehensively covers God's master plan. He embeds answers to the questions posed below.

Chart 1–1: The questions that formulate God's master plan

What went awry?	What did God's Son do to set things right?	What did God promise, and what are the two things people must do to receive it?	How will God's plan be implemented?

John provides answers that will prepare you to read every other book of the New Testament because they create the context for Christianity's story line. They will enable you to see how the elements that other books write about fit into the whole which is crucial for accurate interpretation.

JOHN'S PURPOSE

John states that he wrote the gospel so that you may believe Jesus is the Christ, the Son of God (Jn 20:31 RSV). He wrote his first letter to enable you to receive eternal life (1 Jn 4:30). But to take in the full power of John's transmission, you must take his own words into your mind and heart. Reading and hearing about Jesus from someone who was not with Jesus might reinforce what John says, but how can their testimony be as powerful as one from the eyewitness disciple whom Jesus loved (Jn 21:20 RSV)?

John wanted his audience to come away as believers full of enthusiasm and confidence about their faith journey to God, but therein resides the conundrum. Pastors and scholars alike call John a difficult "read." John certainly wouldn't have intended to be unclear, but parts of his writings are confusing to today's readers. New readers are sometimes told to stay away from John or to just skip over the "difficult" passages. But now there is an answer to why John's writings appear to be difficult, and, at long last, there is a way to present his writings so they are understandable.

These answers are the basis for this book! After two thousand years, it can be explained now. You might ask what took so long. Let's start by looking at who John was writing for.

JOHN'S FIRST-CENTURY AUDIENCE

Few people in the first century could read; they were an oral culture, so John wrote to accommodate them by using repetitive words and concepts to get his message across. John may have been writing in Greek, but his style of writing was rooted in Semitic orality that had existed for over five thousand years.

By contrast, modern readers see only a linear sequence of passages that John wrote in run-on form as was the style in that day. Chapter headings and verse numbering were inserted into John's writings centuries later. Today's readers may see the repetition, but they don't know what to do with it. They expect things to make sense by reading verse number one after verse number two and so on, but this is not the way John's listening audience put his message together! This difference makes or breaks understandability. It explains why readers:

- can be confounded by passages, even whole stories, that appear to be out of order;
- wonder about all the repetition; and
- may not be able to decode theological elements of the story.

However, if readers today could see the passages numbered sequentially as John intended people to hear and match up, there would be no contradictions and misunderstandings. This is what you will see in this book.

EARLY EVIDENCE THAT "SOMETHING ELSE" WAS GOING ON

It wasn't until the late nineteenth century that Richard Moulton, a scholar from the University of Chicago who is considered the father of literary analysis of the Bible, brought some amazing new ideas to the forefront—namely that biblical writers used unseen literary structures to compose their narratives.

Moulton confirmed what John and other biblical writers were doing! They included unseen structures that were identifiable only by auditory cues to convey important ideas. Moulton strongly advocated for making these underlying structures visible so modern readers could understand what they were saying.

The essential thing is that the verse structure should be represented to the eye...where structural arrangement is wanting, no amount of explanation is likely to be of much avail.[2]

TWENTIETH-CENTURY RESEARCH

As scholars began to do extensive research in this area, their theories varied. One of the preeminent Johannine scholars of the last century, Raymond Brown recognized the considerable number of parallel passages—passages with repetitive words—in the Last Discourse.[3] John Breck said that parallel pairs of passages should go together to complete John's thought.[4] In 1980, Peter Ellis converted John's entire gospel into detailed charts of structures to visibly depict its inner workings.[5]

---

[2] Richard G. Moulton, *The Literary Study of the Bible* (London: Heath & Co., 1898) 45.

[3] Raymond E. Brown, S.S., The Anchor Bible, *The Gospel According to John XIII–XXI* (New York: Doubleday, 1970 582–597.

[4] John Breck, *The Shape of Biblical Language: Chiasmus in the Scriptures and Beyond* (St. Vladimir's Seminary Press, 1994) 20.

[5] Peter Ellis, *The Genius of John* (The Liturgical, 1984).

Today, scholars note some of these parallelisms but have treated them as interesting phenomena, not as elements that significantly contribute to overall clarity. Scholars were on the edge of discovery, but they stopped short and, as a result, momentum waned, but it should not have. You never know when a breakthrough will arrive; if Edison had not conducted the last of his experiments, he would not have been the one to have discovered a practical electric light bulb.

BREAKTHROUGH!

The good news is that scholars' efforts established a foundation that enabled us to keep on trying until we finally found the variation that revealed a practical way to see the results of John's approach. Indeed, our work[6] stands on the shoulders of these scholars. This book will present, for the first time, the writings of John with the directness and comprehensibility that he originally intended. You will not have to miss formerly unseen key points and connections; your reading will be easier, more accurate, and more thorough.

Note: unless otherwise annotated, we present John's scriptural text numbered sequentially according to word and idea repetition, as first-century listeners heard and understood it, to facilitate reading and interpretive ease for today's readers. We call this text Revised Standard Aural Version (RSAV) because it converts the highly regarded RSV into aural form. For additional information about aural text, see appendix A. To see the complete RSAV text used in this book, refer to appendix C.

---

[6] See appendix A for technical information and an explanation of the difference between RSV and RSAV text; see appendix C for the complete RSAV text used in this book.

The Organization of
This Book

INTRODUCTION TO THE FOUR PARTS OF THIS BOOK

This book presents the four excerpts of John's eyewitness account that most directly convey the core elements of Christianity. The excerpts follow:

1. *Prologue* of John's Gospel
2. *Testimony of John the Baptist* and *First Disciples*, the two narratives that follow the *Prologue* in the first Chapter of the gospel
3. The Farewell Address, which includes *Last Supper, Farewell Discourse,* and *Farewell Prayer* (Chapters 13, 14–16, and 17) that describe Jesus's preparation of his disciples for his exit from earth and their continuing his mission of eternal life
4. John's three letters, by which he explains how people may receive eternal life

Not included are Chapters 2–12 and 18–21 of John's Gospel because they depict details of Jesus's earthly ministry that are beyond the purpose of this book.

Typically, modern readers wait to discover the ultimate meaning of a work through their reading of it, but Johannine scholar, C. H. Dodd advises the opposite. He says readers of John would benefit from advance knowledge of his major theme.

> *Accurate interpretation of the whole depends upon precise understanding of the text in light of the ultimate meaning of the work.*[7]

Therefore, before we proceed with a description of the four excerpts, we set the stage by covering the overall purpose and theme of this book.

---

[7] C. H. Dodd, *The Interpretation of the Fourth Gospel* (Cambridge University Press, 1953) 3.

THE PURPOSE OF THIS BOOK

Our purpose is two-fold. One is informational; the other is transformational. As for the informational goal, we hope readers will come away with such a clear understanding of the Christian story that if asked, the answers to the following questions could easily roll off their lips as a brief one- to two-minute summary.

1. What went awry?
2. What did God's Son do to set things right?
3. What did God promise, and what are the two things people must do to receive it?
4. How will God's plan be implemented?

The scriptural text that comprises the body of this book provides the in-depth look at the answers, which will pop with clarity because the text is presented in the RSAV format (Revised Standard Aural Version),[8] which enables twenty-first century readers to see what first century listeners understood when they heard the text read or recited to them.

Having the big picture of Christianity in mind and being open to John's own understandable and heartfelt words are ideal catalysts for transformation. If you wish to become closer to God, strengthen your faith journey, and live more faithfully to God's will, John will provide the ideal inspiration. Why? Because these goals line up perfectly with the guiding theme of his writings, which is eternal life.

THE THEME OF JOHN'S WRITINGS PORTRAYED IN THIS BOOK

John wrote to enable his audience to receive the salvation that God sent his Son to bring to the world, which is the restoration of eternal life with God. This is what Adam and Eve lost, not only for themselves but for their progeny, by choosing *not* to love their maker. This is the core sin that has shrouded the world since.

By his love, Jesus reversed this situation and restored access to God's eternal love. John refers to this as *eternal life*. It is the purpose of God's plan

---

[8] The RSAV format is developed from Revised Standard Version of the Bible, 1952, containing the second edition of the New Testament, 1971, which was developed from biblical research of the late-twentieth and early-twenty-first centuries, which included the discovery of the most ancient manuscripts of the Greek New Testament. See appendix A for technical information and an explanation of the difference between RSV and RSAV text; see appendix C for the complete RSAV text used in this book.

and the prevailing theme of John's writings. John defines *eternal life* as he heard Jesus speak of it in his farewell prayer.

> *And this is eternal life, that they **know** thee the only true God, and Jesus Christ whom thou hast sent* (Jn 17:3 RSV).

The particular Greek word *know* as John uses it in this definition means to commune with God and his Son in the most intimate way possible. John often refers to this kind of *knowing* as being within God and his Son and they within the believer.

John refers to eternal life over one hundred times in the scriptural text you will read when you include all of his varied ways of referencing it such as being *born of God, abiding within,* to *know, love perfected,* and others. By sheer volume of repetitions, eternal life is the theme that John returns to time and again to convey the who, what, where, how, and why of such life so his audience may strengthen their faith and live more actively devoted to God's will.

- **What** is the purpose of God's plan—eternal life.
- **Why** did God initiate the plan—because God is love and he loves the world.
- **Who** has the opportunity to receive it—everyone who believes Jesus is the Son of God.
- **How** God implements it—through the incarnation, death, and resurrection of his Son, Jesus Christ.
- **How** to receive it—believe in Jesus and love one another.
- **Where** will it happen—right here on earth where people can show their love of God by their choices.

Each portion of this book uniquely covers these topics so that, by the end, you will have the package of elements that form the Christian message.

THE ORGANIZATION OF THIS BOOK

Now, that we have covered the original and fatal fall that led to the corruption of the world, let's briefly state the three key ideas behind God's salvation plan that govern the organization of this book:

> God's plan is to reinstate eternal life.
>
> ⬇
>
> God will send his Son, Jesus, to launch the plan by proving that love of God overcomes evil, and for those who choose to believe in him and live love-based lives, he will be their access point to eternal life.
>
> ⬇
>
> Jesus will gather and prepare disciples to continue his mission of eternal life after he leaves the earth.

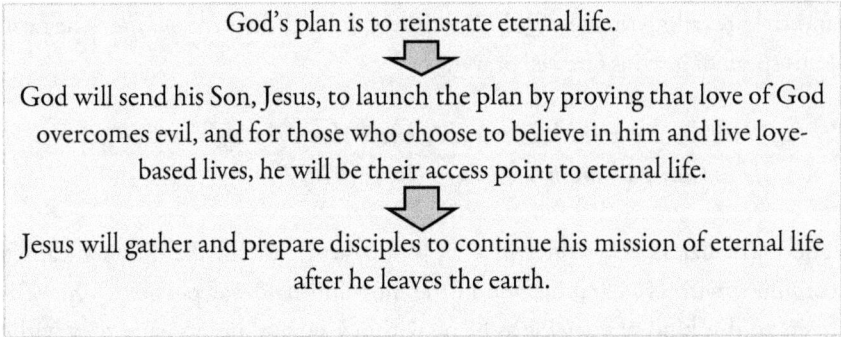

John takes a systematic approach to cover God's plan. This book is organized by four parts that portray God's plan, from announcement to activation to implementation.

1. In stunning grandeur, the verses that comprise "The Prologue" announce and summarize the broad design of God's plan to reinstate eternal life through the incarnation of the Word of life who is Jesus Christ.

2. "The Testimony of John the Baptist" and "The First Disciples" are the following two narratives that portray the announcement of Jesus and his first actions.

    a. In "Testimony of John the Baptist," John the Baptist reveals Jesus as the Son of God to Israel and to two of his own disciples who will become Jesus's first disciples.
    b. In "The First Disciples," Jesus gathers the men who God selected to be his disciples and witnesses from the beginning to the end. They number only five in this narrative because they are representative of the key roles necessary for the implementation of God's plan.

3. We skip the portion of the gospel that deals with Jesus's signs in order to proceed directly to the core elements of Jesus's activation of God's plan. It includes: "Last Supper," "Farewell Discourse," and "Farewell Prayer" that describe Jesus's preparation of his disciples for his exit from earth and for their continuation of his mission to restore eternal life.

4. John's three letters contain God's entire plan in a nutshell. The first letter concisely provides the definitive statement of the entire Christian message.

    a. In 1 John, John explains what the gift of eternal life is, its benefits, and how people may receive it. This letter contains the complete explanation of the New Covenant—what God offers and how people may receive it by fulfilling only two requirements: believe Jesus is the Son of God and live a love-based life.

    b. In 2 John and 3 John, John provides vivid examples of the application of the precepts he covered in his first letter.

2

Gospel of John: Prologue and Testimony (John 1:1–51)

CHAPTER 1

Prologue
John 1:1–16 RSAV

Introduction

God's master plan is introduced in this brief prologue. It is some of the most beautiful writing that you will read in the Bible. Johannine scholar R. Alan Culpepper put it this way:

> *By any standard, the prologue to the Gospel of John is one of the most profound passages in the Bible. As simple as its language and phrases are, its description of Jesus...has exerted a lasting influence on Christian theology.*[9]

The "Prologue" is appreciated as poetry, but it also provides a logical rendition of God's design for humanity. It answers some of Christianity's most fundamental and crucial questions:

- Who is Jesus?
- Why did God send Jesus to the world?
- What did Jesus do?
- Who testified Jesus is the Son of God?
- Who is a child of God?

John answers these core questions by dividing time into three eras—before the fall of Adam and Eve, when all was good; after the fall; and the period after Jesus's glorification. John takes you from a satellite-like view to an on-the-ground view of the ramifications of Jesus's ministry and the response it engendered.

---

[9] R. Alan Culpepper, *The Gospel and Letters of John* (Abingdon Press, 1998), 110.

Jesus's cosmic identity will be portrayed first. Only three verses are needed to explain Jesus's relationship with God. From there, John reveals the coming of the Word as flesh to enlighten the world; he will defeat the instigator of sin and the bringer of death. At the climax, **John will state what it takes to receive the opportunity to have the greatest gift the world has ever been offered—to live in God's loving presence eternally.**

Outline

1. The Word of God
    a. The Word Was in the World That Knew Him Not
    b. The Word Was Coming into the World
    c. God Sent John to Bear Witness That the Word Was God.
2. Two Witnesses of the Word
    a. John the Evangelist Testified That Jesus Is the Son of God
    b. John the Baptist Bore Witness That the Son of God Is Jesus
3. All Who Believe Have the Power to Become Born of God

What to Look For

Consider the following questions as you read in order to deepen your comprehension. There is space to write your answers at the end of the chapter. Our answers are located in appendix D.

1. Who is Jesus?
2. What was Jesus's mission?
3. Who are the three witnesses of Jesus's identity as the Son of God?
4. What does it mean to *know* God?
5. Why will birthright no longer provide automatic child-of-God status?

Prologue
(Jn 1:1–16 RSAV)

The Word of God
The Word Was in the World That Knew Him Not

^{1:1}In the beginning was the Word and the Word was with God. ²He was in the beginning with God; all things were made through him, and without him was not anything made that was made. ³He was in the world, and the world was made through him, yet the world knew him not.

The Word Was Coming into the World

⁴In him was life, and the life was the light of everyone. ⁵The light shines in the darkness, and the darkness has not overcome it. ⁶The true light that enlightens everyone was coming into the world.

God Sent John to Bear Witness That the Word Was God

⁷There was a man sent from God, whose name was John. ⁸He came for testimony, to bear witness to the light. ⁹He was not the light, but came to bear witness to the light, that all might believe through him, that the Word was God and the Word became flesh and dwelt among us.

Two Witnesses of the Word
John the Evangelist Testified That Jesus Is the Son of God

¹⁰We have beheld his glory, glory as of the only Son from the Father full of grace and truth. ¹¹And from his fullness, we have all received, grace upon grace. ¹²Grace and truth came through Jesus Christ, the only Son, who is in the bosom of the Father, he has made him known. ¹³No one has ever seen God, for the law was given through Moses.

John the Baptist Bore Witness That the Son of God Is Jesus

¹⁴John bore witness to him, and cried, "This was he of whom I said, 'He who comes after me ranks before me, for he was before me.'"

> ## All Who Believe Have the Power to Become Born of God
>
> [15]He came to his own home, and his own people received him not. [16]But to all who received him, who believed in his name, he gave power to become children of God; who were born of God, not of blood nor of the will of the flesh nor of the will of man.

Commentary

The Word of God

The Word Was with God and Was in the World Who Knew Him Not

> [1:1]In the beginning was the Word and the Word was with God. [2]He was in the beginning with God; all things were made through him, and without him was not anything made that was made. [3]He was in the world, and the world was made through him, yet the world knew him not.

WHO IS THE WORD?

John opened the "Prologue" by introducing the Word in its primordial existence with God before the world was made. Jesus himself spoke to this in his farewell prayer.

> *"...and now, father, glorify thou me in thy own presence with the glory which I had with thee before the world was made"* (Jn 17:4 RSAV).

In contrast to the synoptic-gospel writers' introductions of Jesus, John placed Jesus at the earliest possible origination point—Jesus is the Word who was with the preexistent God.[10] Mark, the author of the earliest gospel, introduced Jesus as an adult being baptized; the author of the next gospel, Matthew, introduced Jesus at his birth; and Luke, the author of the third gospel, introduced Jesus earlier yet, at his conception. But John, the author of the fourth and last gospel, introduced Jesus as being with God in the beginning as the Word of God at the conception of the world.

---

[10] Gail R. O'Day, *The Gospel of John: Introduction, Commentary, and Reflections*, NIB vvolume IX (Nashville: Abingdon Press, 1995), 516

THE WORLD WAS MADE THROUGH HIM

After announcing the Word's existence, John stated all things were made through him. He was God's active agent[11] in all creation; the Word of God spoke God's intentions into existence.

> *In the beginning...God said...God said...and God saw everything*
> *that he had made, and behold, it was very good* (Gen 1:3–31
> RSV).

The creator Word had been in the world all along; yet those in the world did not *know* him, but how could that be?

THE WORLD LOST THE OPPORTUNITY TO *KNOW* GOD

Adam and Eve *knew* God firsthand in the Garden of Eden and would have continued to know him for eternity, but by their disobedience, they demonstrated their lack of love for God. God banished and destined them to permanent death because the Garden was God's province of love, and people who do not love God could not be there.

> *For this is the love of God, that we keep his commandments...* (1 Jn
> 4:19).

> *...* "*Behold, the man has become like one of us, knowing good and*
> *evil; and now lest he put forth his hand and take also of the tree of*
> *life, and eat, and live forever*"—*therefore the Lord God sent him*
> *forth from the Garden of Eden...*(Gen 2:22–23 RSV).

Afterward, in rare instances, God appeared to special people, but their recognizing God as they did was quite different from *knowing* God. John used a particular Greek word for *knowing*, that conveys *knowing* God as abiding and communing with him in the most intimate way. Even Israel's greatest prophets did not *know* God in this sense.

---

[11] Barclay M. Newman and Eugene A. Nida, *A Handbook on The Gospel of John* (New York: United Bible Societies, 1980), 10.

> *And God said to Moses... "I appeared to Abraham, to Isaac, and to*
> *Jacob as God Almighty, but by my name the LORD I did not make*
> *myself **known** to them"* (Ex 6:2–3 RSV).

When John spoke of this deeper form of *knowing,* he spoke of eternal life.

> *And this is eternal life, that they **know** thee the only true God and*
> *Jesus Christ whom thou hast sent* (Jn 17:3 RSV).

THE BANISHED CONDITION OF THE WORLD

John set the stage for God's new plan to send his Son to save the world by referring to three time periods that track the world's progression from the era when humankind *knew* God to when they faced permanent death to the current era after Jesus restored access to eternal life.

Table 1–1: The world's three time periods in relation to eternal life

#	Time period	Description
1.	The period when the Garden of Eden was accessible	Adam and Eve lived in the Garden in close contact with God for eternity. They *knew* him.
2.	The banishment period when the Garden was not accessible	The world could not live with God to *know* him and have access to the Tree of Life; therefore, everyone was destined to permanent death.
3.	The postresurrection era when access to the Garden is restored.	Access to the Garden of eternal life is available to everyone who believes in Jesus and loves one another as he commanded. Eternal life is exclusively granted by Jesus.

The Word Was Coming into the World

[4]In him was life, and the life was the light of everyone. [5]The light shines in the darkness, and the darkness has not overcome it. [6]The true light that enlightens everyone was coming into the world.

WAS THE WORD ALREADY IN THE WORLD OR COMING INTO THE WORLD?

As the world's co-creator, the Word was already in the world as the sustainer of life, so why did John say the true light was coming into the world? Because during the banishment era the world was not able to see or commune eternally with God.

The Word was coming into the world to become visible for the world to see and receive his saving light. Did John mean the Word would be a light that shines in the darkness in the physical sense? No. John was referring to light in a far more profound way.

THE PAIRING OF LIFE AND THE LIGHT

In John's time, darkness signified evil and death; John used the word *light* to describe Jesus, who was coming to stand down evil and rise victorious to restore eternal life. Those who receive Jesus will be able to stand down the serpent's darkness so as not to be susceptible to his enticement to sin as Adam and Eve were. The eternal life that Jesus grants will protect its recipients from the evil one and will never be taken away.

> *Again Jesus spoke to them, saying, "I am the light of the world; he who follows me will not walk in darkness, but will have the light of life"* (8:12 RSV).

Was Jesus going to wave a wand to automatically grant eternal life? No. The plan was for Jesus himself to show the way to receive eternal life—to enlighten not only Israel but everyone. But how would people realize that Jesus was bringing this opportunity? Generations had come and gone during the banishment era without this being a possibility.

God Sent John to Bear Witness That the Word Was God

[7]There was a man sent from God, whose name was John. [8]He came for testimony, to bear witness to the light. [9]He was not the light, but came to bear witness to the light, that all might believe through him, that the Word was God and the Word became flesh and dwelt among us.

JESUS LOOKED LIKE EVERYONE ELSE

If God had wanted the incarnate Word to be obviously recognized as God's Son, he certainly could have made that happen. The Word could have arrived as a blazing light adorned with Godlike characteristics, but that was not the plan. Instead, Jesus looked like other men, and he dwelt among the people like other men. The plan was for Jesus to show people how to live God's way in the world in order to receive eternal life.

HOW WILL PEOPLE RECOGNIZE JESUS AS THE SON OF GOD?

People would know who Jesus was by testimony, and it started with God himself, who bore witness to his Son when he told John the Baptist how to identify him. God's testimony covered two central aspects of Jesus:

1. Jesus is the Word of God in the flesh who lived among the people.
2. Jesus is the life and the light who will grant eternal life by baptizing with the Holy Spirit.

> *"I myself did not know him; but he who sent me to baptize with water said to me, 'He on whom you see the Spirit descend and remain, this is he who baptizes with the Holy Spirit.'"* (Jn 1:32 RSV).

THE NEED TO BELIEVE

God sent John the Baptist to testify so people could believe Jesus was the Word of God on earth in human form.

> *He...came to bear witness to the light, that all might believe through him the Word was God and the Word became flesh (Jesus) and dwelt among us* (Jn 1:9 RSAV).

Why is it necessary for people to believe? Because it is the way a person loves God. God's plan gives all people the opportunity to receive eternal life, but unlike Adam and Eve, who automatically received eternal life by being in the Garden, God's new plan requires each person to opt in. The way to initiate the process is to believe Jesus is God's Son. Here's why.

If people do *not* believe in Jesus, then his death and resurrection will have no credibility. Jesus must be human for his death to be conceivable, and he must be God's Son to be able to grant eternal life. Therefore, the only way for God's plan to work is for Jesus to be the Word (God) in human form. Without believing this, God's gift of eternal life will not be available.

Excursus: John the Evangelist Is a Witness Too

John the Evangelist Is a Witness

Few people realize the "Prologue" contains the testimony of John the Evangelist, the author of this gospel. He has made powerful statements about Jesus being the Word in the flesh. Why should anyone believe what he says?

He Was with Jesus from the Beginning to the End

We start with the fact John the Evangelist was a disciple of John the Baptist. He not only witnessed John the Baptist's testimony but would have known its basis. You might say John the Evangelist was in the right place at the right time.

> *The next day again John (the Baptist) was standing with two of his disciples; and he looked at Jesus as he walked, and said, "Behold, the Lamb of God!" The two disciples heard him say this, and they followed Jesus* (Jn 1:35–36 RSV).

John the Evangelist was witness to Jesus's entire ministry. He heard John the Baptist's testimony; he saw Jesus's signs, heard his teachings, witnessed Jesus's death on the cross, and was with the other disciples on the third day when the glorified Jesus came to them.

> *"...and you also are witnesses, because you have been with me from the beginning"* (Jn 15:1 RSAV).

At the end of the gospel, John the Evangelist declared that he is this witness.

> *This is the disciple who is bearing witness to these things, and who has written these things; and we know that his testimony is true* (Jn 21:24 RSV).

Two Witnesses of the Word
John the Evangelist Testified That Jesus Is the Son of God

[10]We have beheld his glory, glory as of the only Son from the Father full of grace and truth. [11]And from his fullness, we have all received, grace upon grace. [12]Grace and truth came through Jesus Christ, the only Son, who is in the bosom of the Father, he has made him known. [13]No one has ever seen God, for the law was given through Moses.

WHO BEHELD JESUS'S GLORY?

To behold Jesus's glory is to actually see him as the visible materialization of God.[12] This was what the disciples saw on the third day when the glorified Jesus came and breathed the Holy Spirit on them, granting them eternal life.

> *God raised him on the third day and made him manifest; not to all the people but to us who were chosen by God as witnesses...* (Acts 10:40–41 RSV).

> *On the evening of that day...where the disciples were...Jesus came and stood among them and said to them, "Peace be with you." When he had said this, he showed them his hands and his side...he breathed on them, and said to them, "Receive the Holy Spirit"* (Jn 20:19–20; 22b RSV).

The disciples' personal witness of the glorified Jesus who defeated death and their receipt of eternal life by Jesus corroborated Jesus as the Son of God. In this context, John stated that the grace and truth that completely fill Jesus will be available to all.

- **Grace is** the free and undeserved gifts that Jesus grants. The greatest gift is the restoration of eternal life.
- **The truth is** Jesus is the Son of God who the Father granted the power over all flesh to give eternal life.

> *... "Father, the hour has come, since thou hast given him power over all flesh, so that he can give eternal life..."* (Jn 17:1–2 RSAV).

JESUS PROVIDES A NEW BASIS FOR A RELATIONSHIP WITH GOD

God was distant during the banishment period. The people of Israel never saw God even when the covenant was given because permanent death was theirs and the world's destiny.

> *On the morning of the third day...Moses brought the people out of the camp to meet God...And Mount Sinai was wrapped in smoke, because the LORD descended upon it in fire...and the LORD came to*

---

[12] Raymond E. Brown, *The Gospel According to John, I–XII*, 34

the top of Mount Sinai...called Moses to the top...and said to Moses,
"Go down and warn the people lest they break through to the LORD
to gaze and many of them perish" (Ex 19:16–21 RSV).

Jesus redefined how people are able to relate to God. While on earth, he lived among them in a personal, relational, and available way. From heaven, he continues to be available to assist believers on their journey to eternal life through the Holy Spirit. When believers become born of God, they will ultimately see God face-to-face.

Interestingly, this opportunity for relationship is reflected in the language of the "Prologue" at this point. John shifted to more filial language by his reference to God as the Father and the Word as the Father's only Son, Jesus Christ. He even noted the only Son is in the bosom (heart) of the Father.

John the Baptist Bore Witness That the Son of God Is Jesus

> [14]John bore witness to him, and cried, "This was he of whom I said, 'He who comes after me ranks before me, for he was before me.'

JOHN THE BAPTIST BORE WITNESS
John the Baptist fulfilled his assignment from God. He proclaimed the Son of God was in the world in the person of Jesus.

> *"And I have seen and have borne witness that this is the Son of*
> *God"* (Jn 1:34 RSV).

God had come to the people of the world! Did Israel's religious hierarchy believe him? The author addressed this next.

All Who Believe Have the Power to Become Born of God

> [15]He came to his own home, and his own people received him not. [16]But to all who received him, who believed in his name, he gave power to become children of God; who were born of God, not of blood nor of the will of the flesh nor of the will of man.

WHO REJECTED JESUS?
Was Jesus rejected by all of the Jewish people? No. In the years immediately following his death, most Christians were Jewish. Jesus was Jewish, and he conducted his ministry almost entirely in Israel. It was chiefly the Jewish

leadership who rejected Jesus, which might have been caused by Israel's long history of being punished for worshipping false Gods. To them, Jesus appeared to be saying he was God, and in fact, that was what God's only Son was saying!

> The Jews answered him, "It is not for a good work that we stone you but for blasphemy; because you, being a man, make yourself God."
> (Jn 10:33 RSV)

BEING A CHILD OF GOD BEFORE AND AFTER JESUS'S ARRIVAL

The Israelites never chose to be children of God. God gave them this birthright, but as progeny of Adam and Eve, they like everyone else, died a permanent death.

Before Jesus, permanent death was the destiny of all ⟷ **After Jesus, eternal life was available**

God sent his Son to the world to save everyone, not just the Israelites, from permanent death. However, if all people were to have the opportunity, then acquiring this gift by birthright had to be changed. The new determinants would be for a person to make the freewill choice to believe Jesus is God's Son and to live a love-based life. God sent Jesus to the world to implement this new covenant, which Jesus does by doing the following:

- Restoring the opportunity to receive eternal life by demonstrating once and for all the light of love overcomes the darkness of sin and death
- Granting access to eternal life to those who live according to God's command

The rest of this book will cover John's clear and comprehensive description as to how to activate Jesus's life-giving opportunity.

Conclusion

JOHN'S PURPOSE

This prologue presents the two defining tenants of Christianity:

- Jesus is God's Son
- Jesus restored the opportunity and the power to be saved from the bondage of sin and death.

John wrote this gospel to enable everyone to take the initiating step toward receiving this salvation, which is to believe in and receive Jesus as God's Son. For those who do, Jesus will grant the opportunity and the power to do what it takes to receive eternal life.

THE THREE WHO BEAR WITNESSES TO JESUS AS GOD'S SON

1. God himself brought the first testimony when he appointed John the Baptist to testify.

2. John the Baptist testified to the fact he saw the Spirit descend and remain on Jesus as God said would happen. John the Baptist bore witness to Israel and two of his own disciples about this.

3. John the Evangelist was one of the Baptist's disciples who heard his testimony. John the Evangelist was an eyewitness of Jesus from the beginning of his ministry to his death and of his appearance afterward, when Jesus returned to the disciples in glorified form to grant them eternal life. John was supremely qualified to bear witness to Jesus as he did in this gospel.

THE REDEFINITION OF THE RELATIONSHIP WITH GOD

This prologue laid out God's plan for people to know him for eternity through his Son. Jesus came to the world to give people the chance to know an available and personal God. Jesus made his Father known by his being the true light of love and life that overcomes all darkness. Jesus came to show how everyone can have access to God for eternity.

Review of Key Points

In the introduction, we asked you to consider the following questions. What are your answers? Our answers are located in appendix D.

Table 1–2: What are your answers to these questions?

#	Question	Your Answers
1.	Who is Jesus?	
2.	What was Jesus's mission?	
3.	Who are the three witnesses of Jesus's identity as the Son of God?	
4.	What does it mean to *know* God?	
5.	Why will birthright no longer provide automatic child-of-God status?	

What's Next

The Evangelist has already described the introduction of Jesus by John the Baptist, but there is more to cover on this topic. In the next chapter, John the

Baptist will describe the circumstances that led to his giving the testimony—who he gave it to, where he was, and how he announced who Jesus was.

## CHAPTER 2

Testimony of John the Baptist
John 1:17–34 RSAV

Introduction

You are about to see how God arranged for the introduction of Jesus as befits someone who is the Son of God. The inauguration of great leaders is typically full of pomp and circumstance; what will it be for someone so great as God's Son? Who will announce him? Who will be in attendance? Where has God arranged for this to take place?

John revealed these circumstances, but his indicators may not be obvious to a modern reader who might pass over some words and phrases that carry this information. For example, the Baptist gave testimony to the priests and Levites, but they were not your average priests; they were sent by the Pharisees as specialists in ritual purification.[13] They were members of Israel's religious hierarchy who trekked many miles to witness the expected Messiah, as would be appropriate to honor a great new leader. Here are more examples.

- John the Baptist was the herald—he was the *voice crying in the wilderness*, and he sounded the trumpet, so to speak, to introduce Jesus.
- The location *Bethany beyond the Jordan* was a call back to Israel's entrance into the "promised land," and now, through Jesus, it is a call forward to eternal life.
- A great new leader was typically adorned with special garments, but Jesus's adornment is an interior one—it is the Spirit that remains.

John covered first things first in the midst of these circumstantial descriptions. He clearly identified Jesus as the Son of God whose mission is to take away the sin of the world. The Messiah had arrived!

---

[13] Brown, *Gospel According to John, I–XII*, 43.

Outline

1. **The Jews (Israel) Meet with John the Baptist**
2. **John the Baptist Gives Testimony to the Jews (Israel)**
   a. Jesus Is the Lamb of God
   b. Jesus Baptizes with the Holy Spirit
   c. Jesus Is the Son of God

What to Look For

Consider the following questions as you read to deepen your comprehension. There is space to write your answers at the end of the chapter. Our answers are located in appendix D.

1. Why was John the Baptist's testimony necessary to introduce Jesus as the Son of God?
2. How did he know Jesus was the expected Messiah?
3. Why is Jesus considered the Lamb of God?
4. What is *the sin* of the world?
5. What is Jesus's baptism with the Holy Spirit?

The Testimony of John the Baptist
(Jn 1:17–34 RSAV)

The Jews (Israel) Meet with John the Baptist

[17]And this is the testimony of John, when the Jews sent priests and Levites from Jerusalem to ask him, "Who are you?" [18]They said to him then, "Who are you? Let us have an answer for those who sent us. What do you say about yourself?" [19]He confessed, he did not deny, but confessed, "I am not the Christ." [20] "Are you Elijah?" He said, "I am not." "Are you the prophet?" And he answered, "No." [21]And they asked him, "What then?"

[22]Now they had been sent from the Pharisees. [23]They asked him, "Then why are you baptizing, if you are neither the Christ, nor Elijah, nor the prophet?"

[24]He said, "I am the voice of one crying in the wilderness, 'Make straight the

way of the Lord,' as the prophet Isaiah said." [25]This took place in Bethany beyond the Jordan, where John was baptizing.

John the Baptist Gives Testimony to the Jews (Israel)
Jesus Is the Lamb of God

[26]John answered them, "I baptize with water; but among you stands one whom you do not know, even he who comes after me, the thong of whose sandal I am not worthy to untie." [27]The next day he saw Jesus coming toward him, and said, "Behold, the Lamb of God, who takes away the sin of the world! [28]This is he of whom I said, 'after me comes a man who ranks before me, for he was before me.' [29]For this I came baptizing with water, that he might be revealed to Israel. [30]I myself did not know him."

Jesus Baptizes with the Holy Spirit

[31]"I saw the Spirit descend as a dove from heaven, and it remained on him. [32]He who sent me to baptize with water said to me, 'He on whom you see the Spirit descend and remain, this is he who baptizes with the Holy Spirit.' [33]I myself did not know him."

Jesus Is the Son of God

[34]And John bore witness, "I have seen and have borne witness that this is the Son of God."

Commentary

The Jews (Israel) Meet with John the Baptist

[17]And this is the testimony of John, when the Jews sent priests and Levites from Jerusalem to ask him, "Who are you?" [18]They said to him then, "Who are you? Let us have an answer for those who sent us. What do you say about yourself?" [19]He confessed, he did not deny, but confessed, "I am not the Christ." [20]"Are you Elijah?" He said, "I am not." "Are you the prophet?" And he answered, "No." [21]And they asked him, "What then?"

> [22]Now they had been sent from the Pharisees. [23]They asked him, "Then why are you baptizing, if you are neither the Christ, nor Elijah, nor the prophet?"
>
> [24]He said, "I am the voice of one crying in the wilderness, 'Make straight the way of the Lord,' as the prophet Isaiah said." [25]This took place in Bethany beyond the Jordan, where John was baptizing.

TESTIMONY

John's purpose in writing this gospel is *that you may believe Jesus is the Christ, the Son of God* (Jn 20:31 RSV), so it is fitting that John began this first chapter after the Prologue with John the Baptist's testimony. In John's day, giving testimony was serious business. It had to be based on personal experience and, of course, be the whole truth, nothing but the truth.

THE EMISSARY

Expectations of a coming messiah were in the air, so much so the Pharisees, who kept track of the prophecies, sent the priests and Levites, who were specialists in ritual purification[14], to find out whether John the Baptist was the expected one.

> *As the people were in expectation, and all men questioned in their hearts concerning John, whether perhaps he was the Christ* (Lk 3:15 RSV).

Why did the Pharisees think that John the Baptist could be the Christ? John was baptizing as God told him to do, which the Pharisees took to indicate that the Baptist might be the one. God's plan was working. Israel's high-level dignitaries were there for the launch of Jesus's ministry, as appropriate for someone so auspicious.

JOHN THE BAPTIST IS NOT THE CHRIST

God sent John the Baptist to be the herald, as the coming of a great leader would call for. John the Baptist was the forerunner, the witness, and the messenger to announce Jesus as the Messiah. However, the Baptist was far more than an announcer. He actually identified Jesus as the Son of God and

---

[14] Brown, *Gospel According to John, I–XII*, 43.

said that they should prepare the way for his arrival because of the glory that Jesus would bring.

> *A voice cries: "In the wilderness prepare the way of the Lord, make straight in the desert a highway for our God...And the glory of the Lord shall be revealed, and all flesh shall see it together..."* (Is 40:3–5 RSV).

Table 2–1: The implications of the Isaiah passage (Is 40:3–5 RSV)

#	Element of the Isaiah passage	What it meant to those who heard John the Baptist
1.	*A voice cries:*	The Baptist is the voice who proclaims the need to take heed.
2.	*In the wilderness...make straight in the desert, a highway for our God*	Similar to Isaiah's calling for angels to prepare a way through the desert for God, the Baptist was telling Israel to prepare a way for God through the bleakness of the world.
3.	*The glory of the Lord shall be revealed*	Jesus revealed God's glory through his works, the greatest being his resurrection and return from the dead in glorified form. *We have beheld his glory, glory as of the only Son from the Father* (Jn 1:10 RSAV).
4.	*And all flesh shall see it*	Through the disciples' personal witness and proclamation of the glorified Jesus, the world (all flesh) will become aware that Jesus was the revelation of the glory of God.

THE SIGNIFICANCE OF "BEYOND THE JORDAN"

There couldn't be a more appropriate location for the launch of Jesus's mission than Bethany beyond the Jordan where the Baptist was baptizing. It was the crossing where it was believed that the Israelites entered the Promised

Land, which evokes the following amazing parallels between Jesus and Joshua.[15]

> *Joshua told the people, "Sanctify yourselves; for tomorrow the Lord*
> *will do wonders among you...Joshua said, 'Hereby, you shall know*
> *that the living God is among you...* (Jos 3:5, 10 RSV).

Table 2–2: Parallelism between Joshua and Jesus at the River Jordan

Joshua		Jesus
Joshua led the Israelites to the Promised Land.	⇒	Jesus will restore access to the "promised land" of eternal life to the world.
Joshua instructed the Israelites to ritually purify themselves before they entered the Promised Land.	⇒	Jesus forgives and cleanses believers of sin to prepare them for entrance to eternal life. In his first epistle, John reinforced the need for this preparation when he stated, *And everyone who thus hopes in him purifies himself as he is pure* (1 Jn 5:12 RSAV).
Joshua said the living God was among them and that his miracles would attest to it.	⇒	Jesus was the living Son of God who walked among the people and performed miracles to attest to his identity.

In addition, there is the possibility of symbolism in John's mention of the location as Bethany. This word is derived from a root that means house of witness, testimony, and response, which couldn't be more applicable to the Baptist and the emissary.[16]

---

[15] Brown, *Gospel According to John, I–XII*, 44.

[16] Brown, *Gospel according to John, I–XII*, 45.

John the Baptist Gives Testimony to the Jews (Israel)
Jesus Is the Lamb of God

[26]John answered them, "I baptize with water; but among you stands one whom you do not know, even he who comes after me, the thong of whose sandal I am not worthy to untie." [27]The next day he saw Jesus coming toward him, and said, "Behold, the Lamb of God, who takes away the sin of the world! [28]This is he of whom I said, 'after me comes a man who ranks before me, for he was before me.' [29]For this I came baptizing with water, that he might be revealed to Israel. [30]I myself did not know him."

WHY ARE YOU BAPTIZING?

The Baptist did not tell the emissary that God sent him to baptize; he told them that he was baptizing so he could reveal the Messiah to them. After noting the greatness of the one he would reveal, he cryptically added that the Messiah stood among them now, and they did *not* know who he was. Even the Baptist didn't know Jesus, his kinsman, was the Messiah. In fact, he couldn't have recognized him as such without God's help.

However, now knowing who Jesus was, he had to grasp the mind-boggling fact that the man Jesus was the incarnate Word of God—the very Word who was with God from the beginning!

"BEHOLD THE LAMB OF GOD"

When the Baptist saw Jesus *coming toward him* the next day, it was his cue to announce that Jesus was the Lamb of God. In Greek, to *come toward* means to *become known*. What did the Baptist *make known* by saying Jesus was the Lamb of God? He associated Jesus with the unblemished lambs in Egypt whose blood was smeared on the Israelites' doorposts to save them from the bringer of death. In parallel fashion, God sent Jesus to the world to save it from the permanent death.

> *For God so loved the world that he gave his only Son, that whoever believes in him should not perish but have eternal life* (Jn 3:16 RSV).

THE PASCHAL LAMB OF GOD

The author clearly drew a parallel of Jesus as the Lamb of God to the paschal lamb, the lamb of deliverance that is celebrated at Passover.

1. Jesus was put on the cross on the Day of Preparation of the Passover, which was when the unblemished lambs were killed by the priests. These lambs were not considered to be a sacrifice, nor was Jesus.

    Now it was the day of Preparation of the Passover; it was about the sixth hour (noon)...They cried out, "crucify him!"... (Jn 19:14–15 RSV).

2. The bones of the Passover lambs were not to be broken, and even though the Jews asked Pilate to have the legs of those on the cross broken so they could be taken away before the Sabbath, Jesus's bones were not broken while he was on the cross.

    So the soldiers came and broke the legs of the first, and of the other...but when they came to Jesus and saw that he was already dead, they did not break his legs (Jn 19:32–33 RSV).

3. In Egypt, hyssop was used to smear the lamb's blood on the door, which was the sign to spare the inhabitants from entrance by the destroyer. The sponge of wine given to Jesus while on the cross was made of hyssop.

    Take a bunch of hyssop and dip it in the blood...and touch the lintel and two doorposts...the LORD will pass over the door, and not allow the destroyer to enter...to slay you (Ex 12:22–23 RSV).

    Jesus, knowing that all was now finished, said... "I thirst."...so they put a sponge full of vinegar on hyssop and held it to his mouth (Jn 19:28–29 RSV).

The blood of the unblemished lambs in Egypt brought the freedom for the Israelites to march through the wilderness to the very place on the Jordan River where Joshua proclaimed wonders of God were to come. The Jordan is where John the Baptist launched Jesus's mission to bring the greatest wonder of all—Jesus's resurrection and the restoration of eternal life.

WHAT IS *THE SIN* OF THE WORLD?

Jesus will restore eternal life by taking away *the sin* of the world. What is this singular sin? It was Adam and Eve's fateful decision to turn away from God by eating the forbidden fruit. Their choice led to their banishment from the Garden of Eden and humankind's ensuing loss of eternal life.

Jesus cannot change the fact that Adam and Eve committed *the sin*; therefore, he can't take the sin away—it happened. But he can reverse the consequence of Adam and Eve's unloving action, which he does by his loving willingness to adhere to the Father's will and submit to the cross. Jesus's defeat of death reinstated the opportunity for those who believe in him, to receive eternal life.

JESUS ALSO FORGIVES *THE SINS* OF THE WORLD

Jesus offers ongoing forgiveness of the sins of believers, which is different from his taking away *the sin* of the world. In this case, Jesus forgives the sins of believers who ask him for forgiveness. It is one of the many ways Jesus helps people recover from their mistakes in order to live a loving life more steadfastly.

> *If we confess our sins, he is faithful and just, and will forgive our sins...* (1 Jn 1:9 RSV).

Jesus Baptizes with the Holy Spirit

[31]"I saw the Spirit descend as a dove from heaven, and it remained on him. [32]He who sent me to baptize with water said to me, 'He on whom you see the Spirit descend and remain, this is he who baptizes with the Holy Spirit.' [33]I myself did not know him."

GOD TESTIFIED

By his testimony to John the Baptist, God himself launched his plan for his Son to save the world. God told the Baptist:

- to baptize with water,
- to look for the descent of the Spirit to identify his Son, and
- what his Son's mission would be—to baptize with the Holy Spirit (restore eternal life).

John the Baptist did as instructed and saw and testified to what God told him to expect. The Baptist repeated that he didn't know his kinsman was the One!

WHAT WAS THE SPIRIT THAT REMAINED ON JESUS?

The Spirit that descended to Jesus was the Spirit that God gave to special people during the banishment period. In those times, God sent his Spirit to heighten their abilities so they could accomplish the special assignments he gave them.

> *"But I am full of the courage that the LORD's Spirit gives, and have a strong commitment to justice. This enables me to confront Jacob with its rebellion, and Israel with its sin"* (Mic 3:8 RSV).

> *"...I have filled him with the Spirit of God, with ability and intelligence, with knowledge and all craftsmanship to devise artistic designs..."* (Ex 31:3–4 RSV).

This Spirit remained with Jesus through the remainder of his human life enabling him to manifest God's glory through great and wondrous signs in support of his mission. This Spirit does not provide eternal life, and it did not keep Jesus from suffering on the cross. It leaves when a person dies, which it did upon Jesus's death.

> *...he said, "It is finished," and he bowed his head and gave up his spirit* (19:30b RSV).

WHAT IS BAPTISM WITH THE HOLY SPIRIT?

When God said that the one (Jesus) would baptize with the Holy Spirit, he announced the heart of Jesus's mission, which was to restore eternal life. Unlike a baptism with water, Jesus's baptism with the Holy Spirit grants eternal life. Jesus did *not* baptize with the Holy Spirit during the earthly phase of his mission because he had to be glorified (restored to his original Divine form) to grant it. Only God can restore what God took away.

> *"Out of his heart shall flow rivers of living water."* Now he said this about the Spirit, which those who believed in him were to receive; for as yet the Spirit had not been given, because Jesus was not yet glorified (Jn 7: 38–39 RSV).

THE DISCIPLES WERE THE FIRST TO BE BAPTIZED

After the Father glorified him, Jesus returned to his disciples to show them that he had defeated death. He stood before them in glorified form with the Divine power to restore eternal life, and he granted them eternal life.

They were the first to receive Jesus's baptism with the Holy Spirit, and they would be the only ones who would have the sensate experience of receiving it. Why were they the only ones? It was so they could testify. Indeed, they saw Jesus in his glory; they felt his breath, and they heard his voice when he baptized them, and they testified to it.

> ...He showed them his hands and his side... "As the Father has sent me, even so I send you." and when he had said this, he breathed on them and said to them, "Receive the Holy Spirit" (Jn 20:20–22 RSV).

Jesus *sent* them to carry his mission onward and outward to convey the good news and testify to the truth.

> The life was made manifest, which was with the Father and was made manifest to us. We (the disciples) saw it and testify to it, and proclaim to you the eternal life (1 Jn 1:3 RSAV).

Jesus Is the Son of God

[34]And John bore witness, "I have seen and have borne witness that this is the Son of God."

JOHN THE BAPTIST GAVE TESTIMONY TO ISRAEL

The inauguration of Jesus's mission to save the world was by the Baptist's testimony to the representatives of Israel's religious hierarchy that Jesus is the Son of God. At this moment in history, the only person on earth who could comprehend this was John the Baptist, and it was because God told him. No one else could possibly imagine that God himself would take the form of a man—the *Word became flesh* (Jn 1:14 RSV)—to demonstrate his love of the world; but this is the truth.

Conclusion

In the perfect confluence of the Baptist's witness of the descent of the Spirit on Jesus and the arrival of the priests and Levites, John the Baptist bore witness that Jesus is the Son of God. This was the launch of the first phase of God's plan. John the Baptist, the voice crying in the wilderness, proclaimed Jesus is the one who will liberate people from the bondage of death and restore eternal life. Therefore, the Baptist called to the emissary to prepare the way.

Through John the Evangelist's revelation of Jesus and the symbols he used, he introduced three themes that he would develop through the rest of this gospel.

1. The use of testimony as the means to introduce and initiate faith in Jesus who is the Son of God.
2. Jesus will restore eternal life, and he will grant it by his baptism with the Holy Spirit.
3. The difference between *the sin* of Adam and Eve and the *sins* of the world. Both are obstacles to access to eternal life. Jesus will remove *the sin* upon a person coming to belief in him and *the sins* a believer commits, prior to his or her coming to belief and the sins committed thereafter, when the believer asks Jesus for forgiveness.

Review of Key Points

In the introduction, we asked you to consider the following questions. What are your answers? Our answers are located in appendix D.

Table 2–3: Review questions and your answers

#	Question	Your Answers
1.	Why was John the Baptist's testimony necessary to introduce Jesus as the Son of God?	
2.	How did the Baptist know Jesus was the expected Messiah?	

#	Question	Your Answers
3.	Why is Jesus considered the Lamb of God?	
4.	What is *the sin* of the world?	
5.	What is Jesus's baptism with the Holy Spirit?	

What's Next?

John the Baptist was the voice of the introduction of Jesus. Jesus's disciples would become his messengers of eternal life. In the next chapter, you will read about Jesus's assemblage of these disciples.

CHAPTER 3

First Disciples
John 1:35–52 RSAV

Introduction

John the Baptist had no sooner announced Jesus as the Lamb of God to two of his disciples than they followed Jesus, who uttered his first words of the gospel to them: "What do you seek?" How would you answer? If you were seeking God, you would be following the right person!

This chapter describes five who responded to Jesus's summons to *follow me*. It is the same call to discipleship that activates Christians' souls to this day. Andrew, one of the first to follow, brought his brother Simon to Jesus. Jesus himself sought out Philip, and Philip delivered Nathanael. None of these events were by chance. Jesus's disciples had been preselected by God to play a specific role in the implementation of his plan. For example, Simon Peter would take the leadership helm. The Baptist's disciple who remained unnamed until the end was the beloved disciple, the communicator who penned this gospel.

Even though John the Baptist spoke explicitly of Jesus's divinity, Jesus's new disciples could not comprehend it. They saw him as an extraordinary man, a prophet like Elijah or Moses, and as the Messiah but not the Son of God. No one other than John the Baptist could grasp this until Jesus resurrected. However, when you hear the truth from Jesus's lips at the climax of this narrative, you will gasp for air to take in its power and majesty.

And he said to them, "Truly, truly, I say to you, you will see heaven opened, and the angels of God ascending and descending upon the Son of man" (Jn 1:51 RSV).

Outline

1. **John Gives Testimony to Two of His Disciples**
   a. Andrew and the Unnamed Disciple (Beloved Disciple) Follow Jesus
   b. Andrew Finds His Brother Simon Peter, Who Follows Jesus
2. **Jesus Finds Philip Who Finds Nathanael**
3. **The Son of Man Is the Son of God**

What to Look For

Consider the following questions as you read in order to deepen your comprehension. There is space to write your answers at the end of the chapter. Our answers are located in appendix D.

1. Why did Jesus begin his ministry by gathering his disciples?
2. Why did Jesus rename Simon to Peter?
3. Who did the disciples think Jesus was? Why is it important to get his identity right?
4. How did Jesus reveal his true identity as the Son of God in this narrative?
5. What did Jesus indicate by referring to himself as the Son of man?

The First Disciples
(Jn 1:35–52 RSAV)

John the Baptist Gives Testimony to Two of His Disciples
Andrew and the Unnamed Disciple (Beloved Disciple) Follow Jesus

[1:35]The next day again John was standing with two of his disciples; and he looked at Jesus as he walked, and said, "Behold, the Lamb of God!" [36]The two disciples heard him say this, and they followed Jesus. [37]Jesus turned, and saw them following, and said to them, "What do you seek?" And they said to him, "Rabbi" (which means Teacher), "where are you staying?" [38]He said to them, "Come and see."

Andrew Finds His Brother Simon Peter, Who Follows Jesus

³⁹One of the two who heard John speak and followed him was Andrew, Simon Peter's brother. ⁴⁰He first found his brother Simon, and said to him, "We have found the Messiah" (which means Christ). He brought him to Jesus. ⁴¹Jesus looked at him, and said, "So you are Simon the son of John? You shall be called "Cephas" (which means Peter). ⁴² They came and saw where he was staying; and they stayed with him that day, for it was about the tenth hour.

Jesus Finds Philip Who Finds Nathanael

⁴³The next day Jesus decided to go to Galilee. And he found Philip and said to him, "Follow me." ⁴⁴Now Philip was from Bethsaida, the city of Andrew and Peter.

⁴⁵Philip found Nathanael, and said to him, "We have found him of whom Moses in the law and also the prophets wrote, Jesus of Nazareth, the son of Joseph." ⁴⁶Nathanael said to him, "Can anything good come out of Nazareth?" ⁴⁷Philip said to him, "Come and see."

⁴⁸Jesus saw Nathanael coming to him, and said of him, "Behold, an Israelite indeed, in whom is no guile!" Nathanael said to him, "How do you know me?" ⁴⁹Jesus answered him, "Before Philip called you, when you were under the fig tree, I saw you." ⁵⁰Nathanael answered him, "Rabbi, you are the Son of God! You are the King of Israel!" ⁵¹Jesus answered him, "because I said to you, I saw you under the fig tree do you believe? You shall see greater things than these."

The Son of Man Is the Son of God

⁵²And he said to them, "Truly, truly, I say to you, you will see heaven opened, and the angels of God ascending and descending upon the Son of man."

Commentary

John the Baptist Gives Testimony to Two of His Disciples
Andrew and the Unnamed Disciple (Beloved Disciple) Follow Jesus

> [1:35]The next day again John was standing with two of his disciples; and he looked at Jesus as he walked, and said, "Behold, the Lamb of God!" [36]The two disciples heard him say this, and they followed Jesus. [37]Jesus turned, and saw them following, and said to them, "What do you seek?" And they said to him, "Rabbi" (which means Teacher), "where are you staying?" [38]He said to them, "Come and see."

BEHOLD THE LAMB OF GOD!

The author did not say how the priests and Levites reacted to the Baptist telling them Jesus was the Lamb of God, but when he told two of his own disciples, they followed Jesus to become his disciples. They got John's message: *Jesus is the lamb of deliverance—he is the Messiah.*

Jesus's first words of the gospel were to ask them what they were looking for—an appropriate question for a teacher to ask new disciples. What were they seeking? What would you be seeking? The two responded by addressing Jesus as Rabbi (teacher) and asked where he was staying. In those days, a rabbi's house was the place of study for his disciples.[17] Jesus told them to *come and see.*

Andrew Finds His Brother Simon Peter, Who Follows Jesus

> [39]One of the two who heard John speak and followed him was Andrew, Simon Peter's brother. [40]He first found his brother Simon, and said to him, "We have found the Messiah" (which means Christ). He brought him to Jesus. [41]Jesus looked at him, and said, "So you are Simon the son of John? You shall be called "Cephas" (which means Peter). [42]They came and saw where he was staying; and they stayed with him that day, for it was about the tenth hour.

THE DISCIPLES WERE NOT GATHERED BY CHANCE

After the two saw Jesus's abode, Andrew went to find his brother Simon to tell him they found the Messiah and then took him to Jesus. Was it by chance that these disciples were coming to Jesus? No. An indication of this was Jesus's immediate renaming of Simon to Peter. Jesus "looked deeply" at Simon and

---

[17] http://www.jewishrootsofchristianity.org/jewishroots/discipleship-in-jesus-day.pdf.

renamed him Peter, which means rock, to signify the role he would have as the foundation stone of the church after Jesus leaves the earth.

> *Jesus looked at him, and said, "So you are Simon the son of John?*
> *You shall be called Cephas" (which means Peter)* (Jn 1:42 RSV).

In the Old Testament, when God gave a person a new name, it indicated that person would play an important role in God's plan.

> *No longer shall your name be Abram, but your name shall be*
> *Abraham; for I have made you the father of a multitude of nations*
> (Gen 17:5 RSV).

Later, Jesus himself said that he chose the twelve.

Jesus answered them, *"Did I not choose you, the twelve..."* (Jn 6:70 RSV).

THEY STAYED WITH HIM THAT DAY

The three, Andrew, the unnamed disciple (the beloved disciple), and Peter, stayed that day with Jesus. The author's reference to a detail like the tenth hour may indicate that the hour was pertinent to the timing of their stay, but it could have also been inserted for symbolic meaning. For first-century Jews, the number ten signified the completion of one cycle and the start of a new one. In the end, Jesus would commission them and the rest of his disciples to be the implementation team of God's plan.

Jesus Finds Philip Who Finds Nathanael

[43]The next day Jesus decided to go to Galilee. And he found Philip and said to him, "Follow me." [44]Now Philip was from Bethsaida, the city of Andrew and Peter.

[45]Philip found Nathanael, and said to him, "We have found him of whom Moses in the law and also the prophets wrote, Jesus of Nazareth, the son of Joseph". [46]Nathanael said to him, "Can anything good come out of Nazareth?" [47]Philip said to him, "Come and see."

[48]Jesus saw Nathanael coming to him, and said of him, "Behold, an Israelite indeed, in whom is no guile!" Nathanael said to him, "How do you know me?"

> ⁴⁹Jesus answered him, "Before Philip called you, when you were under the fig tree, I saw you." ⁵⁰Nathanael answered him, "Rabbi, you are the Son of God! You are the King of Israel!" ⁵¹Jesus answered him, "because I said to you, I saw you under the fig tree do you believe? You shall see greater things than these."

JESUS WENT TO FIND PHILIP

Jesus went to Galilee to find Philip, another disciple the Father had designated for him.

> ...thine they were, and thou gave them to me...(Jn 17:5 RSAV).

When Jesus told Philip to *follow him,* it was an invitation to become his disciple.

WHY IS BETHSAIDA MENTIONED?

It is unusual for an out-of-the-way town to be mentioned twice in the gospel, but its mention at this early point set up a link to the contribution Andrew and Philip would make to God's plan near the end of the gospel. Bethsaida was heavily Gentile, which may be why Jews like Andrew and Philip had Greek names.[18] While Jesus was in Jerusalem in his last days, some Greeks approached Philip requesting to see Jesus. Philip told Andrew about it, and they delivered the Greeks' request to Jesus, which led him to state that his *hour* had arrived.

> Now among those who went up to worship at the feast were some
> Greeks. So these came to Philip, who was from Bethsaida in Galilee,
> and said to him, "Sir we wish to see Jesus." Philip went and told
> Andrew; Andrew went with Philip and they told Jesus. And Jesus
> answered them, "The hour has come for the Son of man to be
> glorified" (Jn 12:20–23 RSV).

God's new covenant was not to be exclusively for Israel; the entire world was going to have the opportunity to receive eternal life. The Greeks' request to see Jesus signified that his outreach had gone beyond Israel to the world.

---

[18] Brown, *Gospel According to John, I–XII,* 82.

> *For God **so loved the world** that he gave his only Son, that whoever*
> *believes in him should not perish but have eternal life* (Jn 3:16
> RSV).

PHILIP FOUND NATHANAEL

Philip responded to Jesus's request to *follow him* in the affirmative by going to find Nathanael to tell him they had found the expected prophet! Nathanael was conversant with Scripture, so Philip approached Nathanael by referring to Scripture right away, but Nathanael was skeptical. Nowhere in Scripture had Nazareth been associated with an expected prophet.

> *Nathanael said to him, "Can anything good come out of*
> *Nazareth?"* (Jn 1:46 RSV).

Philip didn't argue. He did what Jesus did earlier—he confidently invited Nathanael to come and see. Before Nathanael reached Jesus, Jesus had already "seen" him under the fig tree and recognized his righteousness.

AN ISRAELITE WITH NO GUILE (DECEIT)

Prior to Jesus's arrival, God's chosen people were predetermined by birthright and sealed by circumcision regardless of their behavior. Calling Nathanael an Israelite with no guile was Jesus's announcement of the new way to become a child of God, and Nathanael was the new template. Birthright would be replaced by righteous behavior.

The benefit of being a child of God under God's new plan was going to be new and spectacular. The new children of God would be sheltered by God's eternal protection and have peace as had been available in the Garden, which the fig tree symbolized.

> *...nation shall not lift up sword against nation...but they shall sit*
> *every man under his vine and under his fig tree, and none shall*
> *make them afraid* (Mic 4:3–4 RSV).

NATHANAEL'S RESPONSE TO JESUS

Nathanael's incredulous response to Jesus's "seeing" powers led him to exclaim that Jesus was the Son of God.

> ... *"Rabbi, you are the Son of God! You are the King of Israel!"*
> (Jn 1:49 RSV).

Did Nathanael actually believe Jesus was the Divine Son of God? If so, his view would have been quite different from that of the other four disciples, but it was not. They saw Jesus as the following:

- Human
- The Messiah
- A prophet like Moses who will liberate the people from bondage
- A prophet like Elijah who will perform miracles

Nathanael's calling Jesus a Son of God was not a divine designation. Davidic kings were adopted human sons of God. Nathanael's placement of *Son of God* between the earthly titles of *rabbi* and *King of Israel* indicates that his view was like that of the others.

WHEN WILL THE DISCIPLES KNOW WHO JESUS IS?

The disciples could not realize Jesus was the Son of God incarnate until he died and resurrected. No one could, other than John the Baptist, and he only knew because God told him so. However, Jesus's new disciples viewed him as so exceptional they were willing to drop everything to follow him. They would know the truth when he returned in glory for them *to hear, see, and touch* (1 Jn 1:1 RASV).

Why is it important to get Jesus's divine identity right? A human cannot grant eternal life—only God can restore what he took away, which is why Jesus had to be restored to his original glory to grant eternal life.

> ... *for as yet the Spirit had not been given, because Jesus was not yet glorified* (Jn 7:39 RSV).

Yet Jesus also had to be human to demonstrate *the way* to God. Jesus chose to live in loving obedience to God's will, which didn't alleviate his suffering and dying a human death. Everyone will suffer during their life and die, but believers who live in a loving state will resurrect as Jesus demonstrated. This opportunity to rise to God is the hope that Jesus brought.

Jesus said to him, "I am the way, and the truth, and the life..." (Jn 14:19 RSAV).

If Jesus had been a god pretending to be a human but who actually had superpowers, as the Greeks and Romans thought of their gods, Jesus's suffering, death, and resurrection would not have been believable. Therefore, for God's plan to work, Jesus had to be God's Son incarnate—a complete human who was at the same time the divine Son of God.

YOU WILL SEE GREATER THINGS

Jesus promised Nathanael and the others that they would see greater things. Indeed, they would! He would turn water into wine, feed five thousand from two fishes and five loaves of bread, and more. People in those days expected to see miracles and healings from their prophets, and Jesus would fulfill their expectations in order to garner the world's attention in preparation for the sign that would fulfill his earthly mission—his resurrection.

The Son of Man Is the Son of God

> [52]And he said to them, "Truly, truly, I say to you, you will see heaven opened, and the angels of God ascending and descending upon the Son of man."

JESUS REVEALS HIS IDENTITY FOR THE FIRST TIME IN THE GOSPEL

Jesus revealed his true identity as the Son of God by referring to a dream that Jacob had of angels ascending and descending to and from heaven. The dream had such an impact on Jacob he declared the *place* where he awoke to be the house of God and the gate of heaven. Jesus paraphrased the dream to state he was now the connection between heaven and earth.

> **Jacob's dream:** *He dreamed that there was a ladder set up on the earth, and the top of it reached to heaven; and behold the angels of God were ascending and descending on it! Then Jacob awoke from his sleep and said, "Surely the LORD is in this **place**...This is none other than the **house of God**; this is the **gate of heaven**"* (Gen 28:12, 16–17 RSV).

> **Jesus's version:** *And he said to them, "Truly, truly, I say to you, you will see heaven opened, and the angels of God ascending and descending upon the Son of man"* (Jn 1:52 RSV).

In Jesus's version, he was the *place* that Jacob identified as the house of God and the gate of heaven. The glory of God would be revealed in Jesus, which he also told the Jews in Jerusalem when he said that his body was the temple of God.

> *Jesus answered them (the Jews), "Destroy this temple, and in three days I will raise it up"...But he spoke of the temple of his body* (2:19, 21 RSV).

As the new *house of God on earth,* Jesus laid claim to being *the gate of heaven,* and he was. He would unlock the gate to eternal life for the new children of God to enter. The Father granted Jesus the key when he gave him authority over all flesh to grant eternal life.

> *"I am the door; if any one enters by me, he will be saved..."* (Jn 10:9 RSV).

WHY DOES JESUS CALL HIMSELF *SON OF MAN?*

Jesus's calling himself the *Son of man* referred to the prophet Daniel's dream in which God (the Ancient of Days) gave the *Son of man* the following:

- **Dominion** over all people, which is power over all flesh to grant eternal life
- **Glory** that will enable Jesus to grant eternal life
- **A kingdom** that shall never be destroyed, which is the eternal life that Jesus will grant

> *"I saw in the night visions...came one like the **son of man**, and he came to the Ancient of Days and was presented before him. And to him was given **dominion and glory and kingdom**, that **all peoples, nations** and languages should serve him; his dominion is an **everlasting dominion**, which shall not pass away, and his kingdom is one that shall **not be destroyed**"* (Dan 7:13–14 RSV).

In his Farewell Prayer to the Father, Jesus stated that the Father had given him the power over all flesh regarding *life,* which is exactly what Daniel's dream revealed.

"Father, the hour has come, since thou hast given him power over all flesh, so that he can give eternal life..." (Jn 17:2 RSAV).

Conclusion

CHRISTIAN THEOLOGY THAT IS PORTRAYED IN THIS NARRATIVE

Jesus had assembled his disciples, who would carry out God's plan after he leaves the earth, and he had conveyed his identity and mission. You might think this would be enough to convey in one narrative, but the author's use of Greek words with multiple meanings, parallel structures, and references to the Old Testament also reveal seven points that convey elements of God's new plan to bring redemption and hope to the world.

1. Jesus's first words in the gospel, "What do you seek?" point straight to the purpose of this gospel—*that you may believe Jesus is the Christ, the Son of God* (Jn 20:31 RSV) because those who seek God will find him through Jesus.

2. When Jesus's new disciples asked where he was *staying* (his physical abode), they were also figuratively touching on the definition of eternal life, which John refers to as the Father and Son *staying* within a believer and the believer in them.

3. The tenth hour marked the beginning of a new era of hope, which is the opportunity for eternal life that will override the permanent death of the banishment era.

4. This chapter describes the first step that Jesus took to set up his future church by assembling disciples to continue the implementation of his mission after he leaves the earth.

5. Jesus redefined who would be eligible to become a child of God by calling Nathanael a true Israelite, one with no deceit. Righteous behavior would replace birthright as the criteria.

   ...everyone who does right is born of him (1 Jn 5:1 RSAV).

6. Jesus's reference to Jacob's dream identified him as the new locus for God and the gate to heaven.

7.   As the Son of man, Jesus was saying he is the access point to heaven because God gave him dominion over all flesh and restored his glory so he could grant access to the kingdom of eternal life.

KEY ATTRIBUTES OF JESUS'S ASSEMBLED DISCIPLES

While Jesus "found" only five disciples in this narrative, they were representative of the others (except Judas). Jesus's assemblage of them was not by chance but in fulfillment of God's plan. As individuals they might *not* appear to be extraordinarily special, but they had attributes needed to carry Jesus's mission onward then and are applicable to disciples even today.

Table 3–1: Attributes of the five disciples

#	Who	Their Role
1.	Andrew former disciple of John the Baptist	**Bringer of key people to Jesus.** He brought his brother Simon to Jesus. Andrew with Philip also brought the request of the Greeks to see Jesus which initiated Jesus's hour.
2.	Philip who Jesus found in Galilee	**Bringer of key people and of lessons for Jesus to teach.** Philip brought Nathanael to Jesus. Philip with Andrew also brought the request of the Greeks to see Jesus. Philip twice demonstrated the need to trust Jesus: first, in regard to supplying the food for the five thousand, and second, by raising the issue that led Jesus to say that when the disciples saw him, they saw the Father.
3.	Nathanael who was sitting under the fig tree.	**The prototype** of the future faithful child of God who will receive eternal life.
4.	Simon, brother of Andrew, renamed Cephas (Peter)	**The leader** —the rock upon which the new church will be built.
5.	The unnamed disciple, the beloved disciple, and former disciple of John the Baptist	**The communicator**—the author of this gospel and three epistles that we include in this book to explain the aspects of God's plan that have become the core theology of Christianity.

Review of Key Points

In the introduction, we asked you to consider the following questions. What are your answers? Our answers are in appendix D.

Table 3–2: Your answers to the review questions

#	Question	Your Answers
1.	Why did Jesus begin his ministry by gathering his disciples?	
2.	Why did Jesus rename Simon to Peter?	
3.	Who did the disciples think Jesus was— human or Divine? Why is it important to get his identity right?	
4.	How did Jesus reveal his true identity as the Son of God in this narrative?	
5.	What did Jesus indicate by referring to himself as the Son of man?	

What's Next?

Since our purpose is to look closely at how God's plan took shape through the eyes of John and how it came to be transmitted through the testimony of the disciples, we move from their selection and introduction to the last day that Jesus would spend with the disciples. We skip the material dedicated to Jesus's signs in order to pick up with the "Last Supper," "Farewell Address," and "Farewell Prayer," where Jesus teaches his final lessons and prays to prepare the disciples for the events that are to come.

3

Gospel of John: Farewell Address (John 13-17)

CHAPTER 4

Last Supper
JOHN 13:1–31 RSAV

Introduction

THE SIGNAL
Prior to this narrative, John described Jesus's launch of his ministry by the gathering of the disciples that God had designated for him. They were witness to his miraculous signs and received his teachings. In this chapter, John picked up when they were gathered in Jerusalem prior to the Passover Feast, when some Greeks requested to see Jesus. This request was the signal that Jesus's *hour* of departure had arrived.

JESUS'S FIRST PREPARATORY ACTIONS
Were his disciples ready? No. Jesus still had a vital lesson to teach and more information to give them. So he interrupted what would be their last supper together to teach the lesson in humility and service that his disciples would need as his forthcoming messengers. Jesus would lay aside his garments, gird himself with a towel, kneel before them (Judas included), and wash their feet. The world would sorely test his disciples, and for them to be able to respond according to God's will, they must remember they would never be greater than their Master, Jesus. After his foot washing, Jesus would send Judas to mobilize the forces who were ready to have Jesus executed.

JUDAS'S BETRAYAL
Jesus orchestrated Judas's departure, such as the offering of a morsel to Judas to fulfill scripture and to time Judas's exit so as to avoid the risk of the disciples' reaction. Upon Judas's departure, Jesus announced his glorification as if it had already happened; for his unstoppable procession to the cross was indeed underway.

Outline

1. **Jesus's Hour Had Come to Return to God**
2. **Jesus Washes the Disciples' Feet**
    a. Jesus Teaches Humility and Service
    b. Jesus Compares "Clean" to "Not Clean"
3. **Jesus Announces One of the Disciples Will Betray Him**
    a. The Morsel Is Given to Judas
    b. Only the Beloved Disciple Knew About Judas's Betrayal
    c. Judas's Exit Leads to Jesus's Glorification
4. **Jesus States, "A Servant Is Not Greater Than His Master"**
5. **Jesus Tells the Disciples (Less Judas) They Have Been Chosen**

What to Look For

Consider the following questions as you read to deepen your comprehension. There is space to write your answers at the end of the chapter. You can find our answers in appendix D.

1. What were the two key lessons Jesus taught by his foot washing?
2. What is the difference between being clean all over, as the disciples were, and not clean, as Judas was?
3. Why did Jesus bring up the fact a disciple would betray him but not tell the disciples who the person was?
4. How is God glorified in Jesus and Jesus glorified by God?

Last Supper
(Jn 13:1–31 RSAV)

Jesus's Hour Had Come to Return to God

[1]Now before the feast of the Passover, when Jesus knew that his hour had come to depart out of this world to the Father, having loved his own who were in the world, he loved them to the end. [2]Jesus knew that the Father had given all things into his hands, and that he had come from God and was going to God.

Jesus Washes the Disciples' Feet
Jesus Teaches Humility and Service

[3]And during supper, when the devil had already put it into the heart of Judas Iscariot, Simon's son, to betray him, he rose from supper, laid aside his garments, and girded himself with a towel. [4]Then he poured water into a basin, and began to wash the disciples' feet, and to wipe them with the towel with which he was girded.

[5]He came to Simon Peter; and Peter said to him, "Lord, do you wash my feet? [6]You shall never wash my feet." Jesus answered him, "If I do not wash you, you have no part in me." [7]Simon Peter said to him, "Lord, not my feet only but also my hands and my head!" [8]Jesus answered him, "What I am doing you do not know now, but afterward you will understand."

[9]When he had washed their feet, and taken his garments, and resumed his place, he said to them, "Do you know what I have done to you? [10]For I have given you an example that you also should do as I have done to you. [11]You call me Teacher and Lord; and you are right, for so I am. [12]If I then, your Lord and Teacher, have washed your feet, you also ought to wash one another's feet."

Jesus Compares "Clean" to "Not Clean"

[13]"He who has bathed does not need to wash, except for his feet, but he is clean all over; and you are clean, but not every one of you." [14]For he knew who was to betray him; that was why he said, "You are not all clean."

Jesus Announces One of the Disciples Will Betray Him
The Morsel Is Given to Judas

[15]When Jesus had thus spoken, he was troubled in spirit, and testified, "Truly, truly, I say to you, one of you will betray me." [16]The disciples looked at one another, uncertain of whom he spoke. [17]One of his disciples, whom Jesus loved, was lying close to the breast of Jesus; [18]so Simon Peter beckoned to him and said, "Tell us who it is of whom he speaks."

[19]So lying thus, close to the breast of Jesus, he said to him, "Lord, who is it?" [19]Jesus answered, "It is he to whom I shall give this morsel when I have dipped it." [20]So when he had dipped the morsel, he gave it to Judas, the son of Simon Iscariot. [21]Then after the morsel, Satan entered into him. Jesus said to him,

"What you are going to do, do quickly." [22]So, after receiving the morsel, he immediately went out; and it was night.

Only the Beloved Disciple Knew About Judas's Betrayal

[23]Now no one at the table knew why he said this to him. [24]Some thought that, because Judas had the money box, Jesus was telling him, "Buy what we need for the feast"; or, that he should give something to the poor.

Judas's Exit Leads to Jesus's Glorification

[25]When he had gone out, Jesus said, "Now is the Son of man glorified, and in him (Jesus) God is glorified; [26]if God is glorified in him (Jesus) God will also glorify him (Jesus) in himself, and glorify him (Jesus) at once."

Jesus States, "A Servant Is Not Greater Than His Master"

[27]"Truly, truly, I say to you, a servant is not greater than his master; nor is he who is sent greater than he who sent him. [28]Truly, truly, I say to you, he who receives any one whom I send receives me; and he who receives me receives him who sent me. [29]If you know these things, blessed are you if you do them."

Jesus Tells the Disciples (Less Judas) They Have Been Chosen

[30]"I am not speaking of you all; I know whom I have chosen; it is that the scripture may be fulfilled, 'He who ate my bread has lifted his heel against me.' [31]I tell you this now, before it takes place, that when it does take place you may believe that I am he."

Commentary

Jesus's Hour Had Come to Return to God

[1]Now before the feast of the Passover, when Jesus knew that his hour had come to depart out of this world to the Father, having loved his own who were in the world, he loved them to the end. [2]Jesus knew that the Father had given all things into his hands, and that he had come from God and was going to God.

JESUS'S *HOUR*

When the Greeks arrived to celebrate Israel's Passover of liberation and asked to see Jesus, it meant that his message of salvation had spread beyond Israel and out to the world as God intended. This was the catalyst for Jesus's departure.

*For God sent the Son...that **the world** might be saved through him* (Jn 3:17 RSV).

The Father had given *all things* to Jesus for his mission, including entrusting the disciples to his caring hands.

*"...thine they were, and **thou gave them to me**..."* (Jn 17:5 RSAV).

The arrival of Jesus's hour meant that their hour had arrived, too. Jesus needed to prepare them for the assignment they would soon receive to continue his mission.

Jesus Washes the Disciples' Feet
Jesus Teaches Humility and Service

³And during supper, when the devil had already put it into the heart of Judas Iscariot, Simon's son, to betray him, he rose from supper, laid aside his garments, and girded himself with a towel. ⁴Then he poured water into a basin, and began to wash the disciples' feet, and to wipe them with the towel with which he was girded.

⁵He came to Simon Peter; and Peter said to him, "Lord, do you wash my feet?" ⁶"You shall never wash my feet." Jesus answered him, "If I do not wash you, you have no part in me." ⁷Simon Peter said to him, "Lord, not my feet only but also my hands and my head!" ⁸Jesus answered him, "What I am doing you do not know now, but afterward you will understand."

⁹When he had washed their feet, and taken his garments, and resumed his place, he said to them, "Do you know what I have done to you? ¹⁰For I have given you an example that you also should do as I have done to you. ¹¹You call me Teacher and Lord; and you are right, for so I am. ¹²If I then, your Lord and Teacher, have washed your feet, you also ought to wash one another's feet."

JESUS'S HOUR WAS ABOUT TO BEGIN

In contrast to the Father "giving" the disciples to Jesus's caring hands, Judas was about to "give" Jesus into the hands of those who would condemn him. Jesus knew what was in Judas's heart; nevertheless, Jesus began his foot washing lesson with Judas included.

THE SON OF GOD WASHED HIS DISCIPLES' FEET!

For a master or teacher to wash his disciples' feet was an extraordinary act. It was what servants did, not masters, when a person entered a house, and it certainly was *not* done during the course of a meal.[19] Therefore, this venue was ideal for the lesson in humility and service that Jesus had in mind.

Peter's objection confirmed how radical it was for his Teacher and Lord to wash their feet. But when Jesus told Peter that he could have no part with (*in*) him if he did not allow Jesus to wash his feet, Peter quickly changed his mind.

WHAT DID THE DISCIPLES UNDERSTAND AFTERWARD?

After his *hour* when Jesus returned to the disciples, they realized the following:

- Their teacher and Lord was the Divine Son of God himself.
- Jesus sending them to carry on his mission was the reason they had been selected.

Did Jesus mean they should wash each other's feet literally? Probably not. It was a representation of the humility and service that Jesus had just demonstrated. The author indicated this next by his reference to who was clean and who was not clean.

Jesus Compares "Clean" to "Not Clean"

> [13]"He who has bathed does not need to wash, except for his feet, but he is clean all over; and you are clean, but not every one of you." [14]For he knew who was to betray him; that was why he said, "You are not all clean."

---

[19]Gail R. O'Day, *The Gospel of John: Introduction, Commentary, and Reflections*, *NIB Volume IX* (Nashville: Abingdon Press, 1995), 722–723.

WHO IS *NOT* CLEAN?

All but the disciple who would betray Jesus were *bathed,* which meant they were clean all over, even in their hearts. They were free of the type of sin that would lead to their permanent death. However, they still had "road dust," nonmortal sins that accumulate by walking on the journey of life. For this, they didn't need to bathe, but they did need to "freshen up."

Judas, however, was not clean. His intention to betray Jesus, even without executing it, was so grave that permanent death would be his destiny.

TWO CATEGORIES OF SIN

Sin at any level needs to be addressed, but some sins are so serious they are deadly if not recanted.

- **Mortal sin:** an intentional action that when committed precludes access to eternal life and leads to permanent death.

    All wrongdoing is sin, but there is sin, which is not mortal (1 Jn 3:28 RSAV).

- **Nonmortal sin (road dust):** an action committed that in itself does not preclude eternal life but is like road dust that needs to be washed.

Jesus Announces One of the Disciples Will Betray Him
The Morsel Is Given to Judas

[15]When Jesus had thus spoken, he was troubled in spirit, and testified, "Truly, truly, I say to you, one of you will betray me." [16]The disciples looked at one another, uncertain of whom he spoke. [17]One of his disciples, whom Jesus loved, was lying close to the breast of Jesus; [18]so Simon Peter beckoned to him and said, "Tell us who it is of whom he speaks."

[19]So lying thus, close to the breast of Jesus, he said to him, "Lord, who is it?" [19]Jesus answered, "It is he to whom I shall give this morsel when I have dipped it." [20]So when he had dipped the morsel, he gave it to Judas, the son of Simon Iscariot. [21]Then after the morsel, Satan entered into him. Jesus said to him, "What you are going to do, do quickly." [22]So, after receiving the morsel, he immediately went out; and it was night.

JESUS DIDN'T SAY WHO THE BETRAYER WAS

After having said one of his disciples was unclean, Jesus elaborated by saying this disciple planned to betray him—to hand him over to the authorities. Of course the disciples would want to know who the betrayer was. Peter turned to the beloved disciple to find out.

When the beloved disciple asked Jesus who the betrayer was, Jesus still didn't say directly but indicated who he was indirectly. In those days, it was not uncommon for the host to dip a select morsel in oil and give it to a guest as a sign of affection.[20] Jesus told the beloved disciple that he would offer a dipped morsel to the betrayer. By this action, Jesus fulfilled scripture. Why was this important? It was so, afterward, the disciples would realize that Jesus orchestrated his betrayal and believe in him as the Son of God.

> "...'He who ate my bread has lifted his heel against me.' I tell you
> this now, before it takes place, that when it does take place you may
> believe that I am he" (Jn 13:18–19 RSV).

JESUS WAS IN CHARGE

The scriptural text doesn't cover this issue any further; instead it focuses on Jesus and Judas. After Judas ate the morsel, Jesus told him to proceed with his betrayal and do it quickly. Judas obeyed; he immediately went into the *night* to do it. This confirms that Jesus knew that Judas was going to betray him and that Jesus was in control of the event. He decided when to give the morsel to Judas and even told Judas to go quickly to betray him.

Only the Beloved Disciple Knew About Judas's Betrayal

[23]Now no one at the table knew why he said this to him. [24]Some thought that, because Judas had the money box, Jesus was telling him, "Buy what we need for the feast"; or, that he should give something to the poor.

WHY DIDN'T JESUS REVEAL WHO WOULD BETRAY HIM?

The narrator, who is the beloved disciple, inserted this passage, noting that the disciples did not know why Jesus told Judas to go quickly. But the beloved disciple knew and did not tell anyone. Why were the other disciples left out? There are two reasons:

---

[20] Brown, *Gospel According to John, I–XII*, 578.

1. Jesus still had much to cover to prepare his disciples for what was coming, but who would be able to listen knowing Judas was the one!
2. Jesus knew any of the other disciples might try to stop the betrayer, which would deter God's plan. In fact, Peter did try! It was after Jesus and his remaining disciples rose from supper and went to the garden where they were confronted by Judas with soldiers seeking Jesus.

So Judas, procuring a band of soldiers...went there...Then Jesus...said to them, "Whom do you seek?" They answered him, "Jesus of Nazareth." Jesus said to them, "I am he." Judas, who betrayed him, was standing with them...Then Simon Peter, having a sword, drew it and struck the high priest's slave...(Jn 18: 3–5, 10 RSV).

Predictably, Peter responded by trying to stop the soldiers.

Judas's Exit Leads to Jesus's Glorification

²⁵When he had gone out, Jesus said, "Now is the Son of man glorified, and in him (Jesus) God is glorified; ²⁶if God is glorified in him (Jesus) God will also glorify him (Jesus) in himself, and glorify him (Jesus) at once."

GLORIFICATION WAS UNDERWAY

Judas's exit from the dinner put Jesus's *hour* into motion. Jesus's reference to being glorified tells us what was about to happen in the future, *not* what had happened at that moment. By calling himself the *Son of man,* Jesus referred to what God gave the *Son of man* in the prophet Daniel's dream (Dan 7:13–14 RSV). It was exactly what Jesus would receive when he ascended to the Father.

- **Dominion** over all people, which is power over all flesh
- **Glory,** which will enable Jesus to grant eternal life
- **A kingdom** that shall never be destroyed, which is eternal life

WHAT DOES THIS MUTUAL GLORIFICATION MEAN?

There is no doubt that these passages about glorification are confusing. We explain them starting with how Jesus glorified God.

1. *...in him (Jesus) God is glorified*: Jesus honored (glorified) God by performing signs during his ministry and adhering to God's will to go to the cross.

2. *...God will glorify him (Jesus) in himself*: When Jesus died on the cross and resurrected, God immediately glorified (honored) Jesus by restoring him to the Divine form he had with God in the beginning.

God's glorification of Jesus enabled him to return to his disciples to grant them eternal life and *send* them out to carry his mission forward, but that was hardly the end of the story. It was the beginning; because Jesus continues to honor God by granting eternal life for the salvation of believers who live love-based lives.

> *... "Father the hour has come; since thou hast given him power over all flesh, so that he can give eternal life...glorify thy Son that the Son may glorify thee"* (Jn 17:1–2 RSAV).

Jesus States, "A Servant Is Not Greater Than His Master"

[27]"Truly, truly, I say to you, a servant is not greater than his master; nor is he who is sent greater than he who sent him. [28]Truly, truly, I say to you, he who receives any one whom I send receives me; and he who receives me receives him who sent me. [29]If you know these things, blessed are you if you do them."

A SERVANT IS NOT GREATER THAN HIS MASTER

After resuming his position at the table, Jesus capped his lesson by reminding the disciples of their need for humility. Knowing that they would soon know he is God himself who has called them to serve as his messengers, he told them to remember that he was willing to disrobe and kneel before them to wash their feet in humble service.

> *"For I have come down from heaven, not to do my own will, but the will of him who sent me..."* (Jn 6:38 RSV).

They will be blessed if they, too, humbly serve God, for those who receive them will be able to receive God through them and be blessed.

Jesus Tells the Disciples (Less Judas) They Have Been Chosen

> ³⁰"I am not speaking of you all; I know whom I have chosen; it is that the scripture may be fulfilled, 'He who ate my bread has lifted his heel against me.' ³¹I tell you this now, before it takes place, that when it does take place you may believe that I am he."

WHY WAS JESUS CONCERNED ABOUT THE DISCIPLES BELIEVING?

Jesus knew that the upcoming events would be so horrific they would test the faith of the most loyal of disciples. How could the real Messiah choose someone like Judas or die in such a disgraceful way? In those days, people believed prophets were proved to be false by the fact they died, and for three days, it would appear that Jesus had died and was a false prophet.

> *"But the prophet who presumes to speak a word in my name which I have not commanded him to speak or who speaks in the name of other gods, that same prophet shall die"* (Dt 18:20 RSV).

Jesus assured the disciples that he knew what he was doing when he chose each of them, even Judas, who was selected to fulfill Scripture. This was so they might believe.

> *Even my bosom friend in whom I trusted, who ate my bread, has lifted his heel against me* (Ps 41:9 RSV).

JESUS HAD TWO GOALS IN REGARD TO THE EVENTS RELATED TO JUDAS

Before we look at Jesus's goals, we review who knew about Judas, when they knew, and who did not know.

- Jesus did not identify Judas as the betrayer when he said one of the disciples would betray him.
- When the beloved disciple asked Jesus who the betrayer was, Jesus responded with an oblique answer.
- The beloved disciple told no one what he knew.
- No one else at the table knew Judas was the betrayer.

In hindsight, we can surmise that Jesus had two goals in regard to who did and did *not* know that Judas was the betrayer. They must have been the following:

1. To keep the disciples from stopping Judas from executing his betrayal
2. To tell the disciples just enough in advance so they would believe afterward

Conclusion

JESUS PUT HIS *HOUR* INTO MOTION

During his last supper with the disciples, Jesus dispatched Judas to put his *hour* into motion. Jesus's announcement to his disciples only revealed that he would be betrayed but not by whom or when. The elements in this narrative could easily have raised questions as to whether Jesus was who he claimed to be, but Jesus walked a tightrope between how much to tell his disciples and not risk having them thwart God's plan, yet still give them a basis to believe in him afterward. We saw the following:

- Why Judas was selected to be a disciple
- Why Jesus announced that one of his disciples would betray him but did not say who he was
- Why Jesus told his betrayer to go do it quickly
- Why Jesus offered the morsel to Judas his betrayer that traditionally was given to a guest of honor

JESUS TAUGHT THE VITAL FINAL LESSON

By washing his disciples' feet, Jesus dramatically demonstrated the humility and service required to avoid the pride that could arrive with the responsibility they would be given. Jesus walked on earth as a humble servant of God. His foot washing foreshadowed the ultimate humiliation he was about to endure on the cross, but it would also lead to the magnificent transformative gift that he was about to bring. Humility and service were indeed the vital lessons.

> *"I do as the Father has commanded me, so that the world may know that I love the Father..."* (Jn 14:31 RSV).

Review of Key Points

In the introduction, we asked you to consider the following questions. What are your answers? Our answers are in appendix D.

Table 4–1: Your answers to the review questions

#	Question	Your Answers
1.	What were the two key lessons Jesus taught by his foot washing?	
2.	What is the difference between being clean all over, as the disciples were, and not clean, as Judas was?	
3.	Why did Jesus bring up the fact that a disciple would betray him but not tell the disciples who the person was?	
4.	How is God glorified in Jesus and Jesus glorified by God?	

What's Next?

Next, Jesus will break the news that he will leave the disciples soon, and they will not be permitted to follow him. Time is short and he still has much to convey, so Jesus will proceed with one of the most poignant dialogues of the Bible that is also the source of most of Christianity's theology.

CHAPTER 5

Farewell Discourse
John 14:1–16:26 RSAV

Introduction

THE SITUATION

Jesus launched his hour when he told Judas to go do what he was going to do. Judas's immediate departure meant that time was of the essence for Jesus to prepare his disciples for the events to come and their ensuing role.

Jesus would assure them that he is the way, the truth, and the life. He would promise to send them a Counselor to be with them forever. He told them, when they asked in his name, they would be assured of receiving what they asked for. He commanded them to love one another, and he encouraged them to bear fruit so that their joy may be full, but the one thing that Jesus couldn't tell them was that he was about to be put to death. Why? Because he knew they couldn't handle it. Instead, Jesus told them he was going to the Father who the disciples presumed was a father on earth.

THE DISCIPLES' PERCEPTION OF JESUS

At this point, the disciples did *not* believe Jesus was the Son of God. This made what he wanted to communicate all the more difficult because they interpreted what he said from their earthly perspective because Jesus was speaking of things that could only be understood after his hour had been completed.

As Jesus continued with his discourse, the disciples came to believe that he did indeed come from God, and at that point they realized that Jesus was speaking plainly! The chart below shows the progression from their *believing* that Jesus was a prophet to *knowing* that Jesus is the Son of God. We discuss this here, in advance of your reading, because John shared his experience with Jesus from his own two perspectives. The perspective of being with Jesus as the events were unfolding and after the resurrection, as someone who had reflected on all that happened and was sharing what he absolutely knew.

THE PROGRESSION FROM BELIEF TO KNOWING

We use the term *to believe* to mean accepting something to be true. This kind of acceptance commonly comes from believing someone else. The term *to know* refers to personally possessing knowledge of something. It carries more certainty because its source is from within.

Table 5–1: The progression in the disciples' perception of Jesus from belief to knowledge

Insufficient belief ⇨	True belief ⇨	Knowledge
Before *Jesus's hour,* the disciples **believed** Jesus to be a prophet and the Messiah.	During this discourse, they came to **believe** Jesus came from God, which was the belief they needed to be qualified to receive eternal life.	When Jesus returned to them in glorified form, they realized that they were face-to-face with God! That was when they **knew** Jesus was the Son of God who granted eternal life because he granted it to them.

The thing to remember is that today's readers have the benefit of the disciples' testimony of Jesus's resurrection as a basis for belief, but what does it mean to believe? The term *belief* is widely used in this gospel; the key is to ask what does the belief refer to. The excursus that follows discusses some of these belief passages to clarify the disciples' progression from belief to absolutely knowing that Jesus is the Son of God.

Excursus: Who Is Jesus?

The Disciples Did *Not* Realize Jesus Was the Son of God Before Jesus Began This Discourse

There is no question that the disciples loved and revered Jesus as a prophet and the Messiah. They viewed him as so exceptional they were willing to drop everything to follow him. They saw him as their Lord and Teacher, but not the Son of God.

Table 5–2: Who the disciples thought Jesus was before his resurrection

Disciple	Jesus was	Reference
Andrew	1. The Messiah	*He first found his brother Simon, and said to him, "We have found the Messiah"* (which means Christ) (Jn 1:41 RSV).
Philip	2. A prophet like Moses, who will liberate the people from bondage 3. A prophet like Elijah, who will perform miracles[21]	... *"We have found him of whom Moses in the law and also the prophets wrote, Jesus of Nazareth, the son of Joseph."* (Jn 1:45 RSV).
Nathanael	4. Rabbi 5. Son of God (Davidic kings were called sons of God, but they were adopted human sons, not Divine.) 6. King of Israel	*Nathanael answered him, "Rabbi, you are the Son of God! You are the King of Israel!"* (Jn 1:49 RSV).

---

[21] Brown, *Gospel According to John, I–XII*, 86.

Passages That Might Cause People to Believe the Disciples Thought Jesus Was the Son of God Before They Actually Did

The following passages include statements about the disciples believing, but what did they believe?

- When Jesus asked the twelve, "Do you wish to go away?" Simon Peter responded by saying Jesus was a Holy One of God. Peter was *not* saying that Jesus was the Son of God but that he was a holy man.

  > *"Lord, to whom shall we go? You have the words of eternal life; and* **we have believed** *and have come to know that you are the Holy One of God."* (Jn 6:68–69 RSV).

- When the disciples saw Jesus's first miracle at Cana, it confirmed that they thought Jesus was a prophet, since prophets perform miracles, but not that he was the Son of God.

  > *This is the first of his signs, Jesus did at Cana in Galilee, and manifested his glory; and* **his disciples believed in him** (Jn 2:11 RSV).

During his discourse, Jesus confirmed that the disciples did *not* believe he was the Son of God.

> *"And now I have told you before it takes place, so that when it does take place, you may believe"* (Jn14:29 RSV).

The Point When the Disciples *Believed* Jesus Came from God

The passage below was when the disciples had their *aha* moment.

> *"Do you now believe?" His disciples said, "Ah, now you are speaking plainly...by this we believe that you came from God"* (Jn 15:31–32 RSAV).

The Point When the Disciples *Knew* Jesus Was the Son of God

The disciples' belief moved to **knowing** that Jesus was the Son of God on the third day, when he returned to them in glorified form. This is when they realized that they were face-to-face with God who granted them by his breath, the honor to receive the Holy Spirit (eternal life)!

*On the evening of **that day**...Jesus came and stood among them and said to them, "Peace be with you." When he had said this, he showed them his hands and his side...And...he breathed on them, and said to them, "Receive the Holy Spirit"* (Jn 20:19–20, 22 RSV).

Outline

1. **Jesus's Hour Had Come**
    a. Jesus Is Leaving Soon
    b. The Disciples Ask for Clarity
        i. **Peter Wants to Go with Him**
        ii. **Philip Wants to See the Father**
        iii. **Thomas Wants to Know Where He Is Going**

2. **Jesus Is the Way to the Father: Believe and Love**
    a. Jesus Is the Way
    b. Believe and Love
    c. Do Not Be Afraid

3. **Jesus Will Send Another Counselor**
    a. The Disciples Will Receive the Holy Spirit (the Spirit of Truth)
    b. The Holy Spirit (the Spirit of Truth) Is Available to Everyone
    c. The Holy Spirit (the Spirit of Truth) Will Bear Witness

4. **Jesus Is Going in a Little While**
    a. What Does "a Little While" Mean?
    b. When Jesus Goes, the Spirit of Truth Comes
    c. Sorrow Turns to Joy

5. **The Disciples Believe Jesus Came from God**
6. **Ask in My Name and You Shall Receive That Your Joy May Be Full**
7. **Jesus Prepares the Disciples for Their Mission**
   a. Abide in Jesus and Bear Fruit
   b. The Disciples Are Clean by the Word
   c. The World Hated Jesus
   d. If They Persecuted Me, They Will Persecute You
   e. Love One Another as I Have Loved You
   f. Bear Fruit That Your Joy May Be Full

What to Look For

Consider the following questions as you read in order to deepen your comprehension. There is space to write your answers at the end of the chapter. You can find our answers in appendix D.

1. Why did the disciples fail to comprehend Jesus's remarks at the beginning of the discourse?
2. What did Jesus mean when he said that he was *the way*?
3. Can everyone receive eternal life?
4. What is new about Jesus's commandment to love one another?
5. How do you know that Jesus was really free to lay down his life? Why is this important?
6. What is *that day*? Why is it significant?
7. How were the disciples able to do greater works than Jesus?
8. What is the role of the disciples in God's plan?
9. How will the disciples be assured of success in fulfilling their role?
10. Did Jesus put an end to the world's tribulation?

Farewell Discourse
(Jn 14:1–16:26 RSAV)

Jesus's Hour Had Come
Jesus Is Leaving Soon

¹⁴:¹"Little children, yet a little while I am with you. You will seek me; and as I said to the Jews so now I say to you, 'Where I am going you cannot come.'"

The Disciples Ask for Clarity
Peter Wants to Go with Him

²Simon Peter said to him, "Lord, where are you going?" Jesus answered, "Where I am going you cannot follow me now." ³Peter said to him, "Lord, why cannot I follow you now? I will lay down my life for you." ⁴Jesus answered, "Will you lay down your life for me? ⁵Truly, truly, I say to you, the cock will not crow, till you have denied me three times, but you shall follow afterward.

⁶In my Father's house are many rooms; if it were not so, would I have told you that I go to prepare a place for you? ⁷And when I go and prepare a place for you, I will come again and will take you to myself, that where I am you may be also."

Philip Wants to See the Father

⁸Philip said to him, "Lord, show us the Father, and we shall be satisfied." ⁹Jesus said to him, "Have I been with you so long, and yet you do not know me, Philip? ⁹He who has seen me has seen the Father; how can you say, 'Show us the Father'? ¹⁰Do you not believe that I am in the Father and the Father in me? ¹¹Believe me that I am in the Father and the Father in me; or else believe me for the sake of the works themselves. ¹²The words that I say to you I do not speak on my own authority; but the Father who dwells in me does his works.

¹³Truly, truly, I say to you, he who believes in me will also do the works that I do. ¹⁴Whatever you ask in my name I will do it. ¹⁵If you ask anything in my name I will do it, that the Father may be glorified in the Son ¹⁶and greater works than these will he do, because I go to the Father."

Thomas Wants to Know Where He is Going

[17]"And you know the way where I am going." [18]Thomas said to him, "Lord, we do not know where you are going; how can we know the way?"

Jesus Is the Way to the Father: Believe and Love
Jesus Is the Way

[19]Jesus said to him, "I am the way, and the truth, and the life; no one comes to the Father, but by me. [20]If you had known me, you would have known my Father also; henceforth you know him and have seen him."

Believe and Love

[21]"Let not your hearts be troubled; believe in God, believe also in me. [22]A new commandment I give to you, that you love one another; that you also love one another even as I have loved you. [23]By this all men will know that you are my disciples, if you have love for one another."

Do Not Be Afraid

[24]"Let not your hearts be troubled, neither let them be afraid. [25]You heard me say to you, `I go away, and I will come to you.' [26]I will no longer talk much with you, for the ruler of this world is coming. He has no power over me. [27]If you loved me, you would have rejoiced, because I go to the Father; for the Father is greater than I. [28]I do as the Father has commanded me, so that the world may know that I love the Father.

[29]And now I have told you before it takes place, so that when it does take place, you may believe."

Jesus Will Send Another Counselor
The Disciples Will Receive the Holy Spirit (the Spirit of Truth)

[30]"If you love me, you will keep my commandments. [31]And I will pray the Father, and he will give you another Counselor, the Spirit of truth, whom the world cannot receive, because it neither sees him nor knows him; you know him, for he dwells with you, and will be in you to be with you forever. [32]In that day you will know that I am in my Father, and you in me, and I in you.

[33]I will not leave you desolate I will come to you. [34]Yet a little while, and the world will see me no more, but you will see me; because I live, you will live also. [35]And the Counselor, the Holy Spirit, whom the Father will send in my name, he will teach you all things, and bring to your remembrance all that I have said to you. [36]Peace I leave with you; my peace I give to you; not as the world gives do I give to you.

[37]He who has my commandments and keeps them, he it is who loves me; and he who loves me will be loved by my Father, and I will love him and manifest myself to him." [38]He who does not love me does not keep my words; and the word which you hear is not mine but the Father's who sent me."

The Holy Spirit (the Spirit of Truth) Is Available to Everyone

[39]Judas (not Iscariot) said to him, "Lord, how is it that you will manifest yourself to us, and not to the world?" [40]Jesus answered him, "If a man loves me, he will keep my word, and my Father will love him, and we will come to him and make our home with him.

[41]These things I have spoken to you, while I am with you."

The Holy Spirit (the Spirit of Truth) Will Bear Witness

[15:1]"But when the Counselor comes, whom I shall send to you from the Father, even the Spirit of truth, who proceeds from the Father, he will bear witness to me; and you also are witnesses, because you have been with me from the beginning.

[2]I did not say these things to you from the beginning, because I was with you. [3]I have said all this to you to keep you from falling away. [4]They will put you out of the synagogues, [5]and they will do this because they have not known the Father, nor me. [5]Indeed, the hour is coming when whoever kills you will think he is offering service to God. [6]I have said these things to you, that when their hour comes you may remember that I told you of them. [7]But because I have said these things to you, sorrow has filled your hearts.

[8]Nevertheless I tell you the truth: it is to your advantage that I go away, for if I do not go away, the Counselor will not come to you; but if I go, I will send him to you. [9]And when he comes, he will convince the world concerning sin and righteousness and judgment: [10]concerning sin, because they do not believe in

me; [11]concerning judgment, because the ruler of this world is judged; [12]concerning righteousness, because I go to the Father, and you will see me no more."

Jesus Is Going in a Little While
What Does "a Little While" Mean?

[13]"Now I am going to him who sent me; yet none of you asks me, 'Where are you going?' [14]A little while, and you will see me no more; again a little while, and you will see me."

[15]Some of his disciples said to one another, "What is this that he says to us, 'a little while, and you will not see me, and again a little while, and you will see me'; and, 'because I go to the Father'?" [16]Jesus knew that they wanted to ask him; so he said to them, "Is this what you are asking yourselves, what I meant by saying, 'A little while, and you will not see me, and again a little while, and you will see me.'"

[17]They said, "What does he mean by 'a little while'? We do not know what he means."

When Jesus Goes, the Spirit of Truth Comes

[18]"I have yet many things to say to you, but you cannot bear them now. [19]When the Spirit of truth comes he will guide you into all the truth; for he will not speak on his own authority, but [20]he will glorify me, for he will take what is mine and declare it to you. [21]All that the Father has is mine; therefore, I said that he will take what is mine and declare it to you. [22]Whatever he hears he will speak, and he will declare to you the things that are to come."

Sorrow Turns to Joy

[23]"Truly, truly, I say to you, you will weep and lament, but the world will rejoice; you will be sorrowful, but your sorrow will turn into joy. [24]So you have sorrow now, but I will see you again and your hearts will rejoice, and no one will take your joy from you.

[25]When a woman is in travail she has sorrow, but when she is delivered of the child, she no longer remembers the anguish because her hour has come for joy

that a child is born into the world.

[26]The hour is coming, indeed it has come, when you will be scattered, every man to his home, and will leave me alone; yet I am not alone, for the Father is with me. I have said this to you, that in me you may have peace. In the world you have tribulation; but be of good cheer, I have overcome the world."

The Disciples Believe Jesus Came from God

[27]"In that day you will ask nothing of me. [28]I have said this to you in figures; I shall no longer speak to you in figures but tell you plainly of the Father. [29]The hour is coming. I came from the Father and have come into the world; again, I am leaving the world and going to the Father. [30]Do you now believe?" [31]His disciples said, "Ah, now you are speaking plainly, not in any figure! Now we know that you know all things, and need none to question you; by this we believe that you came from God."

Ask in My Name and You Shall Receive That Your Joy May Be Full

[32]Jesus answered them, "in that day you will ask in my name, because you have loved me and have believed that I came from the Father. [33]I do not say to you that I shall pray the Father for you; for the Father himself loves you."

[34] "Truly, truly, I say to you, hitherto you have asked nothing in my name; if you ask anything of the Father, he will give it to you in my name. [35]Ask, and you will receive, that your joy may be full."

Jesus Prepares His Disciples
Abide in Jesus and Bear Fruit

[16:1]"Rise, let us go hence. [2]I am the true vine, and my Father is the vinedresser. [3]Every branch of mine that bears no fruit, he takes away and every branch that does bear fruit he prunes, that it may bear more fruit. [4]As the branch cannot bear fruit by itself, unless it abides in the vine, neither can you, unless you abide in me. [5]I am the vine, you are the branches. He who abides in me, and I in him, he it is that bears much fruit, for apart from me you can do nothing. [6]If a man does not abide in me, he is cast forth as a branch and withers; and the branches are gathered, thrown into the fire and burned."

The Disciples Are Clean by the Word

[7]"You are already made clean by the word which I have spoken to you. [8]Abide in me, and I in you. [9]If you abide in me, and my words abide in you, ask whatever you will, and it shall be done for you. [10]By this my Father is glorified, that you bear much fruit, and so prove to be my disciples."

The World Hated Jesus

[11]"If the world hates you know that it has hated me before it hated you; but you are not of the world, because I chose you out of the world, therefore the world hates you. [12]If I had not come and spoken to them, they would not have sin; but now they have no excuse for their sin. [13]If I had not done among them the works which no one else did, they would not have sin; but now they have seen and hated both me and my Father. [14]He who hates me hates my Father also. [15]It is to fulfill the word that is written in their law, 'They hated me without a cause.'"

If They Persecuted Me, They Will Persecute You

[16]"Remember the word that I said to you, 'if they persecuted me, they will persecute you; a servant is not greater than his master', if they kept my word, they will keep yours also. [17]But all this they will do to you on my account, because they do not know him who sent me."

Love One Another as I Have Loved You

[18]"As the Father has loved me, so have I loved you; abide in my love. [19]If you keep my commandments you will abide in my love, just as I have kept my Father's commandments and abide in his love. [20]"This is my commandment, that you love one another as I have loved you. [21]This I command you, to love one another.

[22]Greater love has no man than this that a man lay down his life for his friends. [23]You are my friends if you do what I command you. [24]No longer do I call you servants, for the servant does not know what his master is doing; but I have called you friends, for all that I have heard from my Father I have made known to you."

Bear Fruit That Your Joy May Be Full

²⁵"You did not choose me, but I chose you and appointed you that you should go and bear fruit and that your fruit should abide; so that whatever you ask the Father in my name, he may give it to you.

²⁶These things I have spoken to you, that my joy may be in you, and that your joy may be full."

Commentary

Jesus's Hour Has Come
Jesus Is Leaving Soon

---

¹⁴:¹" Little children, yet a little while I am with you. You will seek me; and as I said to the Jews so now I say to you, 'Where I am going you cannot come.'"

THE DISCIPLES CANNOT GO WITH JESUS

Jesus and his disciples (minus Judas) were still at supper, when this discourse picks up. Jesus got right to the point. He was going to leave them. He did not say where he was going, only that they, like the Jews, could not follow him. But how could they who loved Jesus be like the Jews!

> *"I go away, and you will seek me...where I am going you cannot come...you are of this world; I am not of this world"* (Jn 8:21, 23 RSV).

At this stage, no one could leave the world to go to the Father because everyone in the world—all Jews, gentiles, and even the disciples—were banished from eternal life due to Adam and Eve's fall. The very reason that Jesus was leaving was to rectify this situation. He was going to the Father to restore access to God's kingdom. Jesus would have to go to the cross to do it, and he knew his disciples couldn't bear hearing this.

> *"I have many things to say to you, but you cannot bear them now"* (Jn 15:18 RSV).

THE DISCIPLES ASK FOR CLARITY

The upcoming dialogues reflect Jesus's desire to prepare his disciples, but not to explicitly tell them everything. Even so, they couldn't comprehend how they, who left everything to follow Jesus, could be excluded now?

- Peter asked why he must wait to follow afterward?
- If they can't go to the Father's house, Philip wanted to at least see the Father.
- Thomas wanted to know the way because they didn't know where Jesus was going.

Jesus's responses to their questions confused them all the more. They interpreted what he said in worldly terms, but he spoke to them in relation to what they would understand after they saw him glorified.

The Disciples Ask for Clarity
Peter Wants to Go with Him

²Simon Peter said to him, "Lord, where are you going?" Jesus answered, "Where I am going you cannot follow me now. ³Peter said to him, "Lord, why cannot I follow you now? I will lay down my life for you." ⁴Jesus answered, "Will you lay down your life for me? ⁵Truly, truly, I say to you, the cock will not crow, till you have denied me three times, but you shall follow afterward.

⁶In my Father's house are many rooms; if it were not so, would I have told you that I go to prepare a place for you? ⁷And when I go and prepare a place for you, I will come again and will take you to myself, that where I am you may be also."

PETER WANTED TO FOLLOW JESUS

From Peter's perspective, how could he *not* follow Jesus? Peter promised to protect Jesus—to lay down his life if necessary, and, in fact, Peter did risk his life at Jesus's arrest.

> *Then Simon Peter, having a sword, drew it and struck the high priest's slave...*(Jn 18:10 RSV).

Why would Jesus have responded by bringing up the fact Peter would deny him? When viewed after the fact, Jesus was most likely using this as a teaching moment. Peter did go on to deny Jesus three times before a cock crowed. When Peter snapped out of his oblivion, he realized he had done exactly what Jesus said he would do, and he wept in grief.

> *And Peter remembered the saying of Jesus...And he went out and wept bitterly* (Mt 26:75 RSV).

Jesus's handling Peter this way certainly heightened Peter's awareness of his need for more humility and strength of faith. But we are getting ahead of the story, Jesus had just started his discourse and these events had *not* happened yet.

WHAT WAS THE PLACE JESUS WAS PREPARING FOR THE DISCIPLES?

Jesus promised the disciples they will follow him *afterward* to a place he would prepare. John used three words—*house*, *rooms*, and *place*—that in the Greek refer to both physical and nonphysical spaces. The disciples presumed they would follow him to a physical structure, but Jesus meant a non-physical space. Upon his return in glorified form, he would take the disciples *to himself*, which meant he would grant them eternal life where they would abide eternally with him and the Father.

Philip Wants to See the Father

[8]Philip said to him, "Lord, show us the Father, and we shall be satisfied." [9]Jesus said to him, "Have I been with you so long, and yet you do not know me, Philip? [9]He who has seen me has seen the Father; how can you say, 'Show us the Father'? [10]Do you not believe that I am in the Father and the Father in me? [11]Believe me that I am in the Father and the Father in me; or else believe me for the sake of the works themselves. [12]The words that I say to you I do not speak on my own authority; but the Father who dwells in me does his works.

[13]Truly, truly, I say to you, he who believes in me will also do the works that I do. [14]Whatever you ask in my name I will do it. [15]If you ask anything in my name I will do it, that the Father may be glorified in the Son [16]and greater works than these will he do, because I go to the Father."

SHOW US THE FATHER

Philip asked to see the Father, but Jesus's response was what he had told them in the past. He and the Father dwell within each other; therefore, the disciples have already seen the Father. Through Jesus, they had heard the Father's words and seen his works.

"...I and the Father are one" (Jn 10:30 RSV).

Do the disciples understand? No. It would take Jesus's great "work," his resurrection, to confirm the unfathomable truth that he was the Son of God.

WHO WILL BE ABLE TO PERFORM WORKS?

Did Jesus mean that all who believe will be able to perform miracles (works) as he did? No. Jesus was addressing the disciples specifically at that point. He knew they would soon realize that he was the Son of God, and he promised to do what they asked for, under the conditions that their requests not be small-minded or self-oriented but intended to honor God.

To ask in Jesus's name means that the request is relevant to the continuation of Jesus's work on earth. For example, when the disciples generated new believers after Jesus left, they would glorify (honor) him and the Father.

WHAT IS A GREATER WORK?

The Greek meaning for the word *greater* refers to either quantity or quality. Jesus was not necessarily saying the disciples would perform more marvelous works than he but that they would take his message to a greater quantity of people, and they did. In one day alone, three thousand people became believers.

> *So those who received his (Peter's) word were baptized, and there were added that day about three thousand souls* (Acts 3:41 RSV).

Thomas Wants to Know Where Jesus Is Going

[17]"And you know the way where I am going." [18]Thomas said to him, "Lord, we do not know where you are going; how can we know the way?"

WHAT DID JESUS MEAN "THEY KNEW THE WAY"?

Thomas thought Jesus was talking about a road to the Father's house, not the way to heaven. Jesus could say the disciples knew the way where he was going (to receive eternal life) because they were living love-based lives, which was the way to heaven, but they weren't aware of it.

Jesus Is the Way to the Father: Believe and Love
Jesus Is the Way

> [19]Jesus said to him, "I am the way, and the truth, and the life; no one comes to the Father, but by me. [20]If you had known me, you would have known my Father also; henceforth you know him and have seen him."

HOW IS JESUS *THE WAY* TO THE FATHER?

The Greek word for *way* can refer to either a road, which Thomas was asking about, or a manner of conduct, which Jesus was referring to. Jesus modeled and taught the way of living that leads to eternal life. Here are some examples.

- By following the will of the Father, Jesus demonstrated his love of the Father—"*I always do what is pleasing to him*" (Jn 8:29 RSV).
- He advocated the need to stop sinning when he found the lame man in the temple and told him to "*Sin no more...*" (Jn 5:14 RSV).
- Jesus kept the Father's word—he told the Jews, "*...I do know him and I keep his word.*" (Jn 8:55 RSV).

The disciples, who kept Jesus's word and emulated him as their teacher, actually knew how to conduct themselves in the manner that would make them acceptable to the Father, but they didn't realize it.

> "*Truly, truly, I say to you, if any one keeps my word, he will never see death*" (Jn 8:51 RSV).

WHEN DID THE DISCIPLES KNOW JESUS IS THE TRUTH AND THE LIFE?

When Jesus said *henceforth*, he did not mean the disciples knew at that moment. It wouldn't be until the end of his hour, when Jesus returned to them in glorified form for them to see, hear, and feel his breath as he granted eternal life to them, that they would know the following:

- Jesus is the **truth**—Jesus is the incarnate Word of God, the Son of God.
- Jesus is the **life** because he defeated death and by his resurrection and glorification, grants eternal life.

WHAT DID JESUS MEAN BY "NO ONE COMES TO THE FATHER BUT BY ME"?

Jesus became the sole access point to the Father when the Father glorified him. This was when the Father gave Jesus the authority and power to decide who may receive eternal life.

> *"since thou hast given him **power /authority** over all flesh, to give eternal life..."* (Jn 17:2 RSV).

Believe and Love

> [21]"Let not your hearts be troubled; believe in God, believe also in me. [22]A new commandment I give to you, that you love one another; that you also love one another even as I have loved you. [23]By this all men will know that you are my disciples, if you have love for one another."

WHY WOULD JESUS SAY THE DISCIPLES HAVE TROUBLED HEARTS?

Of course, the disciples were dismayed to hear they couldn't go with him; the disciples left everything to be with Jesus, and they followed him faithfully. In this light, Jesus told them the essential thing to do—believe (*trust*) in God and in him. What were they to believe? The following passage describes it.

> For **God so loved the world** that **he gave his only Son,** that whoever believes in him should not perish but have eternal life (Jn 3:16 RSV).

This passage confirms the following, which serves as the basis for Jesus's new commandment to love one another.

- God is a loving God.
- Jesus is God's Son who he sent to the world; Jesus is the incarnate Word of God.
- God's plan for the world is a loving plan because he offered salvation from the bondage of sin and death.

WHAT IS NEW ABOUT LOVING ONE ANOTHER?

To abide in love had been God's plan for the world all along.

"You shall not take vengeance or bear any grudge against the sons of your own people, but you shall love your neighbor as yourself: I am the LORD" (Lev 19:18 RSV).

But Jesus upped the ante for how to love one another. His call was for the disciples to love one another as he loved them, which would be to their death if necessary. This is the new standard. It doesn't stop with love of a neighbor as oneself; it is to love as Jesus demonstrated.

"I know my own and my own know me, as the Father knows me and I know the Father; and I lay down my life for the sheep" (Jn 10:15 RSV).

Do Not Be Afraid

24 "Let not your hearts be troubled, neither let them be afraid. 25You heard me say to you, `I go away, and I will come to you.' 26I will no longer talk much with you, for the ruler of this world is coming. He has no power over me. 27If you loved me, you would have rejoiced, because I go to the Father; for the Father is greater than I. 28I do as the Father has commanded me, so that the world may know that I love the Father.

29And now I have told you before it takes place, so that when it does take place, you may believe."

THE GRAND PLAN

When Jesus went away, he would rectify the original rupture brought by Adam and Eve. They did not do as the Father commanded because they did not love him, but Jesus would do exactly as the Father commanded him so the world would know of his love for him.

The grand plan was for Jesus to restore access to eternal life with the loving Father by proving that the ruler of the world of sin and death had no power over him or anyone to whom Jesus grants eternal life.

"I do as the Father has commanded me, so that the world may know that I love the Father" (Jn 14:28 RSAV).

If the disciples had been able to comprehend this, they would have been overjoyed about Jesus going to the Father because Jesus was about to liberate the entire world from its locked-in destiny of permanent death. He would put eternal life into destiny's equation for those who choose to believe in him and love as he commanded.

WHY DID JESUS SAY THAT THE FATHER IS GREATER THAN HIM?

Wasn't the Son of God equal to the Father even while in the flesh? *No.* The authority that the Father gave his Son on earth was the right to choose whether or not to follow his commands. Did this mean that Jesus was contradicting himself when he said he and the Father were one? *No.* Jesus's statement was not about a disparity between the essence of him and the Father; his reference was specific to the human role that God gave him.

Only because Jesus was free to choose to lay down his life could the world believe that his obedience to the Father was a freewill act of love. In the reference cited below, the Greek word for power is *exousia,*[22] means having the power of choice.

> *"For this reason the Father loves me, because I lay down my life...No one takes it from me, but I lay it down of my own accord. I have the* **power** *to lay it down, and I have the power to take it up again; this charge I have received from my Father"* (Jn 10:17–18 RSV).

Jesus Will Send Another Counselor
The Disciples Will Receive the Holy Spirit (the Spirit of Truth)

[30]"If you love me, you will keep my commandments. [31]And I will pray the Father, and he will give you another Counselor, the Spirit of truth, whom the world cannot receive, because it neither sees him nor knows him; you know him, for he dwells with you, and will be in you to be with you forever." [32]In that day you will know that I am in my Father, and you in me, and I in you.

[33]I will not leave you desolate I will come to you. [34]Yet a little while, and the world will see me no more, but you will see me; because I live, you will live also. [35]And the Counselor, the Holy Spirit, whom the Father will send in my name, he will teach you all things, and bring to your remembrance all that I have said to you. [36]Peace I leave with you; my peace I give to you; not as the world gives do I give to you.

[37]He who has my commandments and keeps them, he it is who loves me; and he who loves me will be loved by my Father, and I will love him and manifest

---

[22] http://classic.net.bible.org/verse.php?book=Joh&chapter=10&verse=18

> myself to him. [38]He who does not love me does not keep my words; and the word which you hear is not mine but the Father's who sent me."

THE GRANTING OF THE COUNSELOR, THE HOLY SPIRIT

Jesus had just declared that no one could have access to the Father but by him; yet he juxtaposed this to his statement that he was going away. How will people receive access to the Father without Jesus being there?

Jesus answered this question by his mention that he would pray to the Father to give his disciples **another** Counselor (the Holy Spirit) and by saying that on *that day* the disciples would receive eternal life. Jesus described *that day* as the day the disciples would *know* that they, he, and the Father abide within each other. This is also *the day* that Jesus would send the disciples to be his messengers to prepare people to receive the gift of eternal life, by proclaiming and testifying:

- Jesus is the way to the Father,
- Jesus grants eternal life, and
- Jesus does it through the Holy Spirit.

All of this would happen on *that day*.

THAT DAY WAS THE LAUNCH DAY OF THE NEW COVENANT

Biblical writers used the term *that day* or *the third day* not to indicate a twenty-four-hour period but to signify the occurrence of decisive events. *That day* was used to refer to God's granting the Mosaic Covenant when Israel became God's holy nation, and here again, *that day* was used when Jesus launched the New Covenant by manifesting himself to the disciples in Divine form and baptizing them with the Holy Spirit.

IMPLEMENTATION TEMPLATE

Jesus would implement God's plan for the New Covenant using the same template that God used when he implemented the Mosaic Covenant. The table below displays the three stages of the implementation:

1. The parties coming to agreement
2. God coming to earth on *that day, the third day,*
3. God authorizing his designees to be his agents for implementation

Table 5–3: The three stages of implementation

The stage	Mosaic Covenant	New Covenant
1. Agreement / compliance with God's covenant	If Israel obeyed God's voice and kept his commands, he would prosper Israel as his own possession and holy nation. When the people agreed, God granted them that status. *And all the people answered together and said, "All that the LORD has spoken **we will do**"* (Ex 19:8 RSV).	By the time Jesus had resurrected and was glorified, the disciples had reached compliance with God's commandments. They were ready for Jesus to initiate the New Covenant by granting eternal life to them. *"I have manifested thy name to the men whom thou gavest me...and **they have kept thy word**"* (Jn 17:5 RSAV).
2. God came to earth *that day—the third day.*	God told Moses that he was going to **come down to earth on the third day.** *"Go to the people and consecrate them...and let them be ready by the third day...for on the **third day the LORD will come down** upon Mount Sinai... And Mount Sinai was wrapped in smoke, because the LORD descended upon it in fire...* (Ex 19:10–11, 16 RSV).	After being restored to the glory, he originally had with the Father, the Divine **Jesus** descended from heaven and **came to the disciples on the third day.** *On the evening of **that day, Jesus came and stood among them**...Then the disciples were glad when **they saw the Lord*** (Jn 20:19–20 RSV). They saw God (the glorified Jesus) face-to-face.
3. God authorized his messenger(s) to implement his covenant	God told Moses that he would speak so that the people would hear and respect the authority that God gave him (Moses).	Jesus "sent" the disciples to testify about him. *"...As the Father has sent me, even **so I send you**"*...he

The stage	Mosaic Covenant	New Covenant
	"...Lo, I am coming...that the people may hear when I (God) speak with you (Moses)..." (Ex 19:9 RSV).	*breathed on them, and said to them, "Receive the Holy Spirit"* (Jn 20:21–22 RSV).

KEY DIFFERENCES BETWEEN THE TWO COVENANTS

While the stages of implementing the two covenants are the same, they differ in what God grants, to whom he grants it, and the terms of access.

The Mosaic Covenant: God promised to prosper Israel on earth as his holy nation if they kept his commands. This covenant did *not* include access to eternal life. Therefore, in the end, the Israelites had no access to heaven and would never see God face-to-face because they, like the rest of the world at that time died a permanent death.

The New Covenant: God promises everyone in the world, individual-by-individual, the opportunity to know him and his Son eternally when they demonstrate their love for him by keeping his commandments to believe and love. Setting up the covenant this way means that those who receive the gift of this covenant—eternal life in heaven—will see God face-to-face and it will never be rescinded. John will have more to say about this in his first epistle, which we discuss in the chapters to come.

DID THE DISCIPLES ACTUALLY RECEIVE ETERNAL LIFE?

Much of what Jesus said about his return on *that day* makes it clear that he granted the disciples eternal life.

- The Father will give the disciples another Counselor, the Holy Spirit who is the giver of life[23] to **be with them forever.**
- The world will not see him (Jesus) but the disciples will, because they will *know* him. (The author used the particular Greek word for "*know*" that he consistently used to indicate eternal life).
- Jesus will live after death, and **he stated that because he lives, the disciples will also live after death** (Jn 14:34 RSAV).

---

[23] The Nicene Creed

- After Jesus baptized the disciples with the Holy Spirit, they knew and testified that they abide in Jesus and the Father and they in them (this mutual abiding is how John described eternal life throughout the gospel).

The Holy Spirit (the Spirit of Truth) Is Available to Everyone

> [39]Judas (not Iscariot) said to him, "Lord, how is it that you will manifest yourself to us, and not to the world?" [40]Jesus answered him, "If a man loves me, he will keep my word, and my Father will love him, and we will come to him and make our home with him.
>
> [41]These things I have spoken to you, while I am with you."

THE OPPORTUNITY FOR ETERNAL LIFE IS AVAILABLE TO EVERYONE!

Much of this discourse pertains only to the disciples, and it is true that the glorified Jesus manifested himself only to the disciples because they were to carry Jesus's mission out to the world; for without their testimony, no one would have the opportunity to know that Jesus is the Son of God. However, this is also where Jesus states that the opportunity to *know* him and the Father is available to everyone who fulfill two commandments.

THE NEW COVENANT

Jesus announced that he and the Father would *make their home* (grant eternal life) to those who love him and keep his word. Keeping his word comes down to keeping the two commandments shown in the table below. What is in this table is the New Covenant. It states that God sent his Son so people could be in God's home with him again and what people need to do to receive it.

Table 5–4: The New Covenant

Jesus grants	To people who
Eternal life *"...If a man loves me, he will keep my word, and my Father will love him, and we will come to him and make our home with him."* (Jn 14:40 RSAV)	• Believe Jesus is the Christ, the Son of God • Love one another as their ongoing lifestyle *...believe in the name of his Son Jesus Christ and love one another...* (1 Jn 3:23 RSAV).

The Holy Spirit (the Spirit of Truth) Will Bear Witness

15:1"But when the Counselor comes, whom I shall send to you from the Father, even the Spirit of truth, who proceeds from the Father, he will bear witness to me; and you also are witnesses, because you have been with me from the beginning.

2"I did not say these things to you from the beginning, because I was with you. 3I have said all this to you to keep you from falling away. 4They will put you out of the synagogues, 3and they will do this because they have not known the Father, nor me. 5Indeed, the hour is coming when whoever kills you will think he is offering service to God. 6I have said these things to you, that when their hour comes you may remember that I told you of them. 7But because I have said these things to you, sorrow has filled your hearts.

8Nevertheless I tell you the truth: it is to your advantage that I go away, for if I do not go away, the Counselor will not come to you; but if I go, I will send him to you. 9And when he comes, he will convince the world concerning sin and righteousness and judgment: 10concerning sin, because they do not believe in me; 11concerning judgment, because the ruler of this world is judged; 12concerning righteousness, because I go to the Father, and you will see me no more."

JESUS TOLD THE DISCIPLES WHAT WILL HAPPEN

Because the disciples were his eyewitnesses, Jesus warned them of the arduous future they would encounter. Why was he telling them this now? Jesus would not be with them in his human form again, so he would not be present physically to protect them from those who would attempt to make them fall away.

> "...you will see me no more" (Jn 15:12 RSAV).

It was of upmost importance that the disciples continue to believe in him. So he told them directly that he was telling them these things so they could remember him when his opposition tried to make them distrust and desert him.

> "I have said these things to you, that when their hour comes you
> may remember that I told you of them" (Jn 15:6 RSAV).

Jesus acknowledged their sadness and added that the Holy Spirit (the Counselor), who he was sending to them, would proceed from the Father himself. The Spirit had witnessed Jesus from the beginning to the end; he knew Jesus was the Word incarnate.

- **The beginning:** *"I saw the Spirit descend as a dove from heaven, and it remained on him..."* (Jn 1:31 RSAV).
- **The end:** *...He said, "It is finished;" and he bowed his head and gave up his spirit* (Jn 19:30 RSV).

THE COUNSELOR WILL REFUTE THE WORLD'S OPINION ABOUT JESUS

By being in direct communication with the Father, the Counselor would convict the world's sin, pass judgment on them, and defend Jesus's righteousness:

- **The sin:** Jesus was put to death by the court of the world that claimed he sinned, but they were the ones who sinned because they had the opportunity to believe Jesus was the Son of God but chose not to.

  Though he had done so many signs before them, yet they did not believe in him (Jn 12:37 RSV).

- **The judgment:** When Jesus died on the cross, it appeared that the world's ruler had power over him, but he did not; Jesus's resurrection proved otherwise. The world's ruler convicted himself for putting the Son of God to death. Therefore, the judgment was: the ruler (the evil one) has no power over those to whom Jesus grants eternal life.

  "...he who does not believe is condemned already, because he has not believed in the name of the only Son of God" (Jn 3:18 RSV).

- **Righteousness:** Jesus's willingness to go to the cross and ensuing glorification by the Father proved his acceptability to God. Jesus could not have sent the Holy Spirit to the disciples had he not been glorified, nor would he have been permitted to sit at the right hand of the Father had he not been the innocent and righteous one.

He ascended into heaven and is seated at the right hand of the Father (Nicene Creed).

Since the world could not see or hear the Holy Spirit, how would he convince them of the sin, the judgment, and Jesus's righteousness? The plan was for the disciples to tell the world of these things.

Jesus Is Going in a Little While
What Does "a Little While" Mean?

> [13]"Now I am going to him who sent me; yet none of you asks me, 'Where are you going?' [14]"A little while, and you will see me no more; again a little while, and you will see me."
>
> [15]Some of his disciples said to one another, "What is this that he says to us, 'a little while, and you will not see me, and again a little while, and you will see me'; and, 'because I go to the Father'?" [16]Jesus knew that they wanted to ask him; so he said to them, "Is this what you are asking yourselves, what I meant by saying, 'A little while, and you will not see me, and again a little while, and you will see me'".
>
> [17]They said, "What does he mean by 'a little while'? We do not know what he means."

WHAT IS "A LITTLE WHILE"?
Jesus's preparation of the disciples was working. He had told them numerous times that he was going to the Father, and they presumed the Father was on earth, but they had shifted their thinking. The disciples had accepted that he was going away, but now they wanted to know how soon. The answer was very soon. In only moments, Jesus would be arrested, crucified, and entombed.

When Jesus Goes, the Spirit of Truth Comes

> [18]"I have yet many things to say to you, but you cannot bear them now. [19]When the Spirit of truth comes he will guide you into all the truth; for he will not speak on his own authority, but [20]he will glorify me, for he will take what is mine and declare it to you. [21]All that the Father has is mine; therefore, I said that he will take what is mine and declare it to you. [22]Whatever he hears he will speak, and he will declare to you the things that are to come."

THE COMMUNICATIONS CHAIN

As Jesus guided the disciples while he was with them, the Spirit of truth (Holy Spirit) would do the same when Jesus returned to the Father. The divine communication chain of truth was as follows:

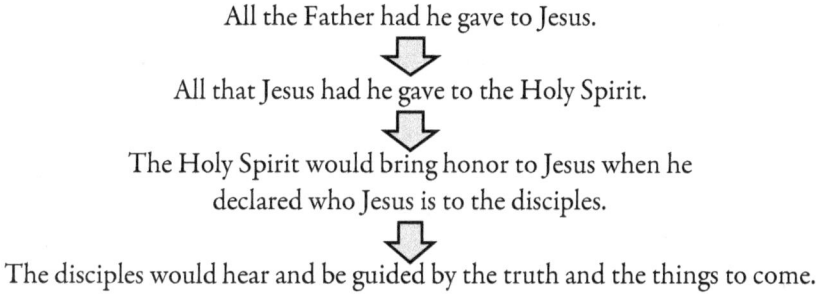

All the Father had he gave to Jesus.

All that Jesus had he gave to the Holy Spirit.

The Holy Spirit would bring honor to Jesus when he declared who Jesus is to the disciples.

The disciples would hear and be guided by the truth and the things to come.

Sorrow Turns to Joy

²³"Truly, truly, I say to you, you will weep and lament, but the world will rejoice; you will be sorrowful, but your sorrow will turn into joy. ²⁴So you have sorrow now, but I will see you again and your hearts will rejoice, and no one will take your joy from you.

²⁵When a woman is in travail she has sorrow, but when she is delivered of the child, she no longer remembers the anguish because her hour has come for joy that a child is born into the world.

²⁶The hour is coming, indeed it has come, when you will be scattered, every man to his home, and will leave me alone; yet I am not alone, for the Father is with me. ²⁷I have said this to you, that in me you may have peace. In the world you have tribulation; but be of good cheer, I have overcome the world."

WHY WILL THE DISCIPLES REJOICE?

Jesus told the disciples they would cry and mourn while the world rejoices but they would rejoice in the end. Why? Jesus's promise to return to them would mean that he succeeded—he overcame the world!

As a mother delivers a child out of her anguish, Jesus's anguish would bring forth freedom from the bondage of sin and death. He would give birth to the new opportunity to live with God in joy and love forever (eternal life). Under God's new plan, once eternal life was granted, no one would take its joy away as happened with Adam and Eve.

GOD'S SALVATION PLAN DOES *NOT* ELIMINATE TRIBULATION

People expected a different kind of salvation than what Jesus brought. God sent his Son to save the world, not from its suffering and afflictions, but from sin and death.

> *"...In me you may have peace. In the world you have tribulation; but be of good cheer, I have overcome the world"* (Jn 16:33 RSV).

The world's troubles will continue, but Jesus's defeat of evil would open the gate to God's kingdom for those believers who keep God's command to love. When they receive eternal life, they will know God's peace even while they are in the world. Jesus is the reason every Christian can have hope, in the face of what the world dishes out.

The Disciples Believe Jesus Came from God

[28]"In that day you will ask nothing of me. [29]I have said this to you in figures; I shall no longer speak to you in figures but tell you plainly of the Father. [30]The hour is coming. I came from the Father and have come into the world; again, I am leaving the world and going to the Father. [31]Do you now believe?" [32]His disciples said, "Ah, now you are speaking plainly, not in any figure! Now we know that you know all things, and need none to question you; by this we believe that you came from God."

WHAT DID THE DISCIPLES BELIEVE?

Jesus finally got through to the disciples. When he asked them if they believed, their answer was yes. What did Jesus say differently to enable them to progress this far in their belief?

Jesus told them that he **came from the Father into the world and would leave the world** to return to the Father. This would have been a totally new thought for the disciples because the world was banished from heaven, so people only knew the dead-end of permanent death—no one could come to the world from the Father and return to the Father again.

However, this was the transformational moment when the disciples finally understood that Jesus's Father did not live down the street; he was in heaven, and they believed Jesus could go back and forth between heaven and the world. With this, the disciples finally believed Jesus came from God.

Ask in My Name and You Shall Receive That Your Joy May Be Full

[33]Jesus answered them, "in that day you will ask in my name, because you have loved me and have believed that I came from the Father. [34]I do not say to you that I shall pray the Father for you; for the Father himself loves you."

[35]"Truly, truly, I say to you, hitherto you have asked nothing in my name; if you ask anything of the Father, he will give it to you in my name. [36]Ask, and you will receive, that your joy may be full."

THE FATHER WILL TRANSFER AUTHORITY TO JESUS

Having told the disciples that they would face difficult times ahead, but he offered them comfort. He told them that the Father himself knew and loved them. He reiterated that whatever they asked in his name, the Father would grant.

While this statement may appear to be a simple offering of support to his disciples after Jesus leaves, its implications were much greater. This was Jesus's announcement of the transfer of authority and power from the Father to him that would happen on *that day*—the day of Jesus's glorification. *That day* was the day when the Father restored Jesus to his original Divine form, and by it, the Father transferred authority and power over all flesh to Jesus so he could give eternal life.

> *"Since thou hast given him power (authority) over all flesh so that*
> *he can give eternal life to all **whom thou has given him**..."* (Jn
> 17:2 RSAV).

Everything related to eternal life would pivot from Jesus from *that day* onward. This is the reason Jesus told the disciples to make their requests to the Father in his name and why their sorrow would turn to joy.

A LOOK AHEAD TO THE NEXT PART OF THIS DISCOURSE

Thus far, Jesus had announced the following:

- His *hour* to leave had arrived.
- He was *the way* to the Father.
- He would send another Counselor, who is the Holy Spirit (the Spirit of truth).
- His exit would bring danger to the disciples.

- He came from the Father into the world and was leaving the world to return to the Father.
- The disciples were loved by the Father, who would grant their requests that are made in Jesus's name.

Now with only moments left, what would Jesus's last words to the disciples be? He had been preparing them to continue his mission since he chose them, so it follows that his focus would be on their upcoming mission.

Jesus Prepares the Disciples for Their Mission
Abide in Jesus and Bear Fruit

> [16:1]"Rise, let us go hence. [2]I am the true vine, and my Father is the vinedresser. [3]Every branch of mine that bears no fruit, he takes away and every branch that does bear fruit he prunes, that it may bear more fruit. [4]As the branch cannot bear fruit by itself, unless it abides in the vine, neither can you, unless you abide in me. [5]I am the vine, you are the branches. He who abides in me, and I in him, he it is that bears much fruit, for apart from me you can do nothing. [6]If a man does not abide in me, he is cast forth as a branch and withers; and the branches are gathered, thrown into the fire and burned."

JESUS IS THE TRUE VINE
Jesus's steps might have appeared to take him closer to his death, but they didn't. They took him to his glorification and his becoming the life-giving vine. So Jesus began to address the disciples' upcoming role by comparing them to the fruit-bearing branches of a vine. New believers are the fruit that will become branches on Jesus's vine. Jesus used this metaphor to emphasize the need for a branch to stay on his vine.

> *"He who abides in me, and I in him, he it is that bears much fruit,*
> *for apart from me you can do nothing"* (Jn 16:5 RSAV).

SOME BRANCHES BEAR FRUIT: SOME DON'T
Becoming a believer puts people on Jesus's vine, but it doesn't mean that they will stay there—that depends on whether they bear fruit. There are two types of branches on Jesus's vine:

1. **Fruit-bearing branches** are believers, and as such, they have access to Jesus's aid. These branches will be pruned (cleansed of useless shoots, a metaphor for being forgiven sin) so they can bear more fruit.

2. **Non-fruit-bearing branches** are people who were once believers but who stopped believing in Jesus. This ended their ability to bear fruit because how could a nonbeliever convince anyone else to believe in Jesus? Therefore, the vinedresser (the Father) will take them away from Jesus's vine to wither, die, and be thrown into the fire.

The Disciples Are Clean by the Word

[7]"You are already made clean by the word which I have spoken to you. [8]Abide in me, and I in you. [9]If you abide in me, and my words abide in you, ask whatever you will, and it shall be done for you. [10]By this my Father is glorified, that you bear much fruit, and so prove to be my disciples."

THE DISCIPLES' MISSION WILL BE SUPPORTED

Jesus reiterated what he told the disciples during the last supper. They were bathed and clean—they were free of all mortal sin.

> *"...and you are clean, but not everyone of you." For he knew who was to betray him; that is why he said, "You are not all clean"* (Jn13:13–14 RSAV).

Therefore, as long as they continue to observe Jesus's words—commands—what they ask will be done for them.

WHAT DOES "PROVE TO BE MY DISCIPLES" MEAN?

The Greek word John used for *disciple* means to be a learner, which was what Jesus's disciples considered themselves to be. They viewed Jesus as their Rabbi and Teacher, but here, Jesus was telling them they had graduated. The time had arrived for them to carry out his lessons in fulfillment of the mission he would give them. This takes discipleship back to its root meaning, which is to become a practitioner of what one learns. Application of what they learned was how disciples would glorify the Father.

The World Hated Jesus

[11]"If the world hates you know that it has hated me before it hated you; but you are not of the world, because I chose you out of the world, therefore the world hates you. [12]If I had not come and spoken to them, they would not have sin; but now they have no excuse for their sin. [13]If I had not done among them the works which no one else did, they would not have sin; but now they have seen and hated both me and my Father. [14]He who hates me hates my Father also. [15]It is to fulfill the word that is written in their law, 'They hated me without a cause.'"

WHY DID THE WORLD HATE JESUS?
Jesus gave the world no cause to hate him.

> *More in number than the hairs of my head are those who **hate me without cause;*** (Ps 69:4 RSV)

At the time that John wrote this gospel, Christians were being persecuted by the Romans and thrown out of the synagogues by the Jews. There is no doubt that John's audience would concur with Jesus's declaration of the world's hatred.[24] By contrast, the essence of God's kingdom is love. So when Jesus said he took his disciples out of the world, he meant their lives were no longer governed by the hatred of the world but by the love of God's kingdom.

WHO HAD NO EXCUSE FOR THEIR SIN?
Hatred was so prevalent, people could easily get caught up in it, but Jesus told them that the way to live was to love one another. It was what God desired. Jesus even showed the world spectacular signs as evidence that he spoke for God; therefore, the world had no excuse for their rejection of him and his works.

> *"... for the works which the Father has granted me to accomplish...*
> *bear me witness that the Father has sent me...you do not believe*
> *him whom he has sent"* (Jn 5:36, 38 RSV).

The world's hatred was the height of irony—those of the world killed the only means of removing their sin and thereby precluded any chance of their receiving eternal life.

---

[24] Brown, *Gospel according to John, XIII–XXI*, 695.

If They Persecuted Me, They Will Persecute You

[16]"Remember the word that I said to you, 'if they persecuted me, they will persecute you. A servant is not greater than his master,' if they kept my word, they will keep yours also. [17]But all this they will do to you on my account, because they do not know him who sent me."

THE DISCIPLES ARE NOT GREATER THAN THEIR MASTER

Jesus told the disciples that they would get the same treatment he did—the good and the bad. If people kept Jesus's word, they would keep the disciples' word; if they pursued, harassed, and mistreated Jesus, they would mistreat them.

Next, Jesus would upgrade the disciples' servant relationship they had with him to that of a friend. However, this won't change how the world would treat them.

Love One Another as I Have Loved You

[18]"As the Father has loved me, so have I loved you; abide in my love. [19]If you keep my commandments you will abide in my love, just as I have kept my Father's commandments and abide in his love. [20]This is my commandment, that you love one another as I have loved you. [21]This I command you, to love one another.

[22]Greater love has no man than this that a man lay down his life for his friends. [23]You are my friends if you do what I command you. [24]No longer do I call you servants, for the servant does not know what his master is doing; but I have called you friends, for all that I have heard from my Father I have made known to you."

THE DISCIPLES WILL BE JESUS'S FRIENDS

As Jesus continued to prepare his disciples, he made sure they knew that he was sharing all that he had heard from the Father with them, including the command to love one another. As Jesus explained it, he was willing to share so much with them because they did what he commanded. Therefore, they were now his friends—associates and allies—no longer his servants. This upgrade in status indicated the importance of their upcoming role in God's plan.

THE BRIDEGROOM'S FRIEND

John the Baptist took the idea of being Jesus's friend a step further than being a well-wishing ally when he called himself such a friend of Jesus that he was like

Jesus's best man.

> *"He who has the bride is the bridegroom (Jesus); the friend (John the Baptist) of the bridegroom, who stands and hears him..."* (Jn 3:29 RSV).

According to Jewish custom, a best man had the responsibility to ask for the hand of the bride. John the Baptist, as the friend (best man), asked for the bride's (Israel's) hand when he gave testimony to the priests and Levites that Jesus was the Son of God. In essence, the Baptist was offering them the opportunity to become God's "bride" under what would be the New Covenant.

When Jesus called the disciples his friends, he was telling them that their job would be to continue what John the Baptist started; however, God's bride would no longer be Israel, but everyone who believes in Jesus. The disciples, as Jesus's *friends* (best men), would testify to him throughout the world.

Table 5–5: The bridegroom, the best man, and the bride

The role	Who	What they do
Bridegroom	Jesus	Offers the opportunity to abide eternally with him and the Father to those who believe in him and commit to live a life of love that he advocates
Friend — Best man	John the Baptist and the disciples	Testify that Jesus is the Son of God and encourage people to believe in Jesus so they have the opportunity to receive eternal life—to be in eternal union with the Father and Son
Bride	People who believe that Jesus is the Son of God	Keep Jesus's commandment to love one another so they can abide with Jesus and the Father eternally

JESUS'S COMMANDMENT

How does a person love Jesus? The answer is straightforward—keep his commandment to love one another.

"This is my commandment, that you to love one another as I have loved you. Greater love has no man than this, that a man lay down his life for his friends" (Jn 16:20, 22 RSAV).

Jesus himself provided the new standard of how to love. It is to love one another (one's friends) to their death if necessary.

Bear Fruit That Your Joy May Be Full

[25]"You did not choose me, but I chose you and appointed you that you should go and bear fruit and that your fruit should abide; so that whatever you ask the Father in my name, he may give it to you.

[26]These things I have spoken to you, that my joy may be in you, and that your joy may be full."

WHAT WERE JESUS'S FINAL WORDS TO HIS DISCIPLES?

Jesus ended his discourse by telling his disciples to go bear fruit that abides. What was this fruit? It was people who believed that Jesus was the Son of God and stuck to it. Jesus told the disciples two more important factors related to this, their mission:

- He chose them for this mission.
- They would be fully supported in that they could ask for whatever they needed in his name and the Father would give it to them.

Jesus's ending on the note of joy was far more than a simple "feel good" conclusion to his making this assignment. He brought an important point of clarity about the two-fold way that joy operates in God's plan. The term *joy* is a reference to the successful completion of a mission assigned by God.

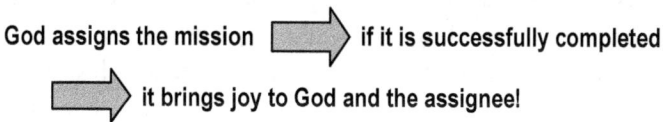

God assigns the mission ➡️ **if it is successfully completed** ➡️ **it brings joy to God and the assignee!**

THE DISCIPLES' JOY

The disciples will know joy two ways, both of which are stated in the passage we cite below.

*"These things I have spoken to you, that **my joy may be in you**, and that **your joy may be full**"* (Jn 16:26 RSAV).

1. **The disciples will know Jesus's joy within them** when he grants eternal life to them. **His victory over death accomplished his God-assigned mission**, and because everyone who receives eternal life abides within the Father and the Son, recipients of eternal life receive Jesus's joy as part of the package.

2. The disciples **will fill-up with more joy** with every new believer they generate as fulfillment of their God (Jesus)-assigned mission.

Conclusion

In this masterpiece, John conveyed Jesus's final lesson to his disciples, in order to:

- Prepare them for the horrific events of his departure to enable them to continue to believe in him.
- Assure them that he would continue to support them after he leaves.
- Prepare them to receive eternal life and to continue his mission of "bearing fruit that abides."

Jesus broke the news that he was leaving, but he couldn't tell the disciples how because he knew they couldn't bear it. So when he began his discourse, the disciples misunderstood much of what he said. If he was leaving and they couldn't go with him, they wanted "real" answers, but Jesus spoke of things they would only understand after he was glorified.

However, Jesus's patience and compassion prevailed such that they finally believed he came from God, enabling Jesus to proceed to discuss their mission to bear fruit and the importance of staying connected to his life-giving vine. Jesus assured them that the Father himself would be available to support them. Jesus concluded with the fact that his own abounding joy from his restoration of eternal life, would be within them and as they have success in their mission, they will generate even more joy.

Throughout this discourse, John brilliantly interwove many core elements of the New Covenant:

- Jesus is *the way* to eternal life; *only* he can unlock the gate to God's kingdom
- Jesus is the truth and the life
- The reason that the glorified Jesus manifested himself only to his disciples
- How to qualify to receive eternal life
- What is new about Jesus's commandment to love one another
- How to demonstrate one's love of God
- What the Counselor (Holy Spirit) provides to believers
- The three who testify to Jesus as being the Son of God
- The divine communications chain of truth: from the Father to Jesus to the Holy Spirit to the disciples
- Why the disciples' witness of Jesus is the linchpin of the continuation of God's plan
- The fact that God's plan does *not* alleviate the world's tribulations and suffering but offers the peace and joy of life eternal with God
- The disciples' God-appointed mission is to bear fruit by developing new believers who stay on Jesus's life-giving vine

This beautifully integrated narrative connected the deep sorrow of Jesus's departure to the height of Jesus's joy that would overflow within the disciples as they carried Jesus's mission onward.

Review of Key Points

In the introduction, we asked you to consider the following questions. What are your answers? Our answers are in appendix D.

Table –5.6: Your answers to the review questions

#	Question	Your answers
1.	Why did the disciples fail to comprehend Jesus's remarks at the beginning of the discourse?	
2.	What did Jesus mean when he said that he was *the way*?	

#	Question	Your answers
	"I am the way... no one comes to the Father, but by me" (Jn 14:19 RSAV).	
3.	Can everyone receive eternal life?	
4.	What is new about Jesus's commandment to love one another?	
5.	How do you know that Jesus was really free to lay down his life? Why is this important?	
6.	What is *that day*? Why is it significant?	
7.	How were the disciples able to do greater works than Jesus?	
8.	What was the role of the disciples in God's plan?	
9.	How would the disciples be assured of success in fulfilling their role?	

#	Question	Your answers
10.	Did Jesus put an end to the world's tribulation?	

What's Next?

Through this discourse, Jesus taught the disciples what they needed to know, but they hadn't yet received eternal life, which they must have to fulfill their mission. Next, Jesus would pray to the Father to be glorified so he could grant eternal life to them.

CHAPTER 6

Farewell Prayer
JOHN 17:1–27 RSAV

Introduction

Since Jesus's disciples were present as he prayed aloud,[25] this prayer is as much a disclosure to them as it was petitions for them and others. Jesus offered this, his priestly prayer, in the same three parts as the high priest Aaron's sacrificial prayer. Aaron prayed for himself, his priestly family, and for the whole people.[26] Jesus prayed for the following:

- His own glorification
- His disciples
- All who believe through the preaching and testimony of his disciples

Jesus's first request was to be restored to his own Divine glory so he could fulfill his mission to grant eternal life. Then, Jesus continued to pray to address the needs of his disciples. He prayed for their safety, sanctification, and receipt of eternal life. They would be his boots on the ground testifying to him. But when they did, they would face the hatred Jesus faced. Yet only through their word would people have the opportunity to know that Jesus is the Son of God who offers eternal escape from the sin and death proffered by the world. The disciples' work would be essential for the future of Christianity.

The poetry of this prayer will carry you to its climatic definition of eternal life. When you see it unfold, the marvel and magnificence of what Jesus offered to the world will be palatable.

---

[25] Brown, *The Gospel According to John, XIII–XXI*, 748
[26] Brown, *The Gospel Accordingl to John, XIII–XXI*, 750

Outline

1. **Jesus Prayed to Be Glorified**
2. **Jesus Prayed for the Disciples**
   a. To Send the Disciples into the World
   b. To Continue to Protect the Disciples from the Evil One
   c. To Give the Glory Jesus Had on Earth to the Disciples
   d. To Give the Disciples Eternal Life
3. **Jesus Prayed for All Who Believe to Have Access to Eternal Life**
4. **John Defined Eternal Life**

What to Look For

Consider the following questions as you read to deepen your comprehension. There is space to write your answers at the end of the chapter. You can find our answers in appendix D.

1. Why does most of this prayer focus on the disciples?
2. Why was Jesus's first request to be glorified?
3. What are the two types of glory mentioned in this prayer?
4. What is eternal life?
5. Who has the opportunity to receive eternal life?

Farewell Prayer
(Jn 17:1–27 RSAV)

Jesus Prayed to Be Glorified

[17:1]When Jesus had spoken these words, he lifted up his eyes to heaven and said, "Father, the hour has come, [2]since thou has given him power over all flesh, so that he can give eternal life to all whom thou has given him. Glorify thy Son that the Son may glorify thee. [3]I glorified thee on earth, having accomplished the work which thou gave me to do; [4]and now, Father, glorify thou me in thy own presence with the glory which I had with thee before the world was made."

Jesus Prayed for the Disciples
To Send the Disciples into the World

[5]"I have manifested thy name to the men whom thou gave me out of the world; thine they were, and thou gave them to me, and they have kept thy word. [6]I am praying for them; I am not praying for the world but for those whom thou has given me, for they are thine; [7]all mine are thine, and thine are mine, and I am glorified in them.

[8]Now they know that everything that thou has given me is from thee; for I have given them the words which thou gave me, and they have received them and know in truth that I came from thee; and they have believed that thou did send me. [9]Sanctify them in the truth; thy word is truth. [10]And for their sake I consecrate myself, that they also may be consecrated in truth. [11]As thou did send me into the world, so I have sent them into the world."

To Continue to Protect the Disciples from the Evil One

[12]"And now I am no more in the world, but they are in the world, and I am coming to thee. [13]I have guarded them, and none of them is lost but the son of perdition, that the scripture might be fulfilled. [14]I have given them thy word; and the world has hated them because they are not of the world, even as I am not of the world. [15]They are not of the world, even as I am not of the world. [16]I do not pray that thou should take them out of the world, but that thou should keep them from the evil one."

To Give the Glory Jesus Had on Earth to the Disciples

[17]"Now I am coming to thee; and these things I speak in the world, that they may have my joy fulfilled in themselves. [18]Holy Father, keep them in thy name, which thou has given me. [19]While I was with them, I kept them in thy name, which thou has given me, that they may be one, even as we are one. [20]The glory which thou has given me I have given to them, that they may be one even as we are one."

To Give the Disciples Eternal Life

[21]"Father, I desire that they also, whom thou has given me, may be with me where I am, to behold my glory which thou has given me in thy love for me

before the foundation of the world. [22]I in them and thou in me, that they may become perfectly one, so that the world may know that thou has sent me and has loved them even as thou has loved me.

[23]O righteous Father, the world has not known thee, but I have known thee; and these know that thou has sent me. [24]I made known to them thy name, and I will make it known, that the love with which thou has loved me may be in them, and I in them."

Jesus Prayed for All Who Believe to Have Access to Eternal Life

[25]"I do not pray for these only, but also for those who believe in me through their word, [26]that they may all be one; even as thou, Father, art in me, and I in thee, that they also may be in us, so that the world may believe that thou has sent me."

John Defined Eternal Life

[27]"And this is eternal life, that they know thee the only true God, and Jesus Christ whom thou has sent."

Commentary

Jesus Prayed to Be Glorified

[17:1]When Jesus had spoken these words, he lifted up his eyes to heaven and said, "Father, the hour has come, [2]since thou has given him power over all flesh, so that he can give eternal life to all whom thou has given him. Glorify thy Son that the Son may glorify thee. [3]I glorified thee on earth, having accomplished the work which thou gave me to do; [4]and now, Father, glorify thou me in thy own presence with the glory which I had with thee before the world was made."

JOHN BEGAN TO NARRATE JESUS FAREWELL PRAYER

The *hour* had arrived for Jesus to conclude what God sent him to do. By his death on the cross and resurrection, he would overcome the power of the evil one to bring the opportunity for enlightenment to everyone (Jn 1:6 RSAV). So what was left to do? Jesus had to be glorified because only when he had been restored to his original Divinity would he have the power and authority to actually grant eternal life by baptizing with the Holy Spirit.

*"He who sent me to baptize with water said to me, 'He on whom you see the Spirit descend and remain, **this is he who baptizes with the Holy Spirit**"* (Jn 1:32 RSAV).

*Now this he said about the Spirit, which those who believed in him were to receive; for as yet **the Spirit had not been given, because Jesus was not yet glorified**"* (Jn 7:39 RSV).

Glorification was Jesus's first request, which would lead to the following:

- Jesus would return to the disciples in glorified form for them to see that he overcame death.
- This is when the disciples would know Jesus is the Son of God.
- Jesus would baptize them with the Holy Spirit, making them the first to receive eternal life that brings ongoing protection from the evil one.
- The disciples would be sanctified and consecrated to be fully prepared to testify and proclaim that Jesus is the Son of God who grants eternal life.

This list of what Jesus would grant to the disciples is a preview of what John described in the scriptural text that follows. However, none of these items would be granted until after Jesus was glorified, even though, as the text was written, it may appear that Jesus was granting or had granted these things. Please keep in mind these things would *not* be consummated until the *third day*, when Jesus returned to the disciples in glorified form. Now with this said, let's return to the prayer and the disciples' status while Jesus was praying for them.

Jesus Prayed for the Disciples
To Send the Disciples into the World

[5]"I have manifested thy name to the men whom thou gave me out of the world; thine they were, and thou gave them to me, and they have kept thy word. [6]I am praying for them; I am not praying for the world but for those whom thou has given me, for they are thine; [7]all mine are thine, and thine are mine, and I am glorified in them.

[8]Now they know that everything that thou has given me is from thee; for I have given them the words which thou gave me, and they have received them and know in truth that I came from thee; and they have believed that thou did send

> me. ⁹Sanctify them in the truth; thy word is truth. ¹⁰And for their sake I consecrate myself, that they also may be consecrated in truth. ¹¹As thou did send me into the world, so I have sent them into the world."

THE DISCIPLES' STATUS

At this point in the prayer, Jesus was praying for his disciples. In his discourse, Jesus had already asked them if they believed, and they said that they believed he came from the Father. So Jesus prayed for their sanctification (to be set apart).

> *"Do you now believe?" His disciples said… "Now we know that you know all things…by this we believe that **you came from God**"* (Jn 15:31–32 RSAV).

The disciples gave Jesus good reasons to pray for their sanctification. They honored Jesus by the following:

- They believed he came from the Father.
- They believed that the Father sent him.
- They received all of Jesus's words and knew that his words came from the Father.

WHAT DOES SANCTIFY IN THE TRUTH MEAN?

Jesus's request to *sanctify* the disciples was for them to be "set apart" from the world—to be made holy bearers of the truth. What is the truth?

Jesus said that God's word was the truth. When God testified to John the Baptist that Jesus is the Son of God who baptizes with the Holy Spirit (grants eternal life), it was the truth. Indeed, the disciples would acquire deep inner knowledge of this truth on the *third day* that will set them apart to be dedicated to this truth, but unlike Israel's priests, their sanctification would not include the granting of holy garments and anointing with oil.

> *"…and put upon Aaron the holy garments, and you shall anoint him and consecrate (sanctify) him, that he may serve me (God) as priest"* (Ex 40:13 RSV).

Jesus's disciples would be sanctified by the Holy Spirit that will be within them. It would be like having a river of living water flowing in their hearts that would bring holiness to their behavior.

WHAT DOES JESUS'S CONSECRATION OF HIMSELF MEAN?

Jesus's consecration of himself was his setting himself apart by his total dedication to God, which he conclusively demonstrated by his willing submission to go to the cross. Jesus said he consecrated himself so his disciples would be able to realize the truth of his being the Son of God and be prepared to proclaim this magnificent truth to the world. Note that what we cite below would indeed happen, but not until the *third day* when Jesus appeared before his disciples.

> *"And for their sake I consecrate (dedicate) myself, that they also may be consecrated (dedicated) in truth. As thou did send me into the world, so I have sent them into the world"* (Jn 17:10–11 RSAV).

To Continue to Protect the Disciples from the Evil One

¹²"And now I am no more in the world, but they are in the world, and I am coming to thee. ¹³I have guarded them, and none of them is lost but the son of perdition, that the scripture might be fulfilled. ¹⁴I have given them thy word; and the world has hated them because they are not of the world, even as I am not of the world. ¹⁵They are not of the world, even as I am not of the world. ¹⁶I do not pray that thou should take them out of the world, but that thou should keep them from the evil one."

JESUS WILL BE UNAVAILABLE TO GUARD THE DISCIPLES

Because the disciples would be set apart—they would be different from those of the world in their dedication to the truth of Jesus as God's Son. Therefore, they would be hated as Jesus was.

> *"...because I chose you out of the world, therefore, the world hates you"* (Jn 16:11 RSAV).

Jesus prayed to the Father to *not* take the disciples out of the world. The world was where they were needed! Instead, he prayed for the Father to keep them safe from the evil one.

THREE PHASES OF PROTECTION

Given the importance of the disciples to God's plan and how vulnerable they would be to the world's hatred, they were protected from the time Jesus selected them to when Jesus left them to go to the Father and, finally, when he granted eternal life to them, which brought eternal protection.

Table 6–1: Three phases of protection of the disciples

Phase	Description	Who protected the disciples
1.	After Jesus selected the disciples and they followed him	Jesus was with them and protected them.
2.	During the period of Jesus's arrest, crucifixion, and ascension to the Father	Jesus would *not* be unavailable, so he asked the Father to protect them.
3.	After the glorified Jesus returned to the disciples and granted eternal life to them	God will eternally protect the disciples and all those who receive eternal life. *We know that anyone born of God does not sin, and the evil one does not touch him* (1 Jn 1:5 RSAV).

To Give the Glory Jesus Had on Earth to the Disciples

> [17]"Now I am coming to thee; and these things I speak in the world, that they may have my joy fulfilled in themselves. [18]Holy Father, keep them in thy name, which thou has given me. [19]While I was with them, I kept them in thy name, which thou has given me, that they may be one, even as we are one. [20]The glory which thou has given me I have given to them, that they may be one even as we are one."

THE DISCIPLES' ROLE

When Jesus said he was coming to the Father, it was actually a reference to the accomplishment of his mission on earth (his death and resurrection). When accomplished, Jesus would transfer his earthly mission to the disciples—he would "send" them. As they fulfilled their mission to bear fruit, the disciples would be vulnerable, so Jesus prayed to the Father to keep the disciples safe in his name. This seems clear, but what did Jesus mean when he said he has given them **his** glory?

THE GLORY JESUS GAVE TO THE DISCIPLES

Jesus said that he gave the disciples the glory that the Father gave him, which, in this case, was *not* the divine glory that the Father gave him. It was a type of glory that is operable in the world that brings a desire to honor each other that Jesus and the Father had. Jesus's glory would enable the disciples to see each other in the light of his loving opinion of them, which would help them cohere as a group and be unified by mutual respect and appreciation.

> *"The glory which thou has given me I have given to them that **they may be one** even as we are one"* (Jn 17:20 RSAV).

Jesus was giving them excellent preparation to be able to live in obedience to God's command to love one another as is required to receive eternal life.

To Give the Disciples Eternal Life

[21]Father, I desire that they also, whom thou has given me, may be with me where I am, to behold my glory which thou has given me in thy love for me before the foundation of the world. [22]I in them and thou in me, that they may become perfectly one, so that the world may know that thou has sent me and has loved them even as thou has loved me.

[23]O righteous Father, the world has not known thee, but I have known thee; and these know that thou has sent me. [24]I made known to them thy name, and I will make it known, that the love with which thou has loved me may be in them, and I in them."

JESUS PRAYED TO GRANT ETERNAL LIFE TO THE DISCIPLES

Jesus not only prayed for the disciples to behold his Divine glory but for them to become perfectly one with him in this glory. Here, Jesus was asking the Father for the disciples to be granted eternal life! When granted, it would fulfill Jesus's mission to restore eternal life, which would launch his ongoing granting of eternal life to believers who live love-based lives.

> *"...I will make it known, that the love with which thou has loved me may be in them, and I in them"* (Jn 17:24 RSAV).

The disciples did behold Jesus's glory! They saw him face-to-face, heard him, and touched him when he returned to them in his Divine glory.

> *...Jesus came and stood among them...he showed them his hands and his side...and...he breathed on them, and said to them "Receive the Holy Spirit* (Jn 20:19–20, 22 RSV).

By their receipt of the Holy Spirit, the disciples would abide in the eternal love and protection of the Son and the Father unceasingly. **This was Jesus's final preparation for them to be sent on their mission of testimony.**

Jesus Prayed for All Who Believe to Have Access to Eternal Life

[25]"I do not pray for these only, but also for those who believe in me through their word, [26]that they may all be one; even as thou, Father, art in me, and I in thee, that they also may be in us, so that the world may believe that thou has sent me.

EVERYONE WHO BELIEVES HAS THE OPPORTUNITY FOR ETERNAL LIFE

Christianity has been and will continue to be disseminated through the words of the disciples. Even if a person heard about Jesus from a family member, friend, or pastor, the foundation of its truth comes from the eyewitness testimony of the disciples. John who wrote this gospel is one of these witnesses.

> *Now Jesus did many other signs in the presence of the disciples, which are not written in this book; but **these are written that you may believe that Jesus is the Christ, the Son of God, and that believing you** may have life in his name* (Jn 20:30 RSV).

Belief is the first step to becoming qualified to receive eternal life, but *not* the only step. In the "Prologue," John said a believer receives the *power* (opportunity) to become born of God but *not* the actual gift of eternal life.

> *But to all who received him, who believed in his name, **he gave the power** to become children of God; who were born of God, not of blood nor of the will of the flesh nor of the will of man* (Jn 1:16 RSAV).

So what does it take to be able receive eternal life as the "new child of God"? The initial step is to believe Jesus is the Son of God; however, it also requires living a love-based life. John will have much more to say about this in subsequent chapters.

John Defined Eternal Life

> ²⁷And this is eternal life, that they know thee the only true God, and Jesus Christ whom thou has sent.

THE WORLD DID NOT *KNOW* GOD, NOT EVEN THE DISCIPLES

To *know* God in the sense that John referred to it here is to *know* God and his Son intimately by being in their ongoing presence. Even the disciples who lived with Jesus before he resurrected did *not know* God in the deep and broad ways that formulate eternal life.

- The Greek word that John used for *life* here connotes a life devoted to God that is real, genuine, full, active, vigorous, and abundantly blessed.

  > *"...I came that they may have life, and have it abundantly"* (Jn 10:10 RSV).

- The Greek word for *eternal* means to be never ceasing. Eternal life is a life defined by love that will always be.
- The Greek word to *know* means to know God not by the five senses but through personal experience. This *knowing* is not a thought, an emotion, a feeling, or a mental perception of God. It is to *know* God by having a felt and intimate involvement with God that Jesus so beautifully modeled.

A person who receives eternal life will live an abundantly blessed life in relation to their devotion to God by *knowing* God experientially and intimately.

THE DIFFERENCE THE NEW COVENANT BROUGHT

Adam and Eve did not make a commitment to love God before they received access to God's home the Garden of Eden; God placed them there. Their life with God was intended to be eternal, but God rescinded it when they chose *not* to love him.

However, those who receive eternal life under God's New Covenant will *not* lose it because believers who receive it will have demonstrated their choice to love God and dedication to doing so, by keeping his commandments before Jesus grants eternal life to them. Therefore, when they receive eternal life, they will be wholeheartedly on board with living a loving life, and by their receipt of eternal life, they will be eternally protected from the temptations of the evil one.

JESUS IS THE WAY TO RECEIVE ETERNAL LIFE NOW

The New Covenant is Jesus based. God sent his Son to save the world and gave him authority over all flesh to grant eternal life.

> *"since thou has given him power over all flesh, so that he can give eternal life..."* (Jn 17:2 RSAV).

To receive eternal life, people must believe that Jesus is the Son of God; if they didn't, how could they believe Jesus would be able to give them eternal life with God? Only God could do that!

WHEN DOES ETERNAL LIFE BEGIN?

As a recipient of eternal life, John made it clear that eternal life begins when Jesus grants it. John stated that eternal life is available while a person is alive, as it was for the disciples. In his first epistle, John acknowledged the young men who were alive and active in his community who had received eternal life because they overcame the evil one.

> *I write to you, young men, because you are strong, and **the word of God abides in you, and you have overcome the evil one**** (1 Jn 2:16 RSAV).

After all, what other lifetime does a person have to obtain eternal life? Pope Emeritus Benedict XVI, an eminent theological scholar, draws the same conclusion.

> *"Eternal life" is not—as the modern reader might immediately assume—life after death, in contrast to this present life, which is transient and not eternal. "Eternal life" is life itself, real life, **which can also be lived in the present age**...and is no longer challenged*

by physical death. This is the point: to seize "life" here and now, real
life that can no longer be destroyed by anything or anyone. [27]

Conclusion

If God did *not* send Jesus to be the healer of every sick and disadvantaged person, what did all of Jesus's signs, healings, teachings, and encounters add up to? God sent Jesus on a larger mission. It was to save the world from sin and death.

> *"I have said to you, that in me you may have peace. In the world you*
> *have tribulation; but be of good cheer, I have overcome the world"*
> (Jn 15:27 RSAV).

Jesus's signs and healings were intended to garner the world's attention for when Jesus's *hour* arrived. Then, he would manifest the quintessence of God's glory by his resurrection, which was the climactic completion of his mission on earth. Jesus's return to the disciples in glorified form to grant eternal life to them confirmed his defeat of death. This was when Jesus *sent* them to continue his mission on earth.

In this prayer, Jesus asked for their success, sanctification, and protection. He knew they would encounter the hatred of many. He also knew that it was only a matter of days before they would receive the ultimate protection from the evil one by his granting them eternal life.

Indeed, Jesus's prayer was answered. He overcame the world, and for all who believe, he provided the opportunity to be granted eternal unity with the love of the Father and Son. Jesus's completion of his earthly mission led to its transfer to his direct disciples to continue to advance it, which continues to this day by disciples who have followed after them.

Review of Key Points

In the introduction, we asked you to consider the following questions. What are your answers? Our answers are in appendix D.

---

[27] Joseph Ratzinger Pope Emeritus Benedict XVI, *Jesus of Nazareth Part Two*, 82.

Table 6–2: Your answers to the review questions

#	Question	Answer
1.	Why does most of this prayer focus on the disciples?	
2.	Why was Jesus's first request to be glorified?	
3.	What are the two types of glory mentioned in this prayer?	
4.	What is eternal life?	
5.	Who has the opportunity to receive eternal life?	

What's Next?

The focus of John's gospel is to enable people to believe that Jesus Christ is the incarnate Word of God who came to save the world by restoring eternal life. However, to receive eternal life, believers must also live a love-based life. John wrote the following three epistles to explain the requirements for receiving eternal life in more detail.

4

1 John

## CHAPTER 7

1 John
John's Proclamation of Eternal Life
1 John 1:1-10 RSAV

Introduction

JOHN'S INTRODUCTION TO THIS LETTER

John wrote to his community of believers to urge them to do what was needed to complete their journey to eternal life. In only ten verses, John recounted how eternal life was lost by Adam and Eve's fall and was irrevocably restored by Jesus. John, the beloved disciple who received eternal life directly from Jesus, compellingly proclaimed and testified to the magnificence of this great gift. He and the other disciples experienced the epitome of the love and joy that comes from having this *fellowship* (eternal life) with God and his Son.

JOHN'S PROPOSITION

As John positioned eternal life, there is no reason to delay in incorporating God's commands into one's day-to-day behavior because the opportunity to receive the assurance of eternal life can be had during a believer's own lifetime. Those who receive it while still living may not yet be able to see God face-to-face, but they will have the opportunity to experience a joyous life with God and his Son while they currently live in the world.

This opportunity may be different from what some Christian denominations say is possible. Should you read this letter? Yes! One important reason is to find out what John says to do to receive eternal life, no matter when it is granted.

Outline

1. **John Testified to Eternal Life**
2. **John Proclaimed Jesus Is the Word of Life**
3. **What John Knew**
4. **The Challenge**

What to Look For

Consider the following questions as you read to deepen your comprehension. There is space to write your answers at the end of the chapter. You can find our answers in appendix D.

1. Who is Jesus?
2. What is fellowship as John refers to it?
3. What qualified John to write of eternal life?
4. What is the difference between how Adam and Eve received eternal life and what believers must do to receive it today?
5. What is the difference between the way the disciples received the Holy Spirit and how believers thereafter receive it?
6. What are the benefits of receiving eternal life while a person is still alive?

John's Proclamation of Eternal Life
(1 John 1:1–10 RSAV)

John Testified to Eternal Life

1:1That which was from the beginning, concerning the word of life, which we have heard, which we have seen with our eyes, which we have looked upon and touched with our hands. 2That which we have seen and heard we proclaim also to you, so that you may have fellowship with us and our fellowship is with the Father and with his Son Jesus Christ.

John Proclaimed Jesus Is the Word of Life

3The life was made manifest, which was with the Father and was made manifest to us. We saw it, and testify to it, and proclaim to you the eternal life.

⁴We are writing this that our joy may be complete.

What John Knew

⁵We know that any one born of God does not sin, and the evil one does not touch him. ⁶He who was born of God keeps him, ⁷and we know that the Son of God has come and has given us understanding to know him who is true; and we are in him who is true.

⁸This is the true God and eternal life his Son Jesus Christ.

The Challenge

⁹We know that we are of God, and the whole world is in the power of the evil one. ¹⁰Little children, keep yourselves from idols.

Commentary

John Testified to Eternal Life

¹:¹That which was from the beginning, concerning the word of life, which we have heard, which we have seen with our eyes, which we have looked upon and touched with our hands. ²That which we have seen and heard we proclaim also to you, so that you may have fellowship with us and our fellowship is with the Father and with his Son Jesus Christ.

WHAT ARE JOHN'S FIRST WORDS?

John immediately recounted his eyewitness of the Divine Jesus, who came to the disciples after he "died" on the cross. They saw with their own eyes the glorified Jesus face-to-face. They heard and touched Jesus in his Divine form. They touched God! Without question, they knew that Jesus defeated death.

> *Jesus came and stood among them and said to them, "Peace be with you"...he showed them his hands and his side...And when he had said*

this, he breathed on them, and said to them, "Receive the Holy Spirit" (Jn 20:19–20, 22 RSV).

From John's experience of receiving the breath of the glorified Jesus (God), he knew the following:

- Eternal life is real.
- He actually received it.
- He was living in that high state with God and his Son.

For these reasons, John was entirely qualified and compelled to write of eternal life.

THE PROPOSITION OF THIS LETTER

John used the term *fellowship* to signify eternal life. John's choice of this term colors eternal life as being relational; it is being in an ongoing and intimate relationship with God and his Son. Having eternal *fellowship* would be like having a loving companion at one's side to protect and share love and joy forever. John intended to explain how believers can take part in this *fellowship*, not after they die but as they live.

John Proclaimed Jesus Is the Word of Life

³The life was made manifest, which was with the Father and was made manifest to us. We saw it, and testify to it, and proclaim to you the eternal life.

⁴We are writing this that our joy may be complete.

THE ESSENTIAL TESTIMONY

John testified that he and the disciples saw Jesus visibly, audibly, and tangibly alive after he died on the cross and ascended to the Father. John and the other disciples witnessed Jesus in glorified form when he returned to grant eternal life to them.

> *God raised him on the third day and made him manifest; **not to all the people but to us who were chosen** by God as witnesses...* (Acts 10:40–41 RSV).

Jesus "sent" his disciples to bear witness so all people have the chance to believe Jesus is God's Son, and in so believing, have the opportunity to receive eternal life. The disciples' declaration of Jesus's return and all that he did was an essential part of God's plan.

> *"I do not pray for those only, but also for those who believe in me through their (the disciples') word, that they may all be one; even as thou, Father, art in me, and I in thee...* (Jn 17:25–26 RSAV).

WHAT IS COMPLETE JOY?

John associated having joy with the successful completion of God's appointed mission. Jesus appointed and sent the disciples to go and bear fruit (bring believers to Jesus's vine).

> *"...I chose you and appointed you that you should go and bear fruit and that your fruit should abide..."* (Jn 16:25 RSAV).

As the disciples fulfilled their mission believer-by-believer, the joy they shared with Jesus would grow more and more complete.

> *"These things I have spoken to you, that my joy may be in you, and that your joy may be full"* (Jn 16:26 RSAV).

John's statement about joy was a pronouncement of the purpose of this letter. John's goal was to generate the three-way joy that would arrive when someone receives eternal life—the recipient, the disciples, and Jesus.

What John Knew

> [5]We know that any one born of God does not sin, and the evil one does not touch him. [6]He who was born of God keeps him, [7]and we know that the Son of God has come and has given us understanding to know him who is true; and we are in him who is true.
>
> [8]This is the true God and eternal life his Son Jesus Christ.

JESUS IS THE TRUE GOD

The disciples described Jesus by many titles during their time with him.

- A holy man
- The Messiah
- A prophet
- A rabbi
- The king of Israel

By the end of Jesus's farewell discourse, the disciples believed that he came from God. Now, having been with the glorified Jesus, the disciples were far beyond belief about Jesus's identity; they absolutely *knew* Jesus was the true God. Thomas uttered this realization when he touched the wounds that the glorified Jesus still carried and exclaimed, "My God!"

*Thomas answered him, "My Lord and **my God!**"...* (Jn 20:28 RSV).

Rudolf Schnackenburg[28] and Raymond Brown,[29] two of the most prominent biblical scholars of the twentieth century recognized and affirmed without reserve the truth of John's reference to Jesus being the true God.

THE DISCIPLES' REALIZATION

Imagine how awesome it must have been for the disciples to realize the following:

- They had been with the Word of God all the while they had walked by Jesus's side.
- They actually saw and touched Jesus in Divine form after he returned to them from the Father.
- They received eternal life through the Holy Spirit from Jesus's very breath.

The disciples were alive, conscious, and able to comprehend these things so they could testify to them.

---

[28] Schnackenburg, *Das Johannesevangelium*, 263; 304.

[29] Raymond E. Brown, S.S., *The Anchor Bible*; *v.* 30, "The Epistles of John" (New York: Doubleday, 1982) 626.

THE DISCIPLES RECEIVED ETERNAL LIFE DIFFERENTLY FROM HOW OTHER BELIEVERS WOULD

The disciples had no doubt that they received Jesus's baptism with the Holy Spirit—they felt Jesus's breath when he infused God's nature (seed) into them. However, unlike the disciples, other believers would *not* know when they received eternal life. Jesus described the process as undetectable when he said that the Spirit would come like the wind.

> *"The wind blows where it wills, and you hear the sound of it, but you do not know whence it comes or whither it goes; so it is with everyone who is born of the Spirit"* (Jn 3:8 RSV).

John will elaborate on what people should do to discern if they are on track to receive eternal life and whether they have received it, throughout the rest of this letter, but the fundamental answer is to *keep* his commandments, which is to pay continual attention to:

- Believing in Jesus so his support is always available and
- Loving God and others in word and deed,

HOW CAN ETERNAL LIFE BE GRANTED TO SOMEONE WHO IS ALIVE?

It is understandable that the disciples received eternal life while they were living because they were chosen and appointed to testify about it. But what about everyone else? If they receive eternal life in advance of their death and then slip up and sin, how could they be allowed to enter God's kingdom? Wouldn't God have to turn them away as he did Adam and Eve? You might think the answer is yes, but the New Covenant addresses this another way.

Before Jesus grants eternal life, believers must demonstrate their love of God by sufficiently keeping his commandments, which they do this by living a love-based lifestyle. Eventually, these believers will reach the point where they simply would *not* choose to commit a "mortal" sin. When a believer reaches this point, Jesus will grant eternal life that will *not* be rescinded.

> *He who was born of God **keeps him**,* (1 Jn 1:6 RSAV).

THE WAY ETERNAL LIFE WORKS

After believers receive eternal life, which is to become born of God, they will be safely in Jesus's fold forever and unsusceptible to the deadly lure of the evil one.

We know that any one born of God does not sin and the evil one does not touch him (1 Jn 1:5 RSAV).

Why would this be God's plan? Logically, we can say it will maximize the love in the world. Believers will be motivated to turn toward love and build love-based habits because the sooner they do, the sooner they will have the opportunity to abide in God's eternal protection, joy, and love. Their love of others will generate more love and harmony in the world and motivate others to pursue a love-based lifestyle. It is a win/win/win proposition all the way around.

ETERNAL LIFE IS AVAILABLE NOW

John based this letter on the premise that it is possible to receive eternal life while a believer is alive, and he wrote to urge believers to turn toward love so they may have confidence on Judgment Day.

Perfect love casts out fear, that we may have confidence for the day of judgment, because as he is so are we in this world (1 Jn 4:17 RSAV).

This core message *of seizing (eternal) life now* continues to be preached to this day. We cite Pope Emeritus Benedict XVI because he is considered to be one of the great biblical scholars of the modern age. He states eternal life is available within one's own lifetime and emphasizes the importance of seizing such "real" life now.

*"Eternal life" is not—as the modern reader might immediately assume—life after death, in contrast to this present life, which is transient and not eternal. "Eternal life" is life itself, real life, which can also be lived in the present age and is no longer challenged by physical death. This is the point: to **seize "life" here and now**, real life that can no longer be destroyed by anything or anyone.*[30]

The Challenge

[9]We know that we are of God, and the whole world is in the power of the evil one. [10]Little children, keep yourselves from idols.

---

[30] Joseph Ratzinger Pope Emeritus Benedict XVI, *Jesus of Nazareth, Part Two*, 82.

IDOLATRY IS THE CHALLENGE—FELLOWSHIP IS THE GOAL

Having received the magnificent gift of eternal life and knowing what being in God's loving realm is like, John was able to see how pervasive and deadly idol worship was. When people choose anything that leads to thoughts, words, and actions that are not love-based, idol worship of some form is behind it. John's advice was to stay away from these false gods!

Conclusion

John opened this letter with a proclamation of the magnificent gift of eternal life. Jesus brought a huge reason to turn toward love. As things stood before Jesus arrived, permanent death was the only option, even for good people. John provided a breathtaking overview of God's plan to restore a glorious new option—eternal life, and he backed it up with proclamations and testimonies that are foundational to Christianity.

- John stated Jesus is the true God who brings the opportunity for eternal fellowship with himself and the Father.
- John clearly stated that believers may have eternal life while alive so that they may have confidence for the Day of Judgment.
- John stated that when a believer receives eternal life (becomes born of God), he or she will keep it.

God offers every believer the opportunity to receive eternal life, but because freewill is always in play, people must choose to opt in. Evil actively operates in the world, and false gods that become idols abound, but the opportunity for salvation gives hope. John encouraged his readers to take advantage of it and seize eternal life now!

Review of Key Points

In the introduction, we asked you to consider the following questions. What are your answers? Our answers are in appendix D.

Table 7–1: **Your answers to the review questions**

#	Question	Your Answers
1.	Who is Jesus?	
2.	What is *fellowship* as John referred to it?	
3.	What qualified John to write of eternal life?	
4.	What is the difference between how Adam and Eve received eternal life and what today's believers must do to receive it?	
5.	What is the difference between the way the disciples received the Holy Spirit and how believers thereafter receive it?	
6.	What are the benefits of receiving eternal life while a person is still alive?	

What's Next?

Next, John addressed what Jesus will do to help believers stay on track for the receipt of eternal life.

CHAPTER 8

The Message
1 John 2:1–3:30 RSAV

Introduction

IS ETERNAL LIFE REAL?

The prior chapter's proclamation of Jesus's restoration of eternal life was revolutionary. Before Jesus arrived, the world's destiny was permanent death. There was no access to heaven except for the most exceptional people, such as Moses. How would John persuade his audience of eternal life's validity? You will see his strategy unfold in this chapter through his declaration and explanation of the promise (*the message*) that Jesus made regarding eternal life.

John will state that eternal life was restored by Jesus's blood, which is such a powerful force of love that it counteracted the dearth of love (the sin) that Adam and Eve instigated and that the world has exhibited ever since. John will explain how Jesus forgives sin in three all-encompassing ways and that he provides the guidance through the Holy Spirit that would enable people to develop the loving lifestyle needed to receive eternal life. John will cover the following: the need to confess sins, the difference between mortal and nonmortal sin, and the key pitfall to avoid in regard to one's sins.

JOHN PROVIDED LIVING EXAMPLES AND NONEXAMPLES

John will identify the fathers and young men in his own community as winners in the match-up against evil. They, as recipients of eternal life, proved its attainability. However, John also issued a dire warning about antichrists, who could stop believers, dead in their tracks if they succumbed to the antichrists' unforgivable sin. Antichrists are still operating today, and John will explain how to identify who they are.

JOHN ANNOUNCED THE NEW COMMANDMENT

The center of this chapter is John's announcement of the New Commandment with tips on how to keep it. John introduced a new prayer support network that is another tool to help people keep the commandment to love one another. John's goal was for all believers to be able to meet Jesus with confidence when he comes again.

Outline

1. **Believe in Jesus**
   a. Jesus Cleanses Us from Sin and All Unrighteousness
   b. Pitfalls to Avoid
   c. Jesus Forgives and Guides Us
   d. Have Confidence in His Coming
2. **Status of the Believing Community**
   a. Believers Born of God
   b. Believers Who Stopped Believing in Jesus (Antichrists)
   c. Believers at Risk of the Temptations of the World
   d. How Believers Can Know Their Status
3. **Believe Jesus is The Son of God**
4. **Love One Another**
   a. Don't Be Like Cain to Be Born of God
   b. The Disciples Know They Are Born of God
   c. How Do Believers Know They Are Born of God?
      i. **Test the Spirits**
      ii. **Keep the New Commandment**
5. **The Gift of Being Born of God: Ask and Receive Prayer**

What to Look For

Consider the following questions to deepen your comprehension of what you read. There is space to write your answers at the end of the chapter. You can find our answers in appendix D.

1. What are the two parts of the New Commandment?
2. What are the three categories of sin that Jesus forgives?
3. What is confession?
4. What does Jesus the advocate do?
5. What is the pitfall that will keep even sincere believers from receipt of eternal life?

6. Who are the antichrists; what is their unforgivable sin?
7. What is the old commandment; how is it now new?
8. What did Cain fail to do that is a lesson for believers today?
9. How do you identify any of the following: a false prophet, the antichrist, and the spirit of error?
10. What is the Ask and Receive Prayer?
11. What is the difference between mortal sin and nonmortal sin?

The Message
(1 Jn 2:1–3:30 RSAV)

Believe in Jesus
Jesus Cleanses Us from Sin and All Unrighteousness

²⁾¹This is the message we have heard from him and proclaim to you; ²that God is light and in him is no darkness at all and the blood of Jesus his Son cleanses us from all sin. ³If we confess our sins, he is faithful and just, and will forgive our sins and cleanse us from all unrighteousness.

Pitfalls to Avoid

⁴If we say we have no sin, we deceive ourselves, and the truth is not in us. ⁵If we say we have not sinned, we make him a liar, and his word is not in us.

⁶If we say we have fellowship with him while we walk in darkness, we lie and do not live according to the truth; ⁷but if we walk in the light, as he is in the light, we have fellowship with one another.

Jesus Forgives and Guides Us

⁸My little children, I am writing this to you so that you may not sin; but if any one does sin, ⁹he is the expiation for our sins, and not for ours only but also for the sins of the whole world.

¹⁰We have an advocate with the Father, Jesus Christ the righteous.

Have Confidence in His Coming

¹¹I am writing to you, little children, because your sins are forgiven for his sake.

[12]And now, little children, abide in him, so that when he appears we may have confidence and not shrink from him in shame at his coming.

Status of the Believing Community
Believers Born of God

[13]I am writing to you, fathers, because you know him who is from the beginning. [14]I write to you, fathers, because you know him who is from the beginning.

[15]I am writing to you, young men, because you have overcome the evil one. [16]I write to you, young men, because you are strong, and the word of God abides in you, and you have overcome the evil one.

[17]I write to you, children, because you know the Father.

Believers Who Stopped Believing in Jesus (Antichrists)

[18]Children, it is the last hour and as you have heard that antichrist is coming, so now many antichrists have come therefore, we know that it is the last hour. [19]They went out from us, but they were not of us; but they went out, that it might be plain that they all are not of us. [20]For if they had been of us, they would have continued with us, [21]but you have been anointed by the Holy One, and you all know. [22]You know that no lie comes from the truth. [23]Who is the liar, but he who denies that Jesus is the Christ. [24]This is the antichrist, he who denies the Father and the Son. [25]No one who denies the Son has the Father. He who confesses the Son has the Father also.

[26]I write to you, not because you do not know the truth, but because you know it.

Believers at Risk of the Temptations of the World

[27]Do not love the world or the things in the world. [28]For all that is in the world is not of the Father but is of the world: [29]the lust of the flesh and the lust of the eyes and the pride of life. [30]And the world passes away, and the lust of it. [31]Let what you heard from the beginning abide in you. [32]If what you heard from the beginning abides in you, then you will abide in the Son and in the Father, [33]and this is what he has promised us, eternal life. [34]As for you, the anointing which

you received from him abides in you, as his anointing teaches you about everything, and is true, and is no lie. [35]You have no need that any one should teach you; just as it has taught you, abide in him.

[36]I write this to you about those who would deceive you.

How Believers Can Know Their Status

[37]And by this we may be sure that we know him, if we keep his commandments. [38]Whoever keeps his word, in him truly love for God is perfected. By this we may be sure that we are in him.

[39]He who says "I know him" but disobeys his commandments, is a liar, and the truth is not in him. [40]He who says he abides in him ought to walk in the same way in which he walked. [41]He who says he is in the light and hates his brother is in the darkness still. [42]He who hates his brother is in the darkness and walks in the darkness, and does not know where he is going, because the darkness has blinded his eyes.

[43]He who loves his brother abides in the light, and in it there is no cause for stumbling.

Believe Jesus Christ Is the Son of God

[44]Beloved, I am writing you no new commandment, [45]yet I am writing you a new commandment which is true in him and in you, [46]and the true light is already shining because the darkness is passing away. [47]Yet an old commandment which you had from the beginning, the old commandment is the word which you have heard.

Love One Another
Don't Be Like Cain to Be Born of God

[3:1]For this is the message, which you have heard from the beginning, that we should love one another, [2]and not be like Cain who was of the evil one and murdered his brother, because his own deeds were evil and his brother's righteous. [3]And why did he murder him? [4]Anyone who hates his brother is a murderer, and you know that no murderer has eternal life abiding in him.

[5]If anyone has the world's goods and sees his brother in need, yet closes his heart against him, how does God's love abide in him? [6]By this we know love that we ought to lay down our lives for the brethren, because he laid down his life for us.

The Disciples Knew They Were Born of God

[7]Do not wonder, brethren, that the world hates you. [8]He who does not love abides in death. [9]We know that we have passed out of death into life, because we love the brethren. [10]And by this we know that he abides in us, by the Spirit, which he has given us.

[11]Beloved don't believe every spirit, but test the spirits to see whether they are of God; for many false prophets have gone out into the world. [12]They are of the world, therefore what they say is of the world, and the world listens to them. [13]We are of God. [14]Whoever knows God listens to us, and he who is not of God does not listen to us. [15]By this we know the spirit of truth and the spirit of error.

How Believers Can Know They Are Born of God
Test the Spirits

[16]By this you know the Spirit of God: every spirit which confesses that Jesus Christ has come in the flesh is of God, [17]and every spirit which does not confess Jesus is not of God. [18]This is the spirit of antichrist, of which you heard that it was coming, and now it is in the world already.

[19]Little children, you are of God, and have overcome them; for he who is in you is greater than he who is in the world.

Keep the New Commandment

[20]Little children, let us not love in word or speech but, in deed and in truth. [21]By this we shall know that we are of the truth, because we keep his commandments and do what pleases him. [22]All who keep his commandments abide in him, and he in them. [23]And this is his commandment, that we should believe in the name of his Son Jesus Christ and love one another, just as he has commanded us.

The Gift of Being Born of God: Ask and Receive

[24]Reassure our hearts before him, whenever our hearts condemn us; for God is greater than our hearts, and he knows everything and we receive from him whatever we ask. [25]Beloved, if our hearts do not condemn us, we have confidence before God.

[26]And this is the confidence, which we have in him; if we ask anything according to his will he hears us. [27]If any one sees his brother committing what is not a mortal sin he will ask, and God will give him life for those whose sin is not mortal. [28]All wrongdoing is sin, but there is sin, which is not mortal. [29]There is sin which is mortal. I do not say that one is to pray for that.

[30]And if we know that he hears us in whatever we ask, we know that we have obtained the requests made of him.

Commentary

Believe in Jesus
Jesus Cleanses Us from Sin and All Unrighteousness

[2:1]This is the message we have heard from him and proclaim to you; [2]that God is light and in him is no darkness at all and the blood of Jesus his Son cleanses us from all sin. [3]If we confess our sins, he is faithful and just, and will forgive our sins and cleanse us from all unrighteousness.

THE FIRST PART OF THE *MESSAGE*

John laid out what he heard directly from Jesus regarding eternal life. He noted its significance by using a particular Greek word *angelia*, which means promise[31] for the term *message*, which John would use only one other time in all of his writings, which was when he returned to continue *the message* later in this chapter. His repetition of this word was how he cued his listening audience to make the connection between what God promises and what believers must do to receive it.

---

[31] http://classic.net.bible.org/strong.php?id=1860

The *message* is God's promise of eternal life that Jesus will restore and make attainable by the cleansing of sin. John began the *message* with the idea that for people to be with God eternally, they must come out of the dark (sin) and into alignment with God's light. God sent his Son to incarnate and create a new means for people to develop a light-filled (sin-free) life.

Table 8–1: The beginning of the *message*

This is the **message**...God is light and in him is no darkness at all...(1Jn 2:1–2 RSAV) The message is that God has sent his Son to restore eternal life but sinfulness bars access.		...and the blood of Jesus his Son **cleanses us from all sin** (1Jn 2:2 RSAV). God sent Jesus to help believers deal with their sin so they may receive eternal life.

WHO ARE THE "US" WHO WILL BE CLEANSED OF ALL SIN?

The answer to this question reveals the key to this *message*. The "us" were those who believed that Jesus is God's Son. If a person does not have the foundational belief that Jesus is the incarnate Word on earth, Jesus's forgiveness of sins and granting of eternal life would not be credible because only God can do those things.

> *And when Jesus saw their faith, he said to the paralytic, "My son your sins are forgiven." Now some scribes were sitting there questioning in their hearts... "It is blasphemy! Who can forgive sins but God alone?"* (Mk 2:5–7 RSV)

John advocated for people to believe in Jesus as the first step to take toward eternal life. John was dealing with the repercussions of some believers who had fallen away and were tempting others to do the same. But before John got to this, he had more to say about the pitfalls of sin and the forgiveness that Jesus offers. The *message* states, Jesus's cleansing is by his blood.

WHAT DID JOHN MEAN BY JESUS'S BLOOD?

Under the New Covenant, Jesus's blood is linked to the granting of eternal life because it represents Jesus's death that led to his resurrection and glorification that enabled him to grant eternal life. Jesus's blood also relates to his forgiveness of sin—all thoughts and deeds that violate God's commands.

> *...And he took the cup... "Drink of it, all of you; for this is **my**
> **blood of the covenant**, which **is poured out for many for**
> **the forgiveness of sins**"* (Mt 26:27–28 RSV).

The table below describes how Jesus covers all the bases of forgiveness.

Table 8–2: Three categories of sin

#	The categories of sin	What Jesus does for believers
1.	The original sin of Adam and Eve	When people come to believe in Jesus, he cancels the consequence of Adam and Eve's sin. By this, Jesus unlocks the gate to heaven, but he does *not* open it until the believer demonstrates the desire and ability to live a love-based life.
2.	All sins committed by new believers prior to their coming to belief	When people come to believe in Jesus, he forgives all sins that they committed up to that moment. If a believer died at that moment, he or she would be pure enough to receive eternal life.
3.	Ongoing sins that believers confess to Jesus	Upon their request, Jesus continues to give believers the opportunity to be cleansed from their nonloving thoughts, words, and deeds so they can live more lovingly.

Scholar Raymond Brown cites four other scholars (Hoskyns, Schneider, B. Weiss, and Wilder) who reinforce points 2 and 3 above as aids to walking in the light.

> *When people first believe and come to the light, their sins are*
> *forgiven. They may sin again; yet if they try to walk in the light, the*
> *blood of Jesus, which cleanses from all sin, cleanses from these sins as*
> *well.* [32]

---

[32] Brown, Notes, and Commentary, *The Anchor Bible: The Epistles of John,* 202.

WHAT CONFESSION IS, AND WHY IS IT NECESSARY?

Because people have freewill, Jesus doesn't automatically wipe a person's slate of sins clean every time they sin unless they expressly ask Jesus to forgive their sins. Confession is the term used for this. To confess a sin is to *stop denying it* and sincerely repent. Confession entails the following:

- Recognizing the sin
- Actually admitting it
- Being willing to acknowledge its harm
- Sincerely intending to not commit the sin again

To confess a sin is an act of faith in Jesus's mercy. It is completely different from a confession in a worldly setting where justice requires punishment for wrongdoing to balance the scales. A confession to Jesus elicits his merciful forgiveness because he is true to God's love and mercy.

FORGIVE AND CLEANSE

Why did John differentiate forgiveness from cleansing? Forgiveness sends a sin away.

> *"For I will be merciful toward their iniquities, and I will remember their sins no more"* (Heb 8:12 RSV).

After the sin is sent away, the sinner may still have residual guilt or a felt loss of dignity and self-esteem. Jesus's forgiveness also cleanses this residue that could interfere with the believer's development of a love-based lifestyle.

Pitfalls to Avoid

[4]If we say we have no sin, we deceive ourselves, and the truth is not in us. [5]If we say we have not sinned, we make him a liar, and his word is not in us.

[6]If we say we have fellowship with him while we walk in darkness, we lie and do not live according to the truth; [7]but if we walk in the light, as he is in the light, we have fellowship with one another.

WHAT *NOT* TO DO

With Jesus available to forgive and cleanse sin, why wouldn't people reach out for his forgiveness? It appears some believers in John's community didn't. Two misunderstandings about eternal life could be behind this.

1. People mistakenly think that when they come to belief, they receive eternal life and are protected from the evil one. Therefore, they presume that they do *not* sin anymore, but this is *not* true.
2. People mistakenly think that because all their past sins were forgiven when they came to belief, Jesus continues to automatically forgive their sins. However, this isn't the case because Jesus honors freewill, which means that believers must expressly ask for Jesus's forgiveness.

Both situations are pitfalls because they lead people down the slippery slope of *not* dealing with their sins.

BOTH GROUPS STILL WALK IN DARKNESS (THEY SIN)

Believers in the first group were either blind to their sin or they deliberately choose *not* to admit their missteps. They were leading themselves astray by their blindness and self-deception.

> *If we say we have no sin, we deceive ourselves, and the truth (God's seed) is not in us* (1 Jn 2:4 RSAV).

People in the second group, who claimed they have not sinned, make Jesus seem like a liar because he promised to grant eternal life to those who do not sin. Maybe they were confused as to when Jesus grants eternal life, or maybe they claimed not to sin because they wanted to look "good," but they didn't fool John or Jesus. John called them out on the pitfall that has them trapped and said the Word was not in them, meaning they did *not* have eternal life.

Both situations are ways people sabotage their chance for having *fellowship* with God (eternal life) by sinning and not admitting it. How do they get out of the dark? Anyone in the first group needs to face the truth; the second group must keep Jesus's word. In both cases, John was telling them to look more closely at their words and deeds and turn to Jesus to forgive their sins.

Jesus Forgives and Guides Us

[8]My little children, I am writing this to you so that you may not sin; but if any one does sin, [9]he is the expiation for our sins, and not for ours only but also for the sins of the whole world.

[10]We have an advocate with the Father, Jesus Christ the righteous.

WHAT IS JESUS'S EXPIATION?

John restated his reason for writing, which was to clarify what believers need to do to have *fellowship* with God and his Son. It comes down to keeping God's commands, but if believers miss the mark and sin, John advised them to turn to Jesus because he is the *expiation* for their sins.

Expiation is what Jesus accomplished by his majestic act of loving obedience to God through his death and resurrection. The love that motivated his action released the consequence of Adam and Eve's sin that destined the world to permanent death. Does this mean that everyone in the world can go to heaven now? Yes, in that everyone has the opportunity, but only if they choose to love God by keeping his commandments to believe and love.

WHAT DOES JESUS THE ADVOCATE DO?

Jesus's saving work for the world did not end with his death and resurrection over two thousand years ago; this is when it began! In the text we are considering, the word *advocate* in Greek refers to a person who functions two ways: as someone who gives aid to another and as someone who pleads another's cause. The Father gave Jesus the power and authority to do both.

> *Since thou hast given him power over all flesh, so he can give eternal life...* (Jn 17:2 RSAV).

- Jesus comes to the aid of believers. He has the **power** to forgive sins, which frees believers from habits of sin and self-recrimination so they can develop a love-based lifestyle.
- Jesus advocates for believers, who are qualified to be granted eternal life.

By his righteousness (willingness to keep God's commands), Jesus ascended to the Father where he is seated at his right hand to act on behalf of his flock of believers. But since Jesus is no longer on earth, how does he come to their aid?

JESUS WORKS THROUGH THE HOLY SPIRIT

This Greek word for *advocate* is also the word John used to refer to the Holy Spirit and the Spirit of truth who are one and the same. Jesus provides aid through the Holy Spirit who is the communications link between him and those on earth.

When the Spirit of truth (the Holy Spirit) comes he will guide you into all the truth; for he will not speak on his own authority, but...he will take what is mine and declare it to you. (Jn 15:19 –20 RSAV).

Jesus will be actively involved in the life of believers through the Holy Spirit; all they need do is ask!

Have Confidence in His Coming

> [11]I am writing to you, little children, because your sins are forgiven for his sake. [12]And now, little children, abide in him, so that when he appears we may have confidence and not shrink from him in shame at his coming.

HOW CAN JOHN SAY YOUR SINS ARE FORGIVEN?

When people come to belief, Jesus forgives all their past sins and continues to forgive the sins that they confess. Therefore, John was telling them to continue to abide in Jesus, so they will be ready for him when he comes again. What do believers need to do to *abide*? Two things:

1. They must not depart from their belief in Jesus as the Son of God; otherwise, he cannot forgive any future sins they may commit and certainly *not* grant them eternal life.
2. They must keep his commandment to love one another by living a love-based life.

John believed that the hour of Jesus's return was near, so he urgently advised his disciples to remain in God's love.

Children...so now many antichrists have come therefore, we know that it is the last hour (1 Jn 2:18 RSAV).

Status of the Believing Community
Believers Who Are Born of God

> [13]I am writing to you, fathers, because you know him who is from the beginning. [14]I write to you, fathers, because you know him who is from the beginning. [15]I am writing to you, young men, because you have overcome the evil one. [16]I write to you, young men, because you are strong, and the word of God abides in you, and you have overcome the evil one.
>
> [17]I write to you, children, because you know the Father.

THE FATHERS AND YOUNG MEN HAVE RECEIVED ETERNAL LIFE

The fathers who *knew* Jesus as the Word of life (who is from the beginning) received eternal life. Because John stated the young men overcame the evil one and that the Word of God (Jesus) *abided* in them, he was stating that they had received eternal life. The fathers and the young men are shining examples of rock-solid faith leading to eternal life.

John showcased the fathers because they were some of the first who were *not* Jesus's direct disciples who had received eternal life. The young men were not old enough to have seen Jesus; so they came to belief through the disciples' word taught by the next generation of teachers, who were most likely the fathers. They are exemplars for believers to emulate.

> *"I do not pray for these (disciples) only, but also for those who believe in me through their word"* (Jn 17:25 RSAV).

The young men were living proof that God's plan was working.

> *Jesus said to him (Thomas), "Have you believed because you have seen me? Blessed are those who have not seen and yet believe"* (Jn 20:29 RSV).

People can be swayed by others in positive ways as the young men were, but people can also be swayed in negative ways, which John took up next.

Believers Who Stopped Believing in Jesus (Antichrists)

[18]Children, it is the last hour and as you have heard that antichrist is coming, so now many antichrists have come therefore, we know that it is the last hour. [19]They went out from us, but they were not of us; but they went out, that it might be plain that they all are not of us. [20]For if they had been of us, they would have continued with us, [21]but you have been anointed by the Holy One, and you all know.

[22]You know that no lie comes from the truth. [23]Who is the liar, but he who denies that Jesus is the Christ. [24]This is the antichrist, he who denies the Father and the Son. [25]No one who denies the Son has the Father. He who confesses the Son has the Father also.

[26]I write to you, not because you do not know the truth, but because you know it.

JOHN'S CONCERN ABOUT THE ANTICHRISTS

Some members of John's community who once believed in Jesus as the Christ and the Son of God changed their minds. Because they had the opportunity to know the truth but rejected it and now denied Jesus, they were antichrists.

> *"If I had not come and spoken to them, they would not have sin; but now they have no excuse for their sin. He who hates me hates my Father also"* (Jn 16:12, 14 RSAV).

Antichrists stand in opposition to God himself. The logic is as follows:

When people deny that Jesus is the Christ, they deny that he is the Son, who God sent to save the world.

This denial means they deny the Son's incarnation as Jesus.

Therefore, they deny Jesus is the Son of God.

Denial of Jesus as God's Son is ultimately a denial of the Father.

They will *not* receive Jesus's forgiveness of sin or be granted eternal life, because they are committing the *unforgivable sin*.

WHAT IS THE UNFORGIVABLE SIN?

The unforgivable sin is the sin of a believer who stops believing Jesus is the Christ and Son of God. This sin is not only against God and his Son, it is also against the Holy Spirit who Jesus grants to believers to guide and support them after they come to belief.

> *"Therefore, I tell you, every sin and blasphemy will be forgiven men,* **but the blasphemy against the Spirit will not be forgiven**" (Mt 12:31 RSV).

Jesus cannot forgive this sin because he honors humanity's freewill to choose whether to believe in him or not. Since God gave Jesus sole authority to forgive sin, these people cannot receive his forgiveness, so they have no hope of eternal life—their fate is permanent death. The only way out is for these unbelievers to choose to change. If they repent, they will receive the all-merciful God's forgiveness.

THE ANTICHRISTS ARE A SERIOUS THREAT

Because the antichrists who John mentioned were community members who could have been neighbors and relatives, John wanted his audience to realize that it was appropriate for those who no longer believed in Jesus to leave. Those who remained would continue to have access to the Holy Spirit to rely on. Therefore, they should let the antichrists go.

> ... *his anointing teaches you about everything, and is true, and is no lie* (1 Jn 2:34 RSAV).

Believers at Risk of the Temptations of the World

²⁷Do not love the world or the things in the world. ²⁸For all that is in the world is not of the Father but is of the world: ²⁹the lust of the flesh and the lust of the eyes and the pride of life. ³⁰And the world passes away, and the lust of it. ³¹Let what you heard from the beginning abide in you. ³²If what you heard from the beginning abides in you, then you will abide in the Son and in the Father. ³³And this is what he has promised us, eternal life. ³⁴As for you, the anointing which you received from him abides in you, as his anointing teaches you about everything, and is true, and is no lie. ³⁵You have no need that any one should teach you; just as it has taught you, abide in him.

³⁶I write this to you about those who would deceive you.

DO *NOT* LOVE THE WORLD

John urged believers *not* to succumb to love of the world, but to hold fast to Jesus the true God, who had restored access to God's great gift of eternal life.

> *That, which was from the beginning, concerning the word of life...We saw it, and testify to it, and proclaim to you the eternal life* (1 Jn 1:1, 3 RSAV).

What is love of the world? John placed it under the blanket of lust and pride. Lust is a longing that generates excessive and depraved desires; pride is failure to trust God.

- **Lust of the flesh** represents the cravings that feed the temporary physical nature of a human as opposed to spiritual nature that is ongoing.

- **Lust of the eyes** represents the desires generated from what one sees. Physical sight only observes the visible, whereas spiritual sight is where the invisible and invincible truth lies.

  Jesus said... "I came into this world, that those who do not see may see, and that those who see may become blind" (Jn 9:39 RSV).

- **Pride of life:** The Greek word for life in this passage, *bios*[33], means biological life, a reference to worldly life, not eternal life. Pride is more than boastful talk or excessive focus on worldly wealth, goods, and accomplishments. A person with pride thinks all life's problems can be solved through his or her own human abilities and ingenuity—that he or she can be self-sufficient without God, as Adam and Eve did.

Lust and pride may bring pleasures, but they always pass away. However, the evil one's toxic formula has not passed away. These deceptions are still effective. How can you discern what to love and who to listen to? Believers have the Holy Spirit who serves as an on-call guide to lead those who choose to listen to him, to know what the true loving choices are.

How Believers Can Know Their Status

[37]And by this we may be sure that we know him, if we keep his commandments. [38]Whoever keeps his word, in him truly love for God is perfected. By this we may be sure that we are in him.

[39]He who says "I know him" but disobeys his commandments, is a liar, and the truth is not in him. [40]He who says he abides in him ought to walk in the same way in which he walked. [41]He who says he is in the light and hates his brother is in the darkness still. [42]He who hates his brother is in the darkness and walks in the darkness, and does not know where he is going, because the darkness has blinded his eyes.

[43]He who loves his brother abides in the light, and in it there is no cause for stumbling.

---

[33] http://classic.net.bible.org/strong.php?id=979.

THE WAY TO BE SURE

Both of the following questions can be answered by keeping God's commandments.

1. How does one receive eternal life?
2. How does one know if Jesus has granted it?

To *keep* his commandments, as John referred to the word *keep* here, is to pay continual attention to the following:

- Never stop believing in Jesus so his support is always available
- Loving God and others in word and deed

WHY DOES JOHN BRING UP HATE?

Hate is basically the opposite of love. Hate is a feeling of such strong dislike that John gives three reasons for its danger:

- It puts people in the darkness—it is an emotion that blindsides reason.
- It leads to walking in the darkness—hate is such a strong emotion it triggers hurtful behavior.
- It leads to not knowing where you are going—hate is blinding because it narrows perception and that leads to mental fog and insensitivity.

The way out is to turn toward the light of God's love, which expands one's perception and triggers empathy and compassion. This plays out as loving one's brother.

Believe Jesus Christ Is the Son of God

[44]Beloved, I am writing you no new commandment, [45]yet I am writing you a new commandment which is true in him and in you, [46]and the true light is already shining because the darkness is passing away. [47]Yet an old commandment which you had from the beginning, the old commandment is the word which you have heard.

Jesus Is the New Element in the Old Commandment

John introduced the "old" commandment to love, in order to convey the difference Jesus makes. When people become believers, they become attached to "Jesus's vine" so they can succeed at loving one another.

> *For this is the message, which you have heard from the beginning, that we should love one another* (1 Jn 3:1 RSAV).

The first and most significant way Jesus made the "old" commandment completely new was by his restoration of eternal life. For the first time since Adam and Eve, people could have the hope of receiving eternal life with the loving God instead of facing permanent death. This is the most powerful reason to choose to bypass the evil lures of the world. However, eternal life was *not* the only reason that John could say that the light was already shining. Jesus also helps believers perfect their love by providing the following:

- Ongoing and personalized guidance through the Holy Spirit
- Forgiveness of sins
- Complete cleansing of unrighteousness

What Is True in Jesus and You?

Jesus made God's love "real" in the world by what he said and did, and this is what people who aspire to follow Jesus's commands must do—make God's love "real" in the world by what they say and do. As they progress toward complete love-based living, their observance of the commandment to love becomes more true to the love that Jesus made visible in the world.

Love One Another
Don't Be like Cain to Be Born of God,

$^{3:1}$For this is the message, which you have heard from the beginning, that we should love one another, ^{2}and not be like Cain who was of the evil one and murdered his brother, because his own deeds were evil and his brother's righteous. ^{3}And why did he murder him? ^{4}Anyone who hates his brother is a murderer, and you know that no murderer has eternal life abiding in him.

^{5}If anyone has the world's goods and sees his brother in need, yet closes his heart against him, how does God's love abide in him? ^{6}By this we know love that we ought to lay down our lives for the brethren, because he laid down his life for us.

THE COMPLETION OF THE *MESSAGE*

This is where John completed the core *message* he introduced at the beginning of this chapter. He alerted his audience to this by repeating the word for "message," *angelia*. In today's lingo, he was saying, "Listen up; I'm about to say more about the *message*, and here it is!"

This part of the *message* states what humanity must do to be "counted in." They must meet God's love with their own deeds of love. John acknowledged loving one another had been God's commandment from the beginning; however, Jesus had brought three new aspects to this commandment.

- Jesus brought ongoing support to believers through his forgiveness and cleansing activities and the guidance of the Holy Spirit so they will be able to be successful in keeping this new commandment.
- Jesus upped the ante in regard to the extent to which a person should be willing to help a fellow believer, which is to be willing to give one's life if necessary.
- Jesus unlocked the gate to heaven that had been closed since Adam and Eve, so the outcome for living a love-based life is to experience life with the loving God forever.

Table 8–3: The *message* in its entirety

This is the message...God is light and in him is no darkness at all...(1 Jn 2:1–2 RSAV) The message is that eternal life is now available, but sinfulness bars access.	*and the blood of Jesus his Son cleanses us from all sin* (1 Jn 2:2 RSAV). God sent Jesus to restore eternal life and help people deal with sin.	*For this is the message you have heard from the beginning, that we should love one another* (1 Jn 3:1 RSAV). Believers must live love-based lives.

WHY DOES JOHN BRING UP CAIN?

Why would John use the Genesis story of Cain, who murdered his brother, to convey the requirement to love one another? While this story confirmed that loving one another had been God's desire from the beginning, John turned this story into an important lesson by identifying where evil initiates its ugly work. This is important because this is where evil must be conquered.

We pick up with Cain after he and his brother made their offering to God. God looked with favor on Abel and his offering but not on Cain and his offering because, as John said, he (Cain) was of the evil one. Was Cain destined to always be evil? The answer is no.

People are at choice, and God gave Cain the key choice. When God saw Cain's anger, he told him that if he did what was right, he (God) would accept him. But if Cain did *not* do what was right, sin would be crouching (lying snake-like[34]) at his door (the entrance to his heart) to conquer him.

> *The LORD said to Cain, "Why are you angry...If you do well, will you not be accepted? And if you do not do well, sin is crouching at the door;* ***its desire is for you, but you must master (subdue) it***" (Gen 4:6–7 RSV).

Cain made his choice—he invited his brother to the field and killed him.

THE POWER OF THOUGHTS AND EMOTIONS

This story illustrates what all believers face on their journey to God. Evil is always ready to "mess with their minds," and their minds are where they can and must conquer evil. John stated that hate is the same as murder because hatred is the evil thought that can close one's heart to love and lead to the evil deed, which, in this example, is murder.

Nonloving thoughts lead to nonloving behavior. Mastery over thoughts and emotions is the way to open one's heart so it can be a loving home for God's love.

THE NEW LEVEL OF LOVING ONE ANOTHER

In contrast to Cain's closed-hearted murder, Jesus's open-hearted love led him to lay down his own life for the people of the world. When believers are able to reach this depth of open-hearted love, Jesus will grant them eternal life.

---

[34] http://classic.net.bible.org/strong.php?id=07257

John forthrightly stated that believers ought to be willing to lay down their own lives for fellow Christians to help brothers in need. John was not saying they would necessarily be called to lay down their lives, but that they ought to consider themselves bound by this level of love. This is the new standard that Jesus brought to the "old" commandment.

The Disciples Knew They Were Born of God

[7]Do not wonder, brethren, that the world hates you. [8]He who does not love abides in death. [9]We know that we have passed out of death into life, because we love the brethren. [10]And by this we know that he abides in us, by the Spirit, which he has given us.

[11]Beloved don't believe every spirit, but test the spirits to see whether they are of God; for many false prophets have gone out into the world. [12]They are of the world, therefore what they say is of the world, and the world listens to them. [13]We are of God. [14]Whoever knows God listens to us, and he who is not of God does not listen to us. [15]By this we know the spirit of truth and the spirit of error.

LOVE TAKES YOU FROM DEATH TO LIFE

For John, the divide between life and death was clear. To hate is the same as murder because neither are of love, and nonlove leads to eternal death. Love, as the *message* states, leads to eternal life. How could John be so sure? Because he and the other disciples received eternal life physically from the glorified Jesus. It was a sensate experience that no one else would receive in the same way.

> *...he breathed on them, and said to them "Receive the Holy Spirit"* (Jn 20:22 RSV).

The disciples knew they were born of God, and they knew the Spirit they received was God's Spirit. Those guided by the spirit of error, such as the antichrists and false prophets, were out there. So John advised his audience to test the spirits they listen to.

How Believers Can Know They Are Born of God
Test the Spirits

[16]By this you know the Spirit of God: every spirit, which confesses that Jesus Christ has come in the flesh is of God, [17]and every spirit which does not confess Jesus is not of God. [18]This is the spirit of antichrist, of which you heard that it was coming, and now it is in the world already.

> [19]Little children, you are of God, and have overcome them; for he who is in you is greater than he who is in the world.

HOW TO TEST THE SPIRITS

The first way to identify false spirits is to listen to what they purport of Jesus. If they do *not* say Jesus is the Christ, the Son of God who came in the flesh, they are the spirit of the antichrist. If the world listens to them, it will be to their own demise because correct belief about Jesus is the essential starting point of the journey to eternal life. The apostle Paul had this to say about the spirit of the antichrist:

> *But I am afraid that as the serpent deceived Eve...your thoughts will be led astray from a sincere and pure devotion to Christ...For such men are false apostles, deceitful workmen, disguising themselves as apostles of Christ* (2 Cor 11:3, 13 RSV).

John told his audience of believers that the Holy One they received upon coming to belief was far greater than that of the antichrists who clearly did not confess Jesus.

Keep the New Commandment

> [20]Little children, let us not love in word or speech but, in deed and in truth. [21]By this we shall know that we are of the truth, because we keep his commandments and do what pleases him. [22]All who keep his commandments abide in him, and he in them. [23]And this is his commandment, that we should believe in the name of his Son Jesus Christ and love one another, just as he has commanded us.

THE QUINTESSENTIAL COMMANDMENT

John synthesized the two core elements of the Christian path to eternal life into the following concise commandment that couples the need to believe in Jesus and love one another.

> *And this is his commandment, that we should **believe in the name of his Son Jesus Christ** and **love one another**...* (1 Jn 3:23 RSAV).

Believers who keep this commandment, not for obedience sake but in the spirit of loving God, will receive eternal life.

THE FINE POINTS OF LOVING ONE ANOTHER

How does a person fulfill the love command? John said people must do the following:

- Base their lives on love such that they love one another as an ongoing lifestyle
- Walk the talk— actualize loving thoughts and words into deeds
- Practice deeds according to what pleases God

Those who desire eternal life must become a people of the covenant, which is *the message* that John stated in this letter.

The Gift of Being Born of God: Ask and Receive Prayer

[22]Reassure our hearts before him, whenever our hearts condemn us; for God is greater than our hearts, and he knows everything and we receive from him whatever we ask. [23]Beloved, if our hearts do not condemn us, we have confidence before God.

[24]And this is the confidence, which we have in him; if we ask anything according to his will he hears us. [25]If any one sees his brother committing what is not a mortal sin he will ask, and God will give him life for those whose sin is not mortal. [26]All wrongdoing is sin, but there is sin, which is not mortal. [27]There is sin which is mortal. I do not say that one is to pray for that.

[28]And if we know that he hears us in whatever we ask, we know that we have obtained the requests made of him

THE PRAYER OF THOSE WHO ARE BORN OF GOD

Those who are born of God receive the gift of prayer that is similar to what Jesus granted to his disciples. The prayer's key feature is that it comes with the assurance of it being fulfilled (in God's timeframe) if presented under the conditions that John set out. Think of this prayer as a power prayer because what is asked for is guaranteed to be granted.

"If you abide in me, and my words abide in you, ask whatever you will, and it shall be done for you" (Jn 16:9 RSAV).

The first condition of its use is that the person who invokes it, is born of God (has received eternal life). Throughout this letter John has plainly told his community how to receive eternal life. Here, he reinforced what he told them before. If they were keeping God's word out of their love for God, they shouldn't let their consciences (heart) play mind games with them! He assured them that God knew the goodness of their hearts, whether they believe it at that moment or not. Therefore, they should not judge themselves too harshly in relation to using this prayer.

THE ELEMENTS OF THE PRAYER

Those who pray this prayer also need to keep in mind that whatever the request may be, it will ultimately bring more "life" to the beneficiary. What is this life? It is *not* eternal life per se because no human can grant eternal life; it is the capacity to live more lovingly.

Table 8–4: The elements of the Ask and Receive Prayer

#	Question	Answer
1.	Who can activate this prayer?	Those who are born of God and are currently clean of nonmortal sin.
2.	What can they pray for?	Anything that is according to God's will. John referred to seeing a brother who commits a nonmortal sin as an example of what to pray for.
3.	What is the one thing that cannot be prayed for?	Mortal sin, which is sin that is deliberate and so severe that it will lead to permanent death, is not covered in this prayer. The person who commits these sins must personally confess them to Jesus.
4.	What does the recipient receive?	The request that will be granted in God's timing, will bring more "life"—a more vigorous and robust loving life, but *not* eternal life, because only Jesus can grant eternal life.

ARE THOSE BORN OF GOD REALLY FREE OF ALL SIN?

Those who are born of God are free of all mortal sin but *not* necessarily all sin. They do sin, but it is *not* the kind of sin that would preclude them from receiving eternal life.

- **Mortal sin** is the deliberate and severe violation of the love and/or belief components of the New Commandment. Such violation leads to permanent death. To get such sin released, believers must **confess** their actions to Jesus, who will provide forgiveness and cleansing.
- **Nonmortal sin** is a less severe or unintentional violation of the New Commandment. It does *not* lead to permanent death.

People who are born of God still commit nonmortal sins, and as John has said, they need to deal with them. They need to be "clean" before using the Ask and Receive Prayer. Jesus referred to this issue when he told his disciples they needed to wash each other's feet. He said they (the disciples) were "clean" and did not need to wash overall, but their feet would collect road dust (sins). This metaphor refers to the accumulation of nonmortal sins precipitated by walking on the dusty road of life.

> *"If I then, your Lord and Teacher, have washed your feet, you also ought to wash one another's feet. He who has bathed does not need to wash, except for his feet, but he is clean all over..."* (Jn 13:12–13 RSAV).

Conclusion

John brought fantastic news in this chapter. He confirmed that generations of people after the disciples have withstood the lures of the antichrists and the lust and the pride of the world to the point of receiving eternal life! John's proclamation of heaven on earth is now attainable because of Jesus. This is the *message* of the New Covenant.

Table 8–5: The *message* in its entirety

Eternal life is available in the here and now through Jesus's death and resurrection, but humanity's sinfulness bars access.		God sent Jesus to restore eternal life and to help people deal with sin to receive this life.		To receive eternal life, people must believe Jesus is the Christ, the Son of God, and live a love-based life.

*And this is his commandment, that we should **believe in the name of his Son Jesus Christ** and **love one another**, just as he has commanded us* (1 Jn 3:23 RSAV).

The way to keep this command is not by words alone but by actualizing words into deeds that formulate a loving lifestyle.

Even when the world's temptations take people off track, John explained how Jesus supports them as their advocate. However, John also made it clear that Jesus's assistance can only be in partnership with those who believe in him. When believers are willing to face and admit their sins, Jesus is ready, willing, and able to forgive and cleanse their unrighteousness.

In addition, Jesus grants the Holy Spirit to believers to provide guidance in all truth. He has even set up a "prayer network" among those who are born of God to support their fellow Christians. Indeed, Jesus has made all things new in regard to humanity's opportunity to be with God eternally.

Had John said all he needed to say? No. Next, he would turn to the big picture of God's plan to further explain how the parts all fit together.

Review of Key Points

In the introduction, we asked you to consider the following questions. What are your answers? Our answers are in appendix D.

Table 8–6: Your answers to the review questions

#	Question	Your Answers
1:	What are the two parts of the New Commandment?	
2.	What are the three categories of sin that Jesus forgives?	
3	What is confession?	
4.	What does Jesus the Advocate do?	
5.	What is the pitfall that will keep even sincere believers from receipt of eternal life?	
6.	Who are the antichrists; what is their unforgivable sin?	
7.	What is the old commandment; how is it now new?	
8.	What did Cain fail to do that is a lesson for believers today?	
9.	How does one identify any of the following: a false prophet, the antichrist, and the spirit of error?	

#	Question	Your Answers
10.	What is the Ask and Receive Prayer?	
11.	What is the difference between mortal sin and nonmortal sin?	

What's Next?

Next, John would provide an overview of the key elements of God's plan: the goal, the approach, and the testimony to substantiate it.

## CHAPTER 9

God's Plan
1 John 4:1–30 RSAV

Introduction

In the prior chapter, John announced Jesus's new version of the old commandment to love one another. In this chapter, John defined the very essence of God as being love. Therefore, believers must meet God's love with their love as the basis of their life. Love is the very foundation of God's plan for the restoration of eternal life.

God has *not* changed nor has his command for people to love him and one another, but Jesus transformed the arrangement. He brought the new magnificent outcome of eternal life to believers who choose the path of love; he demonstrated what love-based living looks like, and he provided new means of support to believers in their quest for living a love-based life.

This chapter will cover how God's plan for the restoration of eternal life came about and how it will work.

- God gave the entire world a love-based alternative to the destiny of permanent death that existed during the banishment era.
- God sent Jesus to demonstrate how the *love begets love* circuit works through his life on earth, death, resurrection, and glorification.
- As a human, Jesus showed the way by lovingly walking step-by-step in alignment with God's will, no matter what the world threw at him, including his death on the cross.
- God put Jesus in charge of all flesh for the granting of the great gift of eternal life.

John concluded this chapter by coming back, full circle, to God's love that led him to send his Son to save the world from a destiny of contending with evil and death. Having faith in the love of God's Son is now the key.

Outline

1. **The Goal: Love One Another to Be Born of God**
2. **The Approach**
   a. God Sent His Son, Jesus
      i. **God's Love was Made Manifest in Jesus, His Son**
      ii. **Obey God's Commands: Love God; Love Your Brother**
      iii. **Perfected Love**
   b. Testimony About Jesus and His Mission
      i. **The Disciples Testify**
      ii. **The Spirit Testifies**
      iii. **True Believers Testify**
   c. Faith in Their Testimony

What to Look For

Consider the following questions as you read to assist in deepening your comprehension. There is space to write your answers at the end of the chapter. You can find our answers in appendix D.

1. What is God's fundamental essence?
2. How is God's love perfected in a person?
3. How does perfected love cast out fear?
4. Who testifies to Jesus?
5. What is faith?

God's Plan
(1 Jn 4:1–30 RSAV)

The Goal: Love One Another to Be Born of God

4:1Beloved, let us love one another; for love is of God since God is love. He who loves is born of God and knows God. 2He who does not love does not know God. 3Beloved, if God so loved us, we also ought to love one another. 4If we love one another, God abides in us and his love is perfected in us.

The Approach
God Sent His Son, Jesus
God's love was made manifest in Jesus, his Son

[5]No man has ever seen God. [6]In this the love of God was made manifest among us that God sent his only Son into the world. [7]In this is love, not that we loved God but that he loved us and sent his Son to be the expiation for our sins so that we might live through him.

Obey God's Commands: Love God; Love Your Brother

[8]Whoever confesses that Jesus is the Son of God, God abides in him, and he in God. [9]God is love, and he who abides in love abides in God, so we know and believe the love God has for us.

[10]We love, because he first loved us. [11]If any one says, "I love God," and hates his brother, he is a liar; for he who does not love his brother whom he has seen, cannot love God whom he has not seen.

[12]And this commandment we have from him, that he who loves God should love his brother also. [13]By this we know that we love the children of God, when we love God and obey his commandments. For this is the love of God, that we keep his commandments. And his commandments are not burdensome.

Perfected Love

[14]Everyone who believes that Jesus is the Christ is a child of God, and everyone who loves the parent loves the child. [15]In this is love perfected with us. [16]There is no fear in love; for fear has to do with punishment, and he who fears is not perfected in love. [17]Perfect love casts out fear that we may have confidence for the day of judgment, because as he is so are we in this world.

Testimony About Jesus and His Mission
The Disciples Testify

[18]By this we know that we abide in him and he in us, because he has given us of his own Spirit. [19]And we have seen and testify that the Father has sent his Son as the Savior of the world.

The Spirit Testifies

[20]This is he who came by water and blood, not with the water only but with the water and the blood Jesus Christ. [21]There are three witnesses, and these three agree, the Spirit, the water, and the blood. [22]And the Spirit is the witness, because the Spirit is the truth. [23]And this is the testimony, God gave us eternal life, and this life is in his Son. [24]He who has the Son has life; he who has not the Son of God has not life.

True Believers Testify

[25]If we receive the testimony of men, the testimony of God is greater; for this is the testimony of God that he has borne witness to his Son. [26]He who does not believe God has made him a liar, because he has not believed in the testimony that God has borne to his Son.

[27]He who believes in the Son of God has the testimony in himself.

Faith in Their Testimony

[28]I write this to you who believe in the name of the Son of God, that you may know that you have eternal life. [29]For whatever is born of God overcomes the world, and who is it that overcomes the world, but he who believes that Jesus is the Son of God. [30]This is the victory that overcomes the world, our faith.

Commentary

The Goal: Love One Another to Become Born of God

[4:1]Beloved, let us love one another; for love is of God since God is love. He who loves is born of God and knows God. [2]He who does not love does not know God. [3]Beloved, if God so loved us, we also ought to love one another. [4]If we love one another, God abides in us and his love is perfected in us.

LOVE IS THE FOUNDATION

Only here, in all Scripture, is God defined as love. This, God's essential identity of love, is the basis for his plan. Since everything in God's realm pivots around the central point of his love, it stands to reason that to know God eternally, people must make love the central point of their lives, which is in concurrence with God's core command to love one another. Love was God's intention from the beginning.

> For God created man for incorruption, and made him in the **image of his own eternity**, but through the devil's envy death entered the world, and those who belong to his party experience it (Wisdom 2:23–24 RSV).

When believers keep God's commandment to love, they will receive eternal life. John defined this cumulation of love as God's love being *perfected*, which means that when a believer lives lovingly so consistently, he or she will have carried through God's command to love completely. It will be considered as accomplished.

The Approach
God Sent His Son, Jesus
God's love was made manifest in Jesus, his Son

[5]No man has ever seen God. [6]In this the love of God was made manifest among us that God sent his only Son into the world. [7]In this is love, not that we loved God but that he loved us and sent his Son to be the expiation for our sins so that we might live through him.

JESUS IS THE MANIFESTATION OF GOD'S LOVE
Out of his love for the world, God sent his Son to incarnate for all to see God's love made visible. Jesus's mission was to show *the way*. He was to demonstrate how to live lovingly according to God's will and what it would bring. By the supreme power of Jesus's love, he defeated evil and death so as to repair the consequential damage of Adam and Eve's lack of love of God (their sin). This damage repair was Jesus's *expiation*.

WHAT DID JESUS'S EXPIATION BRING?
By his expiation, Jesus unlocked the gate to eternal life that had been closed and locked during the banishment period. He became the sole access point to eternal life in that he unlocks the gate for those who believe in him and will open the gate to those he grants eternal life. As such, he made it possible for people to:

- Fathom the possibility of eternal life as a real alternative to the permanent death they faced during the banishment period,
- Realize the magnitude of the benefit that would be available from their choosing to turn to love-based living,
- Receive a fresh start when they accepted Jesus as God's Son, by having all prior sins forgiven, and
- Receive ongoing forgiveness to dislodge the sins that people commit, especially those that are entrenched as unloving habits.

Because Jesus made God's love visible, he gives people hope and an extraordinary reason to love. God did *not* send Jesus to the world because people loved God; it was so they could!

Obey God's Commands: Love God; Love Your Brother

[8]Whoever confesses that Jesus is the Son of God, God abides in him, and he in God. [9]God is love, and he who abides in love abides in God, so we know and believe the love God has for us.

[10]We love, because he first loved us. [11]If any one says, "I love God," and hates his brother, he is a liar; for he who does not love his brother whom he has seen, cannot love God whom he has not seen.

[12]And this commandment we have from him, that he who loves God should love his brother also. [13]By this we know that we love the children of God, when we love God and obey his commandments. For this is the love of God, that we keep his commandments. And his commandments are not burdensome.

WHAT DOES CONFESS JESUS MEAN?

John used the term *confess* differently than many people think of it today. The Greek word for *confess* means to agree. John was saying that the place to start on one's journey to eternal life is to agree with God that Jesus is his Son. When people do this, they will be in agreement with what God told John the Baptist when he said his Son was the one who baptizes with the Holy Spirit (grants eternal life). John the Baptist saw this and bore witness to it.

> *"He (God) who sent me to baptize with water said to me, 'He on whom you see the Spirit descend and remain, this is he who baptizes*

with the Holy Spirit'...I have seen and have borne witness that this is the Son of God" (Jn 1:32–34 RSAV).

WHAT HAPPENS WHEN A PERSON "CONFESSES"?

By the tense of the word *confess,* John indicated this particular "confession" is a one-time event, but that its outcome is ongoing. When a person comes to believe Jesus is the Son of God, Jesus responds by sending the Holy Spirit to him or her to provide ongoing support for the person to develop a love-based lifestyle.

God's plan is for believers to meet his abiding love for them with their own abiding love of him by obeying his commandment to love one another. This is the core requirement for a believer to be granted eternal life by the glorified Jesus.

LOVING ONE ANOTHER IS *NOT* SINGULAR

God's command to love is relational; it is to pay loving attention to others. Since God loved us first by making his love clearly visible through Jesus his Son, John carried the same logic of that approach forward to believers. They must make their love of God clearly visible by demonstrating their love of their fellow Christians (brothers).

> *And this commandment we have from him, that he who loves God should love his brother also.* (1 Jn 4:12 RSAV).

Obeying the commandment to love is not burdensome (*weighty or cruel*), because Jesus provides powerful assistance to help believers turn toward love and ingrain love-based living habits. However, the only way to receive this assistance is to confess that Jesus is the Son of God who grants eternal life.

Perfected Love

[14]Everyone who believes that Jesus is the Christ, is a child of God and everyone who loves the parent loves the child. [15]In this is love perfected with us. [16]There is no fear in love; for fear has to do with punishment, and he who fears is not perfected in love. [17]Perfect love casts out fear that we may have confidence for the day of judgment, because as he is so are we in this world.

GOD'S PLAN IS FOR BELIEVERS TO RECEIVE A NEW BIRTH BY GOD

John discussed who a child of God is at the beginning of his gospel, but he didn't provide the details—he only said that the person who believes in Jesus will be empowered to become a child of God.

> But to all who received him, who believed in his name, **he gave power to become children of God**; who were born, not of...the will of man, but of God (Jn 1:12–13 RSV).

This is where John described what Jesus empowers believers to do in order to become a full-fledged child of God, which means that he or she is a recipient of eternal life. Simply put, eternal life is contingent upon loving God as demonstrated by obeying his commandments to believe in Jesus' name and to love one another.

WHAT HAPPENS WHEN BELIEVERS KEEP GOD'S COMMANDMENT TO LOVE?

When believers make love their central focus, they will anchor loving habits that will eventually trigger a tipping point. [35] The person will "tip" over from a worldly orientation to the side of love as the compass of his or her life— he or she would simply *not* dream of committing a mortal sin.

From this point on, the believer carries God's love so completely that John called it *perfected* in him or her, which is another way to say he or she has received eternal life.

HOW DOES PERFECTED LOVE CAST OUT FEAR?

Since the greatest fear is that of death, people who receive eternal life have no fear because they are completely protected from the grip of the evil one who would try to tempt them to commit mortal sins. They may still be on earth as the disciples were, but they abide in the love and protection that eternal life brings and God keeps them that way.

> We know that any one born of God does not sin and the evil one does not touch him. He who was born of **God keeps him** (1 Jn 1:5–6 RSAV).

---

[35] http://dictionary.reference.com/browse/tipping-point?s=t

They become like Jesus in this world, in that they:

- no longer commit mortal sins and
- will die a physical death, yet live on with God for eternity.

> *Jesus said to her, "I am the resurrection and the life; he who believes in me, though he die, yet shall he live," (Jn 11:25 RSV).*

Jesus's granting of eternal life doesn't come with a physical sensation, so how can people know that Jesus has granted them eternal life? This is where faith comes into play. When believers love others not just in word or speech but in deed and in truth (1 Jn 2:20 RSAV), they will receive eternal life. This they can trust because Jesus keeps his word.

> *And this is his commandment, that we should believe in the name of his Son Jesus Christ and love one another... (1 Jn 3:23 RSAV).*

Testimony About Jesus and His Mission
The Disciples Testify

[18]By this we know that we abide in him and he in us, because he has given us of his own Spirit. [19]And we have seen and testify that the Father has sent his Son as the Savior of the world.

HOW DID THE DISCIPLES KNOW THEY HAD RECEIVED ETERNAL LIFE?
The disciples heard and saw the glorified Jesus when he breathed the Holy Spirit on them. John knew he and the other disciples abided in Jesus's own Holy Spirit—they felt his breath when he granted eternal life to them. Jesus did it this way, so they could testify to it, which was what he "sent" them to do.

> *Jesus said to them again, "Peace be with you. As the Father has sent me, even so I send you."...he breathed on them, and said to them, "Receive the Holy Spirit." (Jn 20:21–22 RSV).*

WHAT IS JESUS'S SALVATION?
To *save* is to remove people from a bad situation and take them to safety. Does this mean that Jesus will remove the toil and suffering in the world? No. Jesus does not offer a more comfortable life, but he does offer a greater life. God sent his Son to do the following:

- Save the world from the evil one
- Save the world from permanent death so people may have the opportunity to live eternally in the presence of God's love and joy

The Spirit Testifies

[20]This is he who came by water and blood, not with the water only but with the water and the blood Jesus Christ. [21]There are three witnesses, and these three agree, the Spirit, the water, and the blood. [22]And the Spirit is the witness, because the Spirit is the truth. [23]And this is the testimony, God gave us eternal life, and this life is in his Son. [24]He who has the Son has life; he who has not the Son of God has not life.

THE SPIRIT WITNESSED JESUS

John and the disciples were not the only eyewitness of Jesus's life and death; the Spirit was a witness, too. John the Baptist witnessed the descent of the Spirit that remained on Jesus that launched his ministry. John (this letter's author) was there when Jesus gave up that Spirit.

> *And John bore witness, "I saw the Spirit descend as a dove from heaven, and **it remained** on him"* (Jn 1:32 RSV).

> *...he said, "It is finished"; and he bowed his head and gave up his **spirit**...But one of the soldiers pierced his side with a spear, and at once there came out **blood and water**. He (John the author) who saw it has borne witness—his testimony is true...* (Jn 19:30, 34–35 RSV).

THE SPIRIT TESTIFIES

The Spirit was granted to Jesus by God. Therefore, his testimony which is stated below is the truth.

> *And the Spirit is the witness, because the Spirit is the truth. And this is the testimony, God gave us eternal life, and this life is in his Son* (1 Jn 4:22–23 RSAV).

This testimony means God sent his Son to incarnate, to die and resurrect, and by his resurrection, Jesus demonstrated that he was eternal life and now had the authority and power to grant it.

THE ONGOING ROLE OF THE SPIRIT

The Spirit may have left Jesus upon his human death, but the Holy Spirit lives on to play a pivotal role in God's plan. When people believe in and receive Jesus as the Son of God, he grants the Holy Spirit to them to provide ongoing testimony and guidance to help them complete the journey to eternal life.

> *But when the Counselor comes, whom I shall sent to you from the Father...he will bear witness to me...* (Jn 15:1 RSAV).

WATER AND BLOOD TESTIFY TO JESUS'S HUMANITY

The *water* and *blood* that spilled out from Jesus confirmed he was human, whose death was the ultimate in human love.

> *...one of the soldiers pierced his side with a spear and at once there came out **blood and water*** (Jn 19:30 RSV).

If Jesus had *not* been human, his resurrection could have been discounted as a mere feat that Roman and Greek gods who pretended to be human could do that didn't apply to humans. That would have spelled failure for Jesus's mission. Instead, Jesus's resurrection showed how eternal life was going to become available to humans—they, too, would die physically but "rise" to live eternally with God.

> *...if Christ has not been raised, then our preaching is in vain and your faith is in vain* (1 Cor 15:14 RSV).

Jesus as human could not grant eternal life while on earth. He needed to be glorified (restored to his Divine form) to restore what God took away. Therefore, he had to die and ascend to the Father in order to be glorified.

> *"... 'Out of his heart shall flow rivers of living water.'" Now he said this about the Spirit, which those who believed in him were to receive; for as yet the **Spirit had not been given, because Jesus was not yet glorified**_* (Jn 7:38–39 RSV).

THE BLOOD AND THE WATER SYMBOLIZE WHAT JESUS DOES FROM HEAVEN

Look closely at the passage cited below to see that John's second reference to *water and blood* includes the prefix "**the**."

> *This is he who came by water and blood, not with the water only but with **the** water and **the** blood Jesus Christ* (1 Jn 4:20 RSAV).

This prefix indicates that John also referred to *water* and *blood* not as the visible earthly substances that spilled from Jesus but as symbols to represent how Jesus would enable humanity to receive eternal life.

- **The blood** represents Jesus's ongoing forgiveness of sins that enables believers to be cleansed of errors that lead to *non*-love-based habits so they can become so steeped in loving behavior that Jesus will grant them eternal life.

  > *...and **the blood of Jesus** his Son cleanses us (believers) from all sin* (1 Jn 1:7 RSV).

- **The water** represents Jesus's granting eternal life, which is his **full** activation of the Holy Spirit within believers.

  > *"...**the water** that I shall give him will become in him a spring of water welling up to **eternal life**"* (Jn 4:14b RSV)

True Believers Testify

[25]If we receive the testimony of men, the testimony of God is greater; for this is the testimony of God that he has borne witness to his Son. [26]He who does not believe God has made him a liar, because he has not believed in the testimony that God has borne to his Son.

[27]He who believes in the Son of God has the testimony in himself.

WHAT IS GOD'S TESTIMONY TO HIS SON?

God bore witness to his Son by telling John the Baptist that Jesus is the one *who baptizes with the Holy Spirit* (grants eternal life).

> "*...but he (God) who sent me to baptize with water said to me,
> 'He on whom you see the Spirit descend and remain, **this is he who
> baptizes with the Holy Spirit.***'" (Jn 1:33 RSV).

Therefore, people who do *not* believe the following about Jesus make God a liar.

- Jesus is the Son of God.
- Jesus has the authority and power to grant access to eternal life.

HOW DO PEOPLE HAVE THIS TESTIMONY WITHIN THEMSELVES?

When people come to believe these things about Jesus, he grants the Holy Spirit to reside in them and bring God's testimony to them. This granting of the Holy Spirit does *not* yet bring eternal life but it does bring guidance to help believers develop a love-based lifestyle needed to receive eternal life. Testimony from the Holy Spirit is far greater than man's testimony because it comes directly from God.

WHAT IS THE VALUE OF THE TESTIMONY OF MEN?

The testimony of men is the way people are introduced to Jesus. John the Baptist initiated it, the disciples followed, and other believers have followed ever since. Believers who testify are the linchpin of the continuation of God's plan. Christianity couldn't have expanded or have continued to expand without them. The rollout of God's plan by testimony is depicted below.

Chart 9–1: The progression of witness to Jesus as the Son of God

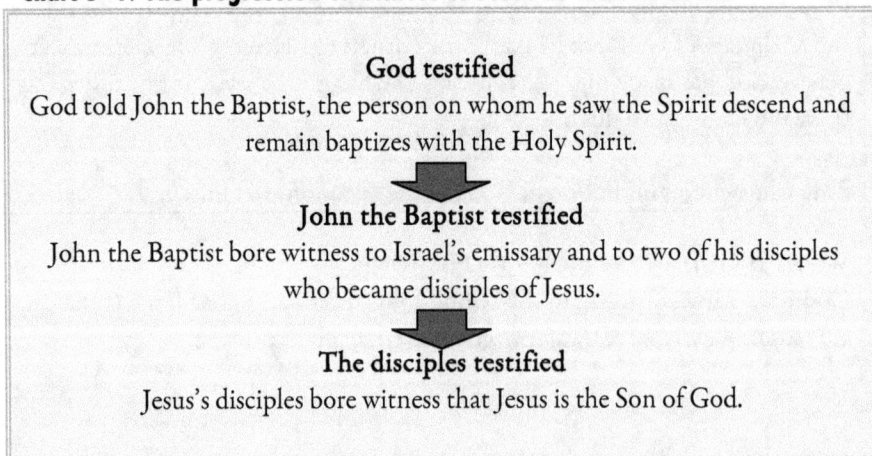

God testified
God told John the Baptist, the person on whom he saw the Spirit descend and remain baptizes with the Holy Spirit.

John the Baptist testified
John the Baptist bore witness to Israel's emissary and to two of his disciples who became disciples of Jesus.

The disciples testified
Jesus's disciples bore witness that Jesus is the Son of God.

Believers testify
When people believe that Jesus is God's Son, they receive the Holy Spirit and become qualified to testify.

Faith in Their Testimony

²⁸I write this to you who believe in the name of the Son of God, that you may know that you have eternal life. ²⁹For whatever is born of God overcomes the world, and who is it that overcomes the world, but he who believes that Jesus is the Son of God. ³⁰This is the victory that overcomes the world, our faith.

JOHN'S PURPOSE WAS TO BUILD FAITH OF HIS AUDIENCE
John wanted his community of believers to reach the point that they knew they had received eternal life. He was telling them, as believers, that when they lived according to their faith in Jesus as God's Son, they would defeat the evil of the world and become born of God and recipients of eternal life.

WHAT IS FAITH?
Faith goes beyond having a belief or an opinion; it is having the unshakable conviction that Jesus is the Son of the God whose essence is love.

> *"Now faith is the assurance of things hoped for, the conviction of things not seen"* (Heb 11:1 RSV).

Faith is what drives behavior when there is no guarantee of the outcome. However, let us point out, people do not lack for faith—the issue is where they choose to place their faith. Is it in Jesus, or is it in the people and things of the world? What does having faith in Jesus mean? John already provided these three key truths to have faith in:

- God so loved the world, he sent his only Son to save it.
- Jesus restored the opportunity to live in God's loving presence forever.
- Jesus grants eternal life to those who believe he is the Son of God and keep his commandment to love one another.

What does a person do with these truths? John took this up in the next chapter.

Conclusion

The key lines of this chapter are its bookends—the opening and ending passages. They state who God is and the basis for his plan to reopen the gate to heaven.

- *. . . for love is of God, since God is love* (1 Jn 4:1 RSAV)
- *This is the victory that overcomes the world, our faith* (1 Jn 4:30 RSAV).

God initiated his plan for the world's salvation when he told John the Baptist how to identify his Son, Jesus, who would restore access to eternal life. Jesus performed this mission on earth and continues to do so from heaven. While on earth, he showed the way of love through his teaching and miraculous signs which climaxed in his resurrection.

After Jesus returned to the Father, the Holy Spirit and the disciples testified to Jesus. Now, ongoing generations of believers continue to carry God's plan onward. This is how a family of God's children, who aspire to be aligned with God's love, extends throughout the world.

The disciples' testimonies, teachings, and writings provide the foundational sources for people to learn the good news that Jesus brought. Those who come to belief through the disciples' word, albeit via people who live generations later, will receive the Holy Spirit who supports their journey to God in three magnificent ways:

- He testifies to Jesus being God's Son and the world's Savior.
- He serves as the communication link between believers on earth and Jesus in heaven.
- He follows Jesus's instructions regarding whom to grant eternal life to and when to grant it.

What follows is a snapshot of God's plan as John portrayed it in this chapter.

Chart 9–2: The schema of God's plan

God so loved the world, he sent his Son to the world to become flesh and show the way to be with God forever.

Those who believe Jesus is the Son of God have the opportunity to receive eternal life.
This belief is crucial because God gave Jesus sole authority over eternal life.

God set up the testimony chain, going from him to John the Baptist to the disciples and to generations of disciples thereafter so people can be introduced to Jesus as the one who grants eternal life.

Those who believe in Jesus as the Son of God receive the Holy Spirit to help them live a love-based life.

Jesus continues to forgive sins, supports believers through the Holy Spirit, and grants God's seed (eternal life) to those who believe in his name and love one another.

Review of Key Points

In the introduction, we asked you to consider the following questions. What are your answers? Our answers are in appendix D.

Table 9–1: Your answers to the review questions

#	Question	Your Answers
1.	What is God's fundamental essence?	
2.	How is God's love perfected in a person?	
3.	How does perfected love cast out fear?	

#	Question	Your Answers
4.	Who testifies to Jesus?	
5.	What is faith?	

What's Next?

John's conclusion comes down to one thing. Choice is the way people of freewill determine their destiny.

CHAPTER 10

Choose
1 John 5:1–14 RSAV

Introduction

Throughout this letter, John has proclaimed eternal life. He has explained why God sent his Son to restore it, what it is, how to receive it, and what it brings. Jesus's restoration of eternal life has given people a choice about their destiny. John is ready to wrap-up by taking his audience to the pivotal question—what destiny will they choose?

> If people do nothing, their destiny will be of the devil, sin, and death.
> But
> those who choose the way of Jesus have the opportunity to become born of God and receive eternal life.

John acknowledged that the world is a lawless place full of deceivers, but he assured his audience that they have the opportunity to be God's children, for two reasons:

- Jesus destroyed the works of the devil, proving love is powerful enough to bring light to the darkness
- Jesus stands by ready and available to cleanse every believer of all unrighteousness and support them on their journey to love.

John would go on to tell his audience that they could become pure as Jesus is pure, fully prepared for his "appearance." But how can anyone be pure as Jesus? John said it is possible and supported this assertion with a description of how everyone can achieve that goal. To begin, they must first choose to abide in Jesus. If they do, Jesus will support them all the way to the finish line and on to eternity!

Outline

1. Children of God or of the Devil
2. Children of God Shall See Jesus
3. Let no One Deceive You

What to Look For

Consider the following questions as you read to assist in deepening your comprehension. There is space to write your answers at the end of the chapter. You can find our answers in appendix D.

1. How does a person become righteous?
2. What does it mean that a believer does not sin and cannot sin?
3. How did Jesus bring hope to the world?
4. How does a person become *pure as Jesus is pure*?
5. What is lawlessness?

Choose
(1 Jn 5:1–14 RSAV)

Children of God or of the Devil

⁵:¹If you know that he is righteous, you may be sure that everyone who does right is born of him. ²He who does right is righteous, as he is righteous; whoever does not do right is not of God, nor he who does not love his brother.

³He who commits sin is of the devil; for the devil has sinned from the beginning. ⁴The reason the Son of God appeared was to destroy the works of the devil. ⁵By this it may be seen who are the children of God, and who are the children of the devil.

Children of God Shall See Jesus

⁶No one born of God commits sin, and he cannot sin because he is born of God; for God's nature abides in him. ⁷See what love the Father has given us,

that we should be called children of God; and so we are. [8]Beloved, we are God's children now; it does not yet appear what we shall be, but we know that when he appears we shall be like him, for we shall see him as he is.

Let No One Deceive You

[9]The reason why the world does not know us is that it did not know him. [10]You know that he appeared to take away sins, and in him there is no sin. [11]No one who abides in him sins; no one who sins has either seen him or known him. [12]And every one who thus hopes in him purifies himself as he is pure. [13]Every one who commits sin is guilty of lawlessness; sin is lawlessness.

[14]Little children, let no one deceive you.

Commentary

Children of God or of the Devil

[5:1]If you know that he is righteous, you may be sure that everyone who does right is born of him. [2]He who does right is righteous, as he is righteous; whoever does not do right is not of God, nor he who does not love his brother.

[3]He who commits sin is of the devil; for the devil has sinned from the beginning. [4]The reason the Son of God appeared was to destroy the works of the devil. [5]By this it may be seen who are the children of God, and who are the children of the devil.

WHAT IS IT TO BE *RIGHTEOUS?*

Righteousness refers to keeping God's commands; therefore, those who know that Jesus is righteous know he spoke truthfully when he said they may have eternal life through him.

> *You search the scriptures because you think that in them you have*
> *eternal life; and it is they that bear witness to me; yet you refuse to*
> *come to me that you may have life* (Jn 5:39 RSV).

In John's day, it would have taken quite a leap of faith for even righteous people to believe they could be born of God and receive eternal life. This had not been possible since the devil got to Adam and Eve. But here, John assured his audience they could trust that Jesus would do what he says because Jesus is righteous. God sent Jesus to save the world, and Jesus did by restoring eternal life.

HOW DO PEOPLE *DO* RIGHT?
If people keep Jesus's commandment to believe in him and love one another, they are righteous—they do right.

> And this is his commandment, that we should **believe in the name of his Son Jesus Christ** and **love one another**, just as he commanded us (1 Jn 3:23 RSAV).

Since John was addressing people who were believers, he emphasized the need for them to love one another. This is the only way to demonstrate their belief in Jesus and love of God because it is only possible to see what a person actually believes by their deeds. Their actions also provide the means for a person to make a clear assessment of his or her own behavior in order to stay on the path of love.

JESUS CHANGED THE PARADIGM!
Jesus changed what the world was able to think possible. Before he arrived, the devil had hold of the world leaving no possibility of having eternal life with God. The situation appeared hopeless, but after Jesus's resurrection, people could have hope because Jesus changed their world view (the paradigm), They were no longer destined to live in the devil's camp of permanent death because Jesus gave them the opportunity to cross over to God's kingdom of eternal love. Jesus, the human who died and rose again, proved this possible, which meant that all people could legitimately be at choice.

Motivated by his love of the Father, Jesus kept the following two commitments, one to God and the other to humanity:

- His commitment to God was to abide by God's will at all times even by going to the cross.
- His commitment to humanity was to grant eternal *life* to those who do right.

> If you know he is righteous, you may be sure that everyone who does right is born of him (1 Jn 5:1 RSAV).

Children of God Shall See Jesus

> [6]No one born of God commits sin, and he cannot sin because he is born of God; for God's nature abides in him. [7]See what love the Father has given us, that we should be called children of God; and so we are. [8]Beloved, we are God's children now; it does not yet appear what we shall be, but we know that when he appears we shall be like him, for we shall see him as he is.

THE ISSUE OF SIN

How do people get out of the devil's lair? There is only one way. Believers must refrain from sin so they can develop the love-based lifestyle that is the definition of a righteous life. When believers make their choice to love one another and commit to it, they will reach a tipping point when they simply wouldn't commit a mortal sin. This is when Jesus responds by granting them God's seed (nature) so they become born of God and full-fledged children of God. They receive eternal life.

Since these believers chose not to sin and upheld their decision, John stated that they now cannot commit mortal sin because they have God's seed in them and as such are protected from the evil one.

> *No one born of God commits sin, and he cannot sin because he is born of God; for God's nature abides in him* (I Jn 5:6 RSAV).

Table 10–1: What happens before and after becoming born of God

Before/After	What happens
Before becoming born of God, they *Choose not to sin*	Believers demonstrate that they love God by choosing not to mortally sin. Through the strength of their faith, love of God, Jesus's forgiveness, and the Holy Spirit's support, they are able to hold their choice. Jesus grants them born-of-God status (eternal life).
After becoming born of God, *Chose not to sin and cannot sin*	Those believers who chose not to sin and became born of God will continually be protected from the evil one who tries to lure people to sin. John was saying that because they are protected, they cannot commit mortal sin. *We know that any one born of God does not sin and the evil one does not touch him* (1 Jn 1:5 RSAV).

HOW IS IT POSSIBLE TO BE PROTECTED FROM THE EVIL ONE?

When John said that eternal life brings ongoing protection from the evil one, he was making an amazing proclamation! Yet, he could proclaim it because he experienced it; he personally knew it was true. John knew that Jesus grants God's seed (nature) to those he grants born-of-God status. John knew that Jesus "fully activates the Holy Spirit" within believers who cross the threshold of sin-free living. John confirmed this when he acknowledged his own receipt of eternal life and pointed out the fathers and the young men in his own community who had received it.

> *I am writing to you, fathers, because you know him who is from the beginning. I am writing to you, young men, because you have overcome the evil one.* (1 Jn 2:13,15 RSAV).

John was telling his community they had the opportunity to know the Father and his Son intimately (receive eternal life) while they were alive. Otherwise, why would he have discussed having ongoing protection from the evil one or assured his audience that they could see Jesus when he appeared again? And there certainly would be no reason to tell them that it would be possible for them to be so like Jesus as to see him as he is when he appears, if they couldn't have received eternal life while they were alive.

> *But we know that when he appears we shall be like him for we shall see him as he is* (1 Jn 5:8 RSAV).
>
> *Blessed are the pure in heart, for they shall see God* (Mt 5:8 RSV).

Let No One Deceive You

[9]The reason why the world does not know us is that it did not know him. [10]You know that he appeared to take away sins, and in him there is no sin. [11]No one who abides in him sins; no one who sins has either seen him or known him. [12]And every one who thus hopes in him purifies himself as he is pure. [13]Every one who commits sin is guilty of lawlessness; sin is lawlessness.

[14]Little children, let no one deceive you.

WHO CAN KNOW JESUS?

After John stated what he absolutely knew, he explained that people of the world could not understand his audience of believers because people of the world chose not to believe in Jesus. So in matters of God, purification, and the opportunity to receive eternal life, why would a believer take advice from someone who does not know or "confess" Jesus?

PURIFY YOURSELF

John's final instruction to those who hope for eternal life was to purify themselves as Jesus is pure. To explain, John brought up lawlessness as the way to look at sin. To be lawless is *not* about violating laws; it is about the absence of love, kindness, and compassion being behind any behavior.

Jesus's purity had to do with living a sacred life by living lovingly. It was by his love of the Father that he kept the Father's commands, and John told his community to do the same—to live according to their love of God. They must choose love as the basis for their thoughts and deeds.

> *But I do as the Father has commanded me, so that the world may know that I love the Father* (Jn 14:28 RSAV).

THE CHOICE

In regard to Jesus's restoration of the opportunity to receive eternal life, everyone has the opportunity to choose to believe in Jesus and love one another. Freewill is the pivot point of their destiny. Which will they choose, eternal life or death? Whichever it is, God will honor it.

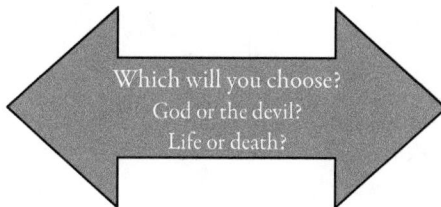

Which will you choose?
God or the devil?
Life or death?

Conclusion

John concluded this, the final chapter of his first letter, with the fact that receipt of eternal life, now that Jesus has been granted authority to grant eternal life, lies in the hands of each individual. A believer's dream of having eternal life with the loving God can come true! Jesus is righteous and comes through with his promise to grant eternal life to his believers who love God and keep his commands.

> *My sheep hear my voice, and I know them, and they follow me; and **I give them eternal life and they shall never perish**, and no one shall snatch them out of my hand* (Jn 10:27–28 RSV).

The devil may connive to test a believer's faith, but the devil is impotent under Jesus's light of love. This is the salvation that God sent Jesus into the world to accomplish, and by his resurrection, he did. At this point, God's plan comes down to humanity's freewill. John urged his audience to choose wisely!

Review of Key Points

In the introduction, we asked you to consider the following questions. What are your answers? Our answers are in appendix D.

Table 10–2: Your answers to the review questions

#	Question	Your Answers
1.	How does a person become righteous?	
2.	What does it mean that a believer does *not* sin and cannot sin? *No one born of God **commits sin;** and he **cannot sin** because he is born of God for God's nature abides in him* (1 Jn 5:6 RSAV).	

#	Question	Your Answers
3.	How did Jesus bring hope to the world?	
4.	How does a person become *pure as Jesus is pure*?	
5.	What is lawlessness?	

What's Next?

In his next two letters, John would provide two "real life" examples of what he covered in his first letter. In 2 John his topic was the issue of whether to welcome or not welcome someone who opposes the truth of who Jesus is.

5

2 and 3 John

CHAPTER 11
2 John

Reject All False Teaching
2 John RSAV

Introduction

John ended his first letter by warning his followers that deceivers who deny Jesus, are out to persuade them to join their side. In this, his second letter, he was concerned about deceivers who wanted to promulgate their false doctrine in another church. John advised the members *not* to admit them or give them any greeting that could be construed as an endorsement.

In his first letter and gospel, John, Jesus's beloved disciple and eyewitness, testified that Jesus was the Christ who came in the flesh, which he backed up with the irrefutable testimony of God himself, John the Baptist, and the disciples. In this letter, the author increased the number of backers to include those who had more recently received eternal life.

John's concern was that if believers succumbed to the lies of the deceivers and denied Jesus, they would face permanent death by committing the unforgivable sin. John's protective love was on full display when he directed the church to do the loving thing by saying "no" to a deceiver who was about to knock on their door.

Outline

1. Walk in the Truth
2. Beware of the Deceiver Who Is the Antichrist
3. Complete Your Journey
4. Walk According to His Commandments

What to Look For

Consider the following questions as you read to assist in deepening your comprehension. There is space to write your answers at the end of the chapter. You can find our answers in appendix D.

1. Who are the elect?
2. John mentioned the people who *know* the truth; who are they?
3. Who are the deceivers? What are the ramifications of believing them?
4. What is the work of God?
5. Can denying someone access to your church be a loving act?

Reject All False Teaching
2 John 1:1–16 RSAV

Walk in the Truth

¹:¹The elder to the elect lady and her children, whom I love in the truth, and not only I but also all who know the truth, ²because of the truth which abides in us and will be with us forever. ³Grace, mercy, and peace will be with us, from God the Father and from Jesus Christ the Father's Son, in truth and love.

⁴Though I have much to write to you, I would rather not use paper and ink, but I hope to come to see you and talk with you face to face, so that our joy may be complete. ⁵The children of your elect sister greet you.

Beware of the Deceiver Who Is the Antichrist

⁶I rejoiced greatly to find some of your children walking in the truth, just as we have been commanded by the Father. ⁷For many deceivers have gone out into the world; men who will not acknowledge the coming of Jesus Christ in the flesh, such a one is the deceiver and the antichrist.

⁸Anyone who goes ahead and does not abide in the doctrine of Christ does not have God; ⁹he who abides in the doctrine has both the Father and the Son. ¹⁰If any one comes to you and does not bring this doctrine, do not receive him into the house or give him any greeting; for he who greets him shares his wicked

work. [12]He who abides in the doctrine has both the Father and the Son.

Complete Your Journey

[13]Look to yourselves that you may not lose what you have worked for, but may win a full reward.

Walk According to His Commandments

[14]And now I beg you, lady, not as though I were writing you a new commandment, but the one we have had from the beginning, that we love one another. [15]This is the commandment, as you have heard from the beginning, that you follow love. [16]And this is love, that we follow his commandments.

Commentary

Walk in the Truth

[1:1]The elder to the elect lady and her children, whom I love in the truth, and not only I but also all who know the truth, [2]because of the truth which abides in us and will be with us forever. [3]Grace, mercy, and peace will be with us, from God the Father and from Jesus Christ the Father's Son, in truth and love.

[4]Though I have much to write to you, I would rather not use paper and ink, but I hope to come to see you and talk with you face to face, so that our joy may be complete. [5]The children of your elect sister greet you.

THE OPENING OF THE LETTER

John was the elder who directed this letter to *the elect lady,* a church and its members. In that era, a church was described as female. The term *elect* indicates that its members were believers because believers have the opportunity to obtain salvation through the receipt of eternal life.[36]

> *Therefore, I endure everything for the sake of the elect, that they also may obtain salvation in Christ Jesus with its eternal glory* (2 Tim 2:10 RSV).

---

[36] Brown, *The Anchor Bible: The Epistles of John,* 654.

John wrote not only out of his own love for this community, but as a representative of the love of all who have received eternal life and know the truth because the Father and Son eternally abide in them. They believe that Jesus is the Son of God. They, like John, can discern who the deceivers are. Therefore, John wasn't standing alone when he issued his warning about the deceivers/antichrists who want to come to talk to this church. He was backed by many others who had received eternal life.

Beware of the Deceiver Who Is the Antichrist

> [6]I rejoiced greatly to find some of your children walking in the truth, just as we have been commanded by the Father. [7]For many deceivers have gone out into the world; men who will not acknowledge the coming of Jesus Christ in the flesh, such a one is the deceiver and the antichrist.
>
> [8]Anyone who goes ahead and does not abide in the doctrine of Christ does not have God; [9]he who abides in the doctrine has both the Father and the Son. [10]If any one comes to you and does not bring this doctrine, do not receive him into the house or give him any greeting; for he who greets him shares his wicked work. [12]He who abides in the doctrine has both the Father and the Son.

JOHN'S CONCERN IS FOR THOSE WHO ARE EN ROUTE

John was not concerned about the members of this community who had received eternal life. They believed Jesus was the Christ and the Son of God and by virtue of being born of God, were protected from the lies of the deceivers.

> *We know anyone born of God does not sin, and the evil one does not touch him* (1 Jn 1:5 RSAV).

It was the others, who were still en route to eternal life, who were of concern to John. Antichrists who were of the same ilk as those who left John's community wanted to visit this church. These deceivers might convince the vulnerable ones to deny Jesus.

> *This is the antichrist, he who denies the Father and the Son. No one who denies the Son has the Father. He who confesses the Son has the Father also* (1 Jn 2:24–25 RSAV).

THE PROBLEM WITH THE DECEIVERS

Anyone who did not believe Jesus is the Christ and Son of God would be destined to permanent death. They would:

- have disobeyed God's command to believe Jesus is his Son,
- made God a liar because God has testified to John the Baptist that Jesus is his Son, and
- not received eternal life because God gave his Son full authority over eternal life to those who believe in him.

"I told you that you would die in your sins...unless you believe that I am he" (Jn 8:24 RSV).

But what would have been worse was that those who no longer believed in Jesus were committing the unforgivable sin; they would have no one to go to for forgiveness because only Jesus forgives sin.

JOHN'S DIRECTIVE IS TO SAY "NO!"

John emphatically advised the church to *not* allow any deceiver to teach, preach, or to try in any other way to impose their false beliefs. John was *not* saying to refrain from having interactions with the deceivers in worldly life or insult them in the process of refusing their admittance. John was saying that the loving act was *not* to allow them in.

Church leaders have an obligation to protect the vulnerable ones under their watch, no differently than parents have an obligation to protect their children.

WHY IS THIS SO IMPORTANT?

Getting the identity of Jesus right is crucial for eternal life. If Jesus, God's Son, did not come in the flesh, it would have meant that he did not really die on the cross or resurrect, and that would have refuted the existence of eternal life itself and the efficacy of God's love. The foundation of Christianity rests on Jesus being the Son of God, the Christ who came in the flesh.

If Christ had not been raised, then our preaching is in vain and your faith is in vain (1 Cor 15:14 RSV).

Protection of this foundation was so important that John said that even those who appear to endorse the deceivers would share in their sin.

Complete Your Journey

> [13]Look to yourselves that you may not lose what you have worked for, but may win a full reward.

WHAT WAS AT STAKE?

In contrast to the deceivers, the person who sticks with Jesus and his teaching has the opportunity to come into an eternal living and loving relationship with both the Father and the Son.

> *If what you heard from the beginning abides in you, then you will*
> *abide in the Son and in the Father, and this is what he has promised*
> *us, eternal life* (1 Jn 2:32–33 RSAV).

WHAT WOULD BELIEVERS SEE WHEN THEY LOOKED TO THEMSELVES?

When John said, *look to yourselves*, it was a reminder to believers that when they came to belief they made a commitment to have faith in Jesus as the Christ and God's Son which translates to keeping his commands.

The Greek meaning of *worked for* is *to commit.* John's treatment of this word indicates a believer's commitment is a one-time promise that continues into the present. The very basis for Jesus granting them the Holy Spirit was to support their journey to eternal life. This was what they were working for; would they give that up?

> ... *"This is the work of God, that you believe in him whom he has sent"* (Jn 6:29 RSV).

John's reference to winning the *full reward* is exactly what will be available to believers who sufficiently abide by Jesus's command to love. When Jesus bestows eternal life, he further activates the Holy Spirit, who believers received upon coming to belief, to grant them the *full reward* of eternal life with God.

Walk According to His Commandments

> [14]And now I beg you, lady, not as though I were writing you a new commandment, but the one we have had from the beginning, that we love one

> another. ¹⁵This is the commandment, as you have heard from the beginning, that you follow love. ¹⁶And this is love, that we follow his commandments.

LOVE IS THE OVERRIDING FOCUS OF JESUS'S TEACHING

While the issue that hastened this letter was the threat to the correct belief in Jesus's identity, John concluded this letter by returning to the command to love.

> *Beloved, let us love one another; for love is of God, since God is love* (1 Jn 4:1 RSAV).

John told the church to love one another as they heard from the beginning. In this case, the love John advocated was tough love that protects those who are still en route to eternal life. This church was facing a challenging situation that required taking the strong and loving stand, which was to ward off those who would attempt to impose false beliefs about Jesus.

Conclusion

The truth was the focus of this letter, and it continues to play out today. Who is Jesus? Was he human? Was he God's Son the Divine? Who should people believe about this? This letter was included in the New Testament to reinforce the truth of this matter. Jesus's eyewitness, the beloved disciple and author of this letter, has stated and restated the truth of Jesus throughout his writings as follows:

Jesus was sent by God on the mission of eternal life.
He was human and Divine.
Jesus is the Christ and the Son of God.

Holding the correct belief about Jesus's identity is crucial to receive eternal life because Jesus is the one who grants it! While on earth, he showed the way to receive it, and from heaven, he continues to support believers in keeping God's command to love. However, this hinges on believing Jesus is the Christ, the Son of God.

A deceiver came knocking on the door of the church addressed in this letter, and a deceiver could come knocking on the door of any believer's heart and mind today. If this happens, shouldn't John's advocacy of tough love apply? He would say to deny any deceiver access to the house of God wherever it may be, even one's heart.

Review of Key Points

In the introduction, we asked you to consider the following questions. What are your answers? Our answers are in appendix D.

Table 11–1: Your answers to the review questions

#	Question	Your answers
1.	Who are the elect?	
2.	John mentioned the people who *know* the truth; who are they?	
3.	Who are the deceivers? What are the ramifications of believing them?	
4.	What is the work of God?	
5.	Can denying someone access to your church be a loving act?	

What's Next?

In his next letter, John provided another example of putting the Father's commandment into practice.

CHAPTER 12
3 John

Love all the Brethren
3 John RSAV

Introduction

This letter concerns the upcoming visit of a missionary to a church whose leader refused to receive him. John had already written to the church about this but had since learned that the leader, who, as John said, put himself first, did not accept John's authority, even to the point of speaking maliciously of him. Therefore, John wrote to Ga'ius, to ask him to provide support to Deme'trius and his fellow missionaries. The people in this letter are as follows.

Table 12–1: The people named in the letter

#	Person	Who they are	Born-of-God status
1.	Ga'ius	A brother to whom John wrote, who has helped missionaries in the past.	He walked in the truth because he is born of God.
2.	Deme'trius	The missionary who was coming to visit the church.	He walked in the truth because he is born of God.
3.	Diot'rephes	The leader of the church who refused to admit the missionaries.	He was *not* born of God. He was still developing a love-based lifestyle.

Outline

1. Greeting
2. Request for Ga'ius to Render Service to Deme'trius
3. Diot'rephes Does Not Welcome the Brethren
4. Imitate God

What to Look For

Consider the following questions as you read to assist in deepening your comprehension. There is space to write your answers at the end of the chapter. You can find our answers in appendix D.

1. What does it mean to follow (walk) in the truth?
2. Who are *friends* as John referred to them?
3. What is the root cause of the evil that John described in this letter?

Love All the Brethren
(3 John 1:1–18 RSAV)

Greeting

[1]The elder to the beloved Ga'ius, whom I love in the truth, [2]I had much to write to you, but I would rather not write with pen and ink; [3]I hope to see you soon, and we will talk together face to face. [4]Peace be to you. The friends greet you. Greet the friends, every one of them by name.

Request for Ga'ius to Render Service to Deme'trius

[5]Beloved, I pray that all may go well with you and that you may be in health; I know that it is well with your soul. [6]For I greatly rejoiced when some of the brethren arrived and testified to the truth of your life, as indeed you do follow the truth. [7]Beloved, it is a loyal thing you do when you render any service to the brethren, [8]especially to strangers, [6a]who have testified to your love before the church. [9]No greater joy can I have than this, to hear that my children follow the truth. [10]So we ought to support such men, that we may be fellow workers in the truth.

[11]You will do well to send them on their journey as befits God's service. [12]For they have set out for his sake and have accepted nothing from the heathen. [13]Deme'trius has testimony from everyone, and from the truth itself; I testify to him too, and you know my testimony is true.

Diot'rephes Does Not Admit the Brethren

[14]I have written something to the church; but Diot'rephes, who likes to put himself first, does not acknowledge my authority. [15]And not content with that, he refuses himself to welcome the brethren, and also stops those that want to welcome them and puts them out of the church. [16]So if I come, I will bring up what he is doing, prating against me with *evil* words. [17]He who does evil has not seen God.

Imitate God

[18]Beloved, do not imitate evil, but imitate good. He who does good is of God.

Commentary

Greeting

[1]The elder to the beloved Ga'ius, whom I love in the truth. [2]I had much to write to you, but I would rather not write with pen and ink. [3]I hope to see you soon, and we will talk together face to face. [4]Peace be to you. The friends greet you. Greet the friends, every one of them by name.

WHO IS GA'IUS?

John knew Ga'ius and loved him as a fellow believer *in the truth*. To be a believer *in the truth* is to be a believer in Jesus as the Son of God because Jesus is the *truth*. John's address of Ga'ius as "beloved" indicated that Ga'ius was someone who followed God's command to love one another. Even from this beginning point, John indicated his purpose for this letter, which was to deal with the issue of treating a fellow brother lovingly.

Ga'ius is or was one of John's disciples. Otherwise, John wouldn't have asked Ga'ius to greet every one of the *friends* by name. These *friends* were brothers who lived in accordance with Jesus's command noted below.

"This is my commandment, that you love one another...You are my
friends if you do what I command you" (Jn 16:20, 23 RSAV).

John's opening may be typical of greetings that were used in those days, but John set the stage for his purpose by his attention to the warmth of the various relationships that stood in strong contrast to what Diot'rephes the church leader said and did.

Request for Ga'ius to Render Service to Deme'trius

⁵Beloved, I pray that all may go well with you and that you may be in health, I know that it is well with your soul. ⁶For I greatly rejoiced when some of the brethren arrived and testified to the truth of your life, as indeed you do follow in the truth. ⁷Beloved, it is a loyal thing you do when you render any service to the brethren; ⁸especially to strangers who have testified to your love before the church. ⁹No greater joy can I have than this, to hear that my children follow the truth. ¹⁰So we ought to support such men, that we may be fellow workers in the truth.

¹¹You will do well to send them on their journey as befits God's service. ¹²For they have set out for his sake and have accepted nothing from the heathen. ¹³Deme'trius has testimony from everyone, and from the truth itself; I testify to him too, and you know my testimony is true.

JOHN ASKS GA'IUS TO SUPPORT THE MISSIONARY WHO IS ARRIVING

John not only knew Ga'ius was a beloved brother, he also commended him for his recent service to the brethren, especially the strangers. Missionaries who went out to counteract the opponents of Christ depended upon people like Ga'ius for support because they didn't receive anything from the heathen (people who do not follow Christ).

So John asked Ga'ius to bankroll the soon-to-arrive missionary Deme'trius as "befits those who do service to God." John added that by Ga'ius's support, he would become a collaborator in God's work.

DEME'TRIUS'S CREDENTIALS ARE IMPECCABLE

Since Ga'ius didn't know Deme'trius, John recounted those who testified of his worthiness:

- Everyone, who were fellow brothers who knew Deme'trius.

- The *truth* that abides in Deme'trius, which Deme'trius demonstrated by the holiness of his life and soundness of his preaching.[37]
- John himself, the beloved disciple of Jesus.

Having established Deme'trius as a "good guy," John laid out the problem.

Diot'rephes Does Not Welcome the Brethren

[14]I have written something to the church; but Diot'rephes, who likes to put himself first, does not acknowledge my authority. [15]And not content with that, he refuses himself to welcome the brethren, and also stops those that want to welcome them and puts them out of the church. [16]So if I come, I will bring up what he is doing, prating against me with *evil* words. [17]He who does evil has not seen God.

THE PROBLEM

Diot'rephes, the leader of the house-church where Deme'trius was headed, posed problems:

- He did *not* accept John's authority; he even spoke disrespectfully of John.
- He refused to welcome (receive) the missionaries.
- He did *not* allow members of his church to receive the missionaries and expelled them if they did.

Clearly, the church leader who was not yet born of God had fallen prey to evil. John planned to deal with him and his evil prating when he was there in person; however, what should people do in the meantime?

Imitate Good

Beloved, do not imitate evil, but imitate good. He who does good is of God.

THE CRUX OF THE LETTER

---

[37] Brown, *The Anchor Bible: The Epistles of John*, 724.

John closed this letter with his final argument to Ga'ius to do the right thing, which was to welcome Deme'trius who was of God. He was the one to imitate.

> *By this it may be seen who are the children of God, and who are the children of the devil; whoever does **not** do right is **not** of God, nor he who does **not** love his brother* (1 Jn 3:10 RSV).

John encouraged Ga'ius to take the high road—to *not* follow the lead of this leader, but to continue his service to God as a supporter of Deme'trius, a true brother.

Conclusion

This letter addresses the ongoing challenge of making love-based choices. Evil strikes where ever there is an opening. Diot'rephes, a church leader, opened the door to evil, both in his heart and his church, by choosing to put himself first. He even provided fertile ground for evil to continue to do its work because he refused feedback from Jesus's beloved disciple! John chose to deal with this situation with a stopgap measure until he could get there to confront Diot'rephes face-to-face (heart-to-heart).

However, the forces for good were also at work, even in a situation like this:

- Brothers, known and unknown, loved one another and went to bat for them.
- Brothers recognized each other's good deeds and commended them.
- Inspiring good works took place and were worthy of imitation.
- Support of anyone's good works offered the opportunity to be a coworker of God's work.

John brought the high note of love into this letter, even in face of evil at work. He showed there are ways for believers to walk in the truth of love, even in a difficult environment.

Review of Key Points

In the introduction, we asked you to consider the following questions. What are your answers? Our answers are in appendix D.

Table 12–2: Your answers to the review questions

#	Question	Your answers
1.	What does it mean to follow (walk) in the truth?	
2.	Who are *friends* as John referred to them?	
3.	What is the root cause of the evil that John described in this letter?	

6

Appendices

Appendix A
The Breakthrough

POSSIBILITIES WERE IN THE AIR

In the "Introduction," we contended that literary analysis in the twentieth century brought exciting possibilities to alleviate the confusion that revolves around John's writings. Scholars had confirmed that first-century authors, like John and Matthew, wrote with hearable organizational markers. However, scholars stopped short of making their discoveries practical. There simply wasn't enough value in the presentation of literary structures for the effort it took for readers to use them. Scholars who were doing this research were meeting resistance from all directions—their peers, superiors, and those they wrote for.

It is always difficult to introduce new ideas, but was it time to give up? This situation was similar to what scientists who discovered the light bulb faced a century earlier when they proved that they could get carbon to glow, but the light didn't last long enough to be practical. If Thomas Edison hadn't picked up on their discovery and pursued it, he wouldn't have eventually discovered how to make the light bulb long lasting, which would transform the way the world operated from that point on.[38]

WHAT WOULD IT TAKE TO MAKE JOHN'S WRITINGS CLEAR?

We asked ourselves, what if instead of changing the words of scripture to today's common language, as scholars do today to make it more clear, we arranged the passages to avail modern readers of the aural markers that first-century listeners used to understand what John was saying? This wasn't a completely new idea; scholars had considered and even recommended it, but didn't pursue it.

*The essential thing is that the **verse structure should be represented to the eye**...where structural arrangement is wanting, no amount of explanation is likely to be of much avail.*[39]

---

[38] http://edison.rutgers.edu/newsletter9.html
[39] Richard G. Moulton, *The Literary Study of the Bible* (London: Heath & Co., 1898) 45.

We can only speculate as to why the idea didn't take off. One reason could have been that it went against prevailing norms, a classic roadblock to the pursuit of new ideas, as Galileo found when he supported the theory of a sun-centered solar system.[40] However, our quest for a practical and value-added way to make John's writings clear led us to pick up where other scholars left off and do the "unthinkable."

While retaining the English translation that is very close to the original Greek, we aligned the passages to coincide with what first-century listeners were able to comprehend. This simple and logical next step in scholarly research reveals:

- The repetitive passages that appear in John's text served a valuable purpose for first century listeners,
- Misalignments in John's logic that scholars have been pointing out for centuries occur because the text in our Bibles is not aligned the way John intended for it to be comprehended, and
- The passages that appear contradictory of each other are not contradictory when parallelism is taken into consideration.

The aural text we present in this book is the breakthrough. It is a practical and replicable delivery vehicle that brings clarity and reading ease that Johannine scholars had been looking for all along! It heightens coherence, reveals valuable new insights, and solves mysteries scholars have pondered for centuries.

WHAT IS AURAL (RSAV) TEXT?

The scriptural text in this book is presented in the RSAV format—Revised Standard Aural Version. It uses the RSV second edition for the New Testament, copyright 1977, for translation from Greek to English for two reasons:

1. It is considered to be closer to the original Greek writings than many other translations
2. It incorporates the more recently discovered ancient manuscripts in Greek of the New Testament.[41]

---

[40] http://www.biography.com/people/galileo-9305220#reaction-by-the-church

[41] *The New Oxford Annotated Bible with the Apocrypha*, Revised Standard Version, Containing the Second Edition of the New Testament, Edited by Herbert G. May & Bruce Metzger, (New York, Oxford University Press, 1977)

HOW COULD JOHN'S FIRST-CENTURY LISTENERS "HEAR" SOMETHING DIFFERENT FROM WHAT PEOPLE READ TODAY?

The answer to this question is based on the fact that context determines the meaning of what a person hears and reads. This axiom is used to teach reading comprehension in grammar schools today. Students are taught to find "context clues" from the words and phrases that surround a point that is in question, which is what John's listeners did in the first century! They knew how to recognize context clues writers of their time meant for them to catch, but today's readers don't catch the clues because they don't realize they are there or are confused by them.

John provided two types of "context clues" for his listeners. He deliberately repeated words and ideas to lead his listeners to the information that would help them interpret what they heard. It was natural for this oral society to recognize words and concepts repeated in other parts of the text because writers had used this kind of parallelism for centuries. However, today's readers depend upon the words and verses that follow each other in the sequence verses were numbered in the mid-sixteenth century, to provide their contextual clues. But this isn't how first-century writers wrote!

Next, we provide two simple examples to explain first-century parallelism. Unfortunately, these examples won't give you the whole picture because John's use of these techniques was so layered and intricate that we dedicate technical booklets to explain them, which are available on Amazon.com.

AN EXAMPLE OF IDEA REPETITION FROM MATTHEW

The example we provide below is commonly referred to by scholars because it firmly establishes that writers in the first century, including John, deliberately used aural cues that modern readers simply wouldn't recognize as such. The passage we cite below, as it appears in RSV text, suggests that the swine trample on the pearls and turn to attack you. Is this correct? No.

> *"Do not give dogs what is holy; and do not throw your pearls before swine, lest they trample them under foot and turn to attack you."*
> (Mt 7:6 RSV)

Dogs are far more likely to attack a person, but today's readers who interpret this passage as it is sequenced would miss the point. People in the first century would have recognized the two parallel ideas that refer to the two animals who do separate things—dogs attack; swine trample. The first-century listeners would have mentally arranged the elements of this passage as follows:

> *"Do not give **dogs** what is holy lest they turn and **attack you;***
> *do not throw your pearls before **swine** lest they **trample** them under foot"*
> (Mt 7:6 RSAV)

This is why we say first-century listeners heard and understood things differently than modern readers do. Why didn't Matthew write this verse as the RSAV text displays? We can only conclude that first-century listeners understood the passage as he presented it because it was what that particular oral culture did.

If modern readers read this passage in RSV text, they have reason to pause and wonder about the meaning or they might just blow by it, but Matthew was relaying quite a profound statement. However, our purpose here is *not* to explain Matthew's text; it is to illustrate how people in the first century would have mentally construed the very same words that modern readers read to come up with a different answer.

AN EXAMPLE OF WORD REPETITION FROM JOHN

The following example illustrates John's "repetitive words" technique. In this case, the common word is *sin* that is used in relation to being *born of God*. The question this passage raises is, does a person born of God have the potential to sin or not? The question is, can you **not** sin when you are born of God? One phrase says a person "does not sin" which implies that they have the potential to sin, where the next phrase says they cannot sin, which implies they do not have the potential to sin.

> *No one born of God commits sin; for God's nature abides in him,*
> *and he cannot sin because he is born of God* (1 Jn 3:9 RSV)

First-century listeners would have mentally placed the two repetitive passages together as shown in RSAV text below.

> ***No one born of God commits sin,** and **he cannot sin because he is***
> ***born of God;** for God's nature abides in him* (1 Jn 5:6 RSAV).

John made a huge theological point in this verse, and it is now possible to understand it.

- **In phase one**, in order to become born of God (receive eternal life), a person chooses to *not* commit (mortal) sin.
- **In phase two**, after a person receives eternal life (is born of God), the person can *no* longer sin mortally because he or she receives God's nature (his seed).

Again, why didn't John write it this way in the first place? Because first-century listeners understood it as he wrote it. This particular verse has many additional implications, which are covered in detail in chapter 10. For now, we encourage you to read the aural text in this book that is for the first time, available for today's readers to "see" what John's direct audience heard and understood. We want you to join them in receiving the information and inspiration that John actually conveyed.[42]

---

[42] Those interested in understanding the entire body of structures that lead to aural text, please contact the authors.

Outline of RSAV Text

A. Gospel of John (John 1:13–17 RSAV)
    a. Prologue (1:1–16 RSAV)
        i. The Word of God
            1. The Word was in the world that knew him not
            2. The Word was coming into the world
            3. God sent John to bear witness so that all could believe the word was God, became flesh and dwelt among us
        ii. Two witnesses
            1. John the Evangelist testified that Jesus is the Son of god
            2. John the Baptist bore witness that the Son of God is Jesus
        iii. All who believe have the power to become born of God

    b. The Testimony of John the Baptist (1:17–34 RSAV)
        i. The Jews (Israel) meet with John the Baptist
        ii. John the Baptist gives testimony to the Jews (Israel)
            1. Jesus is "the Lamb of God"
            2. Jesus baptizes with the Holy Spirit
            3. Jesus is the Son of God

    c. The First Disciples (1:35–52 RSAV)
        i. John gives testimony to two of his disciples
            1. Andrew and the unnamed disciple (beloved disciple) follow Jesus
            2. Andrew finds his brother Simon Peter, who follows Jesus
        ii. Jesus finds Philip who finds Nathanael
        iii. The Son of man is the Son of God

    d. The Last Supper (John 13:1–31 RSAV)

      i. Jesus's hour had come to return to God

     ii. Jesus washes the disciples' feet

          1. Jesus teaches humility and service

          2. Jesus compares "clean" to "not clean"

    iii. Jesus announces one of the disciples will betray him

          1. The morsel is given to Judas

          2. Only the beloved disciple knew about Judas's betrayal

          3. Judas's exit leads to Jesus's glorification

    iv. Jesus states, "a servant is not greater than his master"

     v. Jesus tells the disciples (less Judas) they have been chosen

e. The Farewell Discourse (John 14–16 RSAV)

      i. Introduction

     ii. Jesus's hour had come

          1. Jesus is leaving soon

          2. The disciples ask for clarity

              a. Peter wants to go with him

              b. Philip wants to see the Father

              c. Thomas wants to know where he is going

    iii. Jesus is the way to the Father: believe and love

          1. Jesus is the way

          2. Believe and love

          3. Do not be afraid

    iv. Jesus will send another Counselor

          1. The disciples will receive the Holy Spirit (the Spirit of Truth)

          2. The Holy Spirit (the Spirit of Truth) is available to everyone

          3. The Holy Spirit (the Spirit of Truth) will bear witness

     v. Jesus is going in a little while

          1. What does a little while mean?

          2. When Jesus goes the Spirit of Truth comes

          3. Sorrow turns to joy

    vi. The disciples believe Jesus came from God

     vii. Ask in my name and you shall receive that your joy may be full

    viii. Jesus prepares the disciples

        1. Abide in Jesus and bear fruit

        2. The disciples are clean by the Word

        3. The world hated Jesus

        4. If they persecuted me, they will persecute you

        5. Love one another as I have loved you

        6. Bear fruit that your joy may be full

f. The Farewell Prayer (John 17:1–27 RSAV)

    i. Jesus prays to be glorified

    ii. Jesus prays for the disciples

        1. To send the disciples into the world

        2. To continue to protect the disciples from the evil one

        3. To give the glory Jesus had on earth to the disciples

        4. To give the disciples eternal life

    iii. Jesus prays for all who believe to provide access to eternal life

    iv. John defines eternal life

B. 1 John (1:1–5:14 RSAV)

  a. John's Proclamation of Eternal Life (1:1–10 RSAV)

    i. John testifies to eternal life

    ii. John proclaims Jesus is the Word of life

    iii. What John now knows

    iv. The challenge

  b. The Message (2:1–3:30 RSAV)

    i. Believe in Jesus

        1. Jesus cleanses us from sin and all unrighteousness

        2. Pitfalls to avoid

        3. Jesus forgives and guides us

        4. Have confidence in his coming

  ii. Status of the believing community
    1. Believers born of God
    2. Believers who stopped believing in Jesus (the antichrists)
    3. Believers at risk of the temptations of the world
    4. How believers know their status
  iii. Believe Jesus Christ is the Son of God
  iv. Love one another
    1. Don't be like Cain to be born of God
    2. The disciples know they are born of God
    3. How do believers know they are born of God?
      a. Test the spirits
      b. Keep the new commandment
    4. The gift of being born of God: ask and receive

c. God's Plan (4:1–32 RSAV)
  i. The goal: love one another to be born of God
  ii. The approach
    1. God sent his Son Jesus
      a. God's love was made manifest in Jesus, his Son
      b. Obey God's commands: love God; Love your brother
      c. Perfected love
    2. Testimony about Jesus and his mission
      a. The disciples testify
      b. The Spirit testifies
      c. True believers testify
    3. Faith in their testimony

d. Choose (5:1–14 RSAV)
  i. Children of God or of the devil
  ii. Children of God shall see Jesus
  iii. Let no one deceive you

238 • Jesus's Beloved Disciple Calling

C. 2 John (1:1–16 RSAV)

    a. Walk in the truth

    b. Beware of the deceiver who is the antichrist

    c. Complete your journey

    d. Walk according to His commandments

D. 3 John (1:1–18 RSAV)

    a. Greeting

    b. Request for Gaius to render service to Deme'trius

    c. Diot'rephes does not welcome the brethren

    d. Imitate good

E. Appendices

    a. Description of the development of RSAV text (Revised Standard Aural Version) from RSV text

    b. Outline of RSAV text included in this book

    c. RSAV texts: John 1, 13–17; 1 John, 2 John, 3 John

    d. Review questions and answers

Appendix C
RSAV Text

Part II: Gospel of John: Prologue and Testimony
(John 1:1–51)

The Prologue
(Jn 1:1–16 RSAV)

The Word of God
The Word Was in the World That Knew Him Not

¹:¹In the beginning was the Word and the Word was with God. ²He was in the beginning with God; all things were made through him, and without him was not anything made that was made. ³He was in the world, and the world was made through him, yet the world knew him not.

The Word Was Coming into the World

⁴In him was life, and the life was the light of everyone. ⁵The light shines in the darkness, and the darkness has not overcome it. ⁶The true light that enlightens everyone was coming into the world.

God Sent John to Bear Witness That the Word Was God

⁷There was a man sent from God, whose name was John. ⁸He came for testimony, to bear witness to the light. ⁹He was not the light, but came to bear witness to the light, that all might believe through him, that the Word was God and the Word became flesh and dwelt among us.

Two Witnesses of the Word
John the Evangelist Testified That Jesus Is the Son of God

¹⁰We have beheld his glory, glory as of the only Son from the Father full of grace and truth. ¹¹And from his fullness, we have all received, grace upon grace.

[12]Grace and truth came through Jesus Christ, the only Son, who is in the bosom of the Father, he has made him known. [13]No one has ever seen God, for the law was given through Moses.

John the Baptist Bore Witness That the Son of God Is Jesus

[14]John bore witness to him, and cried, "This was he of whom I said, 'He who comes after me ranks before me, for he was before me.'"

All Who Believe Have the Power to Become Born of God

[15]He came to his own home, and his own people received him not. [16]But to all who received him, who believed in his name, he gave power to become children of God; who were born of God, not of blood nor of the will of the flesh nor of the will of man.

The Testimony of John the Baptist
(Jn 1:17–34 RSAV)

The Jews (Israel) Meet with John the Baptist

[17]And this is the testimony of John, when the Jews sent priests and Levites from Jerusalem to ask him, "Who are you?" [18]They said to him then, "Who are you? Let us have an answer for those who sent us. What do you say about yourself?" [19]He confessed, he did not deny, but confessed, "I am not the Christ." [20]"Are you Elijah?" He said, "I am not." "Are you the prophet?" And he answered, "No." [21]And they asked him, "What then?"

[22]Now they had been sent from the Pharisees. [23]They asked him, "Then why are you baptizing, if you are neither the Christ, nor Elijah, nor the prophet?"

[24]He said, "I am the voice of one crying in the wilderness, 'Make straight the way of the Lord,' as the prophet Isaiah said. [25]This took place in Bethany beyond the Jordan, where John was baptizing.

John the Baptist Gives Testimony to the Jews (Israel)
Jesus Is the Lamb of God

[26]John answered them, "I baptize with water; but among you stands one whom you do not know, even he who comes after me, the thong of whose sandal I am not worthy to untie." [27]The next day he saw Jesus coming toward him, and said, "Behold, the Lamb of God, who takes away the sin of the world! [28]This is he of whom I said, 'after me comes a man who ranks before me, for he was before me.' [29]For this I came baptizing with water, that he might be revealed to Israel. [30]I myself did not know him."

Jesus Baptizes with the Holy Spirit

[31]"I saw the Spirit descend as a dove from heaven, and it remained on him. [32]He who sent me to baptize with water said to me, 'He on whom you see the Spirit descend and remain, this is he who baptizes with the Holy Spirit.' [33]I myself did not know him."

Jesus Is the Son of God

[34]And John bore witness, "I have seen and have borne witness that this is the Son of God."

The First Disciples
(Jn 1:35–52 RSAV)

John the Baptist Gives Testimony to Two of His Disciples
Andrew and the Unnamed Disciple (Beloved Disciple) Follow Jesus

[1:35]The next day again John was standing with two of his disciples; and he looked at Jesus as he walked, and said, "Behold, the Lamb of God!" [36]The two disciples heard him say this, and they followed Jesus. [37]Jesus turned, and saw them following, and said to them, "What do you seek?" And they said to him, "Rabbi" (which means Teacher), "where are you staying?" [38]He said to them, "Come and see."

Andrew Finds His Brother Simon Peter, Who Follows Jesus

[39]One of the two who heard John speak and followed him was Andrew, Simon

Peter's brother. [40]He first found his brother Simon, and said to him, "We have found the Messiah" (which means Christ). He brought him to Jesus. [41]Jesus looked at him, and said, "So you are Simon the son of John? You shall be called "Cephas" (which means Peter). [42] They came and saw where he was staying; and they stayed with him that day, for it was about the tenth hour.

Jesus Finds Philip Who Finds Nathanael

[43]The next day Jesus decided to go to Galilee. And he found Philip and said to him, "Follow me." [44]Now Philip was from Bethsaida, the city of Andrew and Peter.

[45]Philip found Nathanael, and said to him, "We have found him of whom Moses in the law and also the prophets wrote, Jesus of Nazareth, the son of Joseph." [46]Nathanael said to him, "Can anything good come out of Nazareth?" [47]Philip said to him, "Come and see."

[48]Jesus saw Nathanael coming to him, and said of him, "Behold, an Israelite indeed, in whom is no guile!" Nathanael said to him, "How do you know me?" [49]Jesus answered him, "Before Philip called you, when you were under the fig tree, I saw you." [50]Nathanael answered him, "Rabbi, you are the Son of God! You are the King of Israel!" [51]Jesus answered him, "because I said to you, I saw you under the fig tree do you believe? You shall see greater things than these."

The Son of Man Is the Son of God

[52]And he said to them, "Truly, truly, I say to you, you will see heaven opened, and the angels of God ascending and descending upon the Son of man."

Part III: Gospel of John: Farewell Address (John 13–17 RSAV)

Last Supper
(Jn 13:1–31 RSAV)

Jesus's Hour Had Come to Return to God

[1]Now before the feast of the Passover, when Jesus knew that his hour had come to depart out of this world to the Father, having loved his own who were in the world, he loved them to the end. [2]Jesus knew that the Father had given all things into his hands, and that he had come from God and was going to God.

Jesus Washes the Disciples' Feet
Jesus Teaches Humility and Service

[3]And during supper, when the devil had already put it into the heart of Judas Iscariot, Simon's son, to betray him, he rose from supper, laid aside his garments, and girded himself with a towel. [4]Then he poured water into a basin, and began to wash the disciples' feet, and to wipe them with the towel with which he was girded.

[5]He came to Simon Peter; and Peter said to him, "Lord, do you wash my feet? [6]You shall never wash my feet." Jesus answered him, "If I do not wash you, you have no part in me." [7]Simon Peter said to him, "Lord, not my feet only but also my hands and my head!" [8]Jesus answered him, "What I am doing you do not know now, but afterward you will understand."

[9]When he had washed their feet, and taken his garments, and resumed his place, he said to them, "Do you know what I have done to you? [10]For I have given you an example that you also should do as I have done to you. [11]You call me Teacher and Lord; and you are right, for so I am. [12]If I then, your Lord and Teacher, have washed your feet, you also ought to wash one another's feet."

Jesus Compares "Clean" to "Not Clean"

[13]"He who has bathed does not need to wash, except for his feet, but he is clean all over; and you are clean, but not every one of you." [14]For he knew who was to betray him; that was why he said, "You are not all clean."

Jesus Announces One of the Disciples Will Betray Him
The Morsel Is Given to Judas

[15]When Jesus had thus spoken, he was troubled in spirit, and testified, "Truly, truly, I say to you, one of you will betray me." [16]The disciples looked at one another, uncertain of whom he spoke. [17]One of his disciples, whom Jesus loved, was lying close to the breast of Jesus; [18]so Simon Peter beckoned to him and said, "Tell us who it is of whom he speaks."

[19]So lying thus, close to the breast of Jesus, he said to him, "Lord, who is it?" [19]Jesus answered, "It is he to whom I shall give this morsel when I have dipped it." [20]So when he had dipped the morsel, he gave it to Judas, the son of Simon Iscariot. [21]Then after the morsel, Satan entered into him. Jesus said to him, "What you are going to do, do quickly." [22]So, after receiving the morsel, he immediately went out; and it was night.

Only the Beloved Disciple Knew About Judas's Betrayal

[23]Now no one at the table knew why he said this to him. [24]Some thought that, because Judas had the money box, Jesus was telling him, "Buy what we need for the feast"; or, that he should give something to the poor.

Judas's Exit Leads to Jesus's Glorification

[25]When he had gone out, Jesus said, "Now is the Son of man glorified, and in him (Jesus) God is glorified; [26]if God is glorified in him (Jesus) God will also glorify him (Jesus) in himself, and glorify him (Jesus) at once."

Jesus States, "A Servant Is Not Greater Than His Master"

[27]"Truly, truly, I say to you, a servant is not greater than his master; nor is he who is sent greater than he who sent him. [28]Truly, truly, I say to you, he who receives any one whom I send receives me; and he who receives me receives him who sent me. [29]If you know these things, blessed are you if you do them."

Jesus Tells the Disciples (Less Judas) They Have Been Chosen

[30]"I am not speaking of you all; I know whom I have chosen; it is that the scripture may be fulfilled, 'He who ate my bread has lifted his heel against me.'

³¹I tell you this now, before it takes place, that when it does take place you may believe that I am he."

Farewell Discourse
(Jn 14:1–16:26 RSAV)

Jesus's Hour Had Come
Jesus Is Leaving Soon

^{14:1}"Little children, yet a little while I am with you. You will seek me; and as I said to the Jews so now I say to you, 'Where I am going you cannot come.'"

The Disciples Ask for Clarity
Peter Wants to Go with Him

²Simon Peter said to him, "Lord, where are you going?" Jesus answered, "Where I am going you cannot follow me now." ³Peter said to him, "Lord, why cannot I follow you now? I will lay down my life for you." ⁴Jesus answered, "Will you lay down your life for me? ⁵Truly, truly, I say to you, the cock will not crow, till you have denied me three times, but you shall follow afterward.

⁶In my Father's house are many rooms; if it were not so, would I have told you that I go to prepare a place for you? ⁷And when I go and prepare a place for you, I will come again and will take you to myself, that where I am you may be also."

Philip Wants to See the Father

⁸Philip said to him, "Lord, show us the Father, and we shall be satisfied." ⁹Jesus said to him, "Have I been with you so long, and yet you do not know me, Philip? ⁹He who has seen me has seen the Father; how can you say, 'Show us the Father'? ¹⁰Do you not believe that I am in the Father and the Father in me? ¹¹Believe me that I am in the Father and the Father in me; or else believe me for the sake of the works themselves. ¹²The words that I say to you I do not speak on my own authority; but the Father who dwells in me does his works.

¹³Truly, truly, I say to you, he who believes in me will also do the works that I do. ¹⁴Whatever you ask in my name I will do it. ¹⁵If you ask anything in my name I will do it, that the Father may be glorified in the Son ¹⁶and greater works than these will he do, because I go to the Father."

Thomas Wants to Know Where He is Going

[17]"And you know the way where I am going." [18]Thomas said to him, "Lord, we do not know where you are going; how can we know the way?"

Jesus Is the Way to the Father: Believe and Love
Jesus Is the Way

[19]Jesus said to him, "I am the way, and the truth, and the life; no one comes to the Father, but by me. [20]If you had known me, you would have known my Father also; henceforth you know him and have seen him."

Believe and Love

[21]"Let not your hearts be troubled; believe in God, believe also in me. [22]A new commandment I give to you, that you love one another; that you also love one another even as I have loved you. [23]By this all men will know that you are my disciples, if you have love for one another."

Do Not Be Afraid

[24]"Let not your hearts be troubled, neither let them be afraid. [25]You heard me say to you, `I go away, and I will come to you.' [26]I will no longer talk much with you, for the ruler of this world is coming. He has no power over me. [27]If you loved me, you would have rejoiced, because I go to the Father; for the Father is greater than I. [28]I do as the Father has commanded me, so that the world may know that I love the Father.

[29]And now I have told you before it takes place, so that when it does take place, you may believe."

Jesus Will Send Another Counselor
The Disciples Will Receive the Holy Spirit (the Spirit of Truth)

[30]"If you love me, you will keep my commandments. [31]And I will pray the Father, and he will give you another Counselor, the Spirit of truth, whom the world cannot receive, because it neither sees him nor knows him; you know him, for he dwells with you, and will be in you to be with you forever. [32]In that day you will know that I am in my Father, and you in me, and I in you.

[33]I will not leave you desolate I will come to you. [34]Yet a little while, and the world will see me no more, but you will see me; because I live, you will live also. [35]And the Counselor, the Holy Spirit, whom the Father will send in my name, he will teach you all things, and bring to your remembrance all that I have said to you. [36]Peace I leave with you; my peace I give to you; not as the world gives do I give to you.

[37]He who has my commandments and keeps them, he it is who loves me; and he who loves me will be loved by my Father, and I will love him and manifest myself to him." [38]He who does not love me does not keep my words; and the word which you hear is not mine but the Father's who sent me."

The Holy Spirit (the Spirit of Truth) Is Available to Everyone

[39]Judas (not Iscariot) said to him, "Lord, how is it that you will manifest yourself to us, and not to the world?" [40]Jesus answered him, "If a man loves me, he will keep my word, and my Father will love him, and we will come to him and make our home with him.

[41]These things I have spoken to you, while I am with you."

The Holy Spirit (the Spirit of Truth) Will Bear Witness

[15:1]"But when the Counselor comes, whom I shall send to you from the Father, even the Spirit of truth, who proceeds from the Father, he will bear witness to me; and you also are witnesses, because you have been with me from the beginning.

[2]I did not say these things to you from the beginning, because I was with you. [3]I have said all this to you to keep you from falling away. [4]They will put you out of the synagogues, [3]and they will do this because they have not known the Father, nor me. [5]Indeed, the hour is coming when whoever kills you will think he is offering service to God. [6]I have said these things to you, that when their hour comes you may remember that I told you of them. [7]But because I have said these things to you, sorrow has filled your hearts.

[8]Nevertheless I tell you the truth: it is to your advantage that I go away, for if I do not go away, the Counselor will not come to you; but if I go, I will send him to you. [9]And when he comes, he will convince the world concerning sin and righteousness and judgment: [10]concerning sin, because they do not believe in

me; [11]concerning judgment, because the ruler of this world is judged; [12]concerning righteousness, because I go to the Father, and you will see me no more."

Jesus Is Going in a Little While
What Does "a Little While" Mean?

[13]"Now I am going to him who sent me; yet none of you asks me, 'Where are you going?' [14]A little while, and you will see me no more; again a little while, and you will see me."

[15]Some of his disciples said to one another, "What is this that he says to us, 'a little while, and you will not see me, and again a little while, and you will see me'; and, 'because I go to the Father'?" [16]Jesus knew that they wanted to ask him; so he said to them, "Is this what you are asking yourselves, what I meant by saying, 'A little while, and you will not see me, and again a little while, and you will see me.'"

[17]They said, "What does he mean by 'a little while'? We do not know what he means."

When Jesus Goes, the Spirit of Truth Comes

[18]"I have yet many things to say to you, but you cannot bear them now. [19]When the Spirit of truth comes he will guide you into all the truth; for he will not speak on his own authority, but [20]he will glorify me, for he will take what is mine and declare it to you. [21]All that the Father has is mine; therefore, I said that he will take what is mine and declare it to you. [22]Whatever he hears he will speak, and he will declare to you the things that are to come."

Sorrow Turns to Joy

[23]"Truly, truly, I say to you, you will weep and lament, but the world will rejoice; you will be sorrowful, but your sorrow will turn into joy. [24]So you have sorrow now, but I will see you again and your hearts will rejoice, and no one will take your joy from you.

[25]When a woman is in travail she has sorrow, but when she is delivered of the child, she no longer remembers the anguish because her hour has come for joy

that a child is born into the world.

²⁶The hour is coming, indeed it has come, when you will be scattered, every man to his home, and will leave me alone; yet I am not alone, for the Father is with me. I have said this to you, that in me you may have peace. In the world you have tribulation; but be of good cheer, I have overcome the world."

The Disciples Believe Jesus Came from God

²⁷"In that day you will ask nothing of me. ²⁸I have said this to you in figures; I shall no longer speak to you in figures but tell you plainly of the Father. ²⁹The hour is coming. I came from the Father and have come into the world; again, I am leaving the world and going to the Father. ³⁰Do you now believe?" ³¹His disciples said, "Ah, now you are speaking plainly, not in any figure! Now we know that you know all things, and need none to question you; by this we believe that you came from God."

Ask in My Name and You Shall Receive That Your Joy May Be Full

³²Jesus answered them, "in that day you will ask in my name, because you have loved me and have believed that I came from the Father. ³³I do not say to you that I shall pray the Father for you; for the Father himself loves you."

³⁴ "Truly, truly, I say to you, hitherto you have asked nothing in my name; if you ask anything of the Father, he will give it to you in my name. ³⁵Ask, and you will receive, that your joy may be full."

Jesus Prepares the Disciples
Abide in Jesus and Bear Fruit

¹⁶:¹"Rise, let us go hence. ²I am the true vine, and my Father is the vinedresser. ³Every branch of mine that bears no fruit, he takes away and every branch that does bear fruit he prunes, that it may bear more fruit. ⁴As the branch cannot bear fruit by itself, unless it abides in the vine, neither can you, unless you abide in me. ⁵I am the vine, you are the branches. He who abides in me, and I in him, he it is that bears much fruit, for apart from me you can do nothing. ⁶If a man does not abide in me, he is cast forth as a branch and withers; and the branches are gathered, thrown into the fire and burned."

The Disciples Are Clean by the Word

[7]"You are already made clean by the word which I have spoken to you. [8]Abide in me, and I in you. [9]If you abide in me, and my words abide in you, ask whatever you will, and it shall be done for you. [10]By this my Father is glorified, that you bear much fruit, and so prove to be my disciples."

The World Hated Jesus

[11]"If the world hates you know that it has hated me before it hated you; but you are not of the world, because I chose you out of the world, therefore the world hates you. [12]If I had not come and spoken to them, they would not have sin; but now they have no excuse for their sin. [13]If I had not done among them the works which no one else did, they would not have sin; but now they have seen and hated both me and my Father. [14]He who hates me hates my Father also. [15]It is to fulfill the word that is written in their law, 'They hated me without a cause.'"

If They Persecuted Me, They Will Persecute You

[16]"Remember the word that I said to you, 'if they persecuted me, they will persecute you; a servant is not greater than his master', if they kept my word, they will keep yours also. [17]But all this they will do to you on my account, because they do not know him who sent me."

Love One Another as I Have Loved You

[18]"As the Father has loved me, so have I loved you; abide in my love. [19]If you keep my commandments you will abide in my love, just as I have kept my Father's commandments and abide in his love. [20]"This is my commandment, that you love one another as I have loved you. [21]This I command you, to love one another.

[22]Greater love has no man than this that a man lay down his life for his friends. [23]You are my friends if you do what I command you. [24]No longer do I call you servants, for the servant does not know what his master is doing; but I have called you friends, for all that I have heard from my Father I have made known to you."

Bear Fruit That Your Joy May Be Full

[25]"You did not choose me, but I chose you and appointed you that you should go and bear fruit and that your fruit should abide; so that whatever you ask the Father in my name, he may give it to you.

[26]These things I have spoken to you, that my joy may be in you, and that your joy may be full."

Farewell Prayer
(Jn 17:1–27 RSAV)

Jesus Prayed to Be Glorified

[17:1]When Jesus had spoken these words, he lifted up his eyes to heaven and said, "Father, the hour has come, [2]since thou has given him power over all flesh, so that he can give eternal life to all whom thou has given him. Glorify thy Son that the Son may glorify thee. [3]I glorified thee on earth, having accomplished the work which thou gave me to do; [4]and now, Father, glorify thou me in thy own presence with the glory which I had with thee before the world was made."

Jesus Prayed for the Disciples
To Send the Disciples into the World

[5]"I have manifested thy name to the men whom thou gave me out of the world; thine they were, and thou gave them to me, and they have kept thy word. [6]I am praying for them; I am not praying for the world but for those whom thou has given me, for they are thine; [7]all mine are thine, and thine are mine, and I am glorified in them.

[8]Now they know that everything that thou has given me is from thee; for I have given them the words which thou gave me, and they have received them and know in truth that I came from thee; and they have believed that thou did send me. [9]Sanctify them in the truth; thy word is truth. [10]And for their sake I consecrate myself, that they also may be consecrated in truth. [11]As thou did send me into the world, so I have sent them into the world."

To Continue to Protect the Disciples from the Evil One

[12]"And now I am no more in the world, but they are in the world, and I am coming to thee. [13]I have guarded them, and none of them is lost but the son of perdition, that the scripture might be fulfilled. [14]I have given them thy word; and the world has hated them because they are not of the world, even as I am not of the world. [15]They are not of the world, even as I am not of the world. [16]I do not pray that thou should take them out of the world, but that thou should keep them from the evil one."

To Give the Glory Jesus Had on Earth to the Disciples

[17]"Now I am coming to thee; and these things I speak in the world, that they may have my joy fulfilled in themselves. [18]Holy Father, keep them in thy name, which thou has given me. [19]While I was with them, I kept them in thy name, which thou has given me, that they may be one, even as we are one. [20]The glory which thou has given me I have given to them, that they may be one even as we are one."

To Give the Disciples Eternal Life

[21]"Father, I desire that they also, whom thou has given me, may be with me where I am, to behold my glory which thou has given me in thy love for me before the foundation of the world. [22]I in them and thou in me, that they may become perfectly one, so that the world may know that thou has sent me and has loved them even as thou has loved me.

[23]O righteous Father, the world has not known thee, but I have known thee; and these know that thou has sent me. [24]I made known to them thy name, and I will make it known, that the love with which thou has loved me may be in them, and I in them."

Jesus Prayed for All Who Believe to Have Access to Eternal Life

[25]"I do not pray for these only, but also for those who believe in me through their word, [26]that they may all be one; even as thou, Father, art in me, and I in thee, that they also may be in us, so that the world may believe that thou has sent me."

John Defined Eternal Life

[27]"And this is eternal life, that they know thee the only true God, and Jesus Christ whom thou has sent."

Part IV: 1 John (1 Jn 1–5 RSAV)

John's Proclamation of Eternal Life
(1 John 1:1–10 RSAV)

John Testified to Eternal Life

[1:1]That which was from the beginning, concerning the word of life, which we have heard, which we have seen with our eyes, which we have looked upon and touched with our hands. [2]That which we have seen and heard we proclaim also to you, so that you may have fellowship with us and our fellowship is with the Father and with his Son Jesus Christ.

John Proclaimed Jesus Is the Word of Life

[3]The life was made manifest, which was with the Father and was made manifest to us. We saw it, and testify to it, and proclaim to you the eternal life.

[4]We are writing this that our joy may be complete.

What John Knew

[5]We know that any one born of God does not sin, and the evil one does not touch him. [6]He who was born of God keeps him, [7]and we know that the Son of God has come and has given us understanding to know him who is true; and we are in him who is true.

[8]This is the true God and eternal life his Son Jesus Christ.

The Challenge

[9]We know that we are of God, and the whole world is in the power of the evil one. [10]Little children, keep yourselves from idols.

The Message
(1 Jn 2:1–3:30 RSAV)

Believe in Jesus

Jesus Cleanses Us from Sin and All Unrighteousness

²:¹This is the message we have heard from him and proclaim to you; ²that God is light and in him is no darkness at all and the blood of Jesus his Son cleanses us from all sin. ³If we confess our sins, he is faithful and just, and will forgive our sins and cleanse us from all unrighteousness.

Pitfalls to Avoid

⁴If we say we have no sin, we deceive ourselves, and the truth is not in us. ⁵If we say we have not sinned, we make him a liar, and his word is not in us.

⁶If we say we have fellowship with him while we walk in darkness, we lie and do not live according to the truth; ⁷but if we walk in the light, as he is in the light, we have fellowship with one another.

Jesus Forgives and Guides Us

⁸My little children, I am writing this to you so that you may not sin; but if any one does sin, ⁹he is the expiation for our sins, and not for ours only but also for the sins of the whole world.

¹⁰We have an advocate with the Father, Jesus Christ the righteous.

Have Confidence in His Coming

¹¹I am writing to you, little children, because your sins are forgiven for his sake. ¹²And now, little children, abide in him, so that when he appears we may have confidence and not shrink from him in shame at his coming.

Status of the Believing Community
Believers Born of God

¹³I am writing to you, fathers, because you know him who is from the

beginning. [14]I write to you, fathers, because you know him who is from the beginning.

[15]I am writing to you, young men, because you have overcome the evil one. [16]I write to you, young men, because you are strong, and the word of God abides in you, and you have overcome the evil one.

[17]I write to you, children, because you know the Father.

Believers Who Stopped Believing in Jesus (Antichrists)

[18]Children, it is the last hour and as you have heard that antichrist is coming, so now many antichrists have come therefore, we know that it is the last hour. [19]They went out from us, but they were not of us; but they went out, that it might be plain that they all are not of us. [20]For if they had been of us, they would have continued with us, [21]but you have been anointed by the Holy One, and you all know. [22]You know that no lie comes from the truth. [23]Who is the liar, but he who denies that Jesus is the Christ. [24]This is the antichrist, he who denies the Father and the Son. [25]No one who denies the Son has the Father. He who confesses the Son has the Father also.

[26]I write to you, not because you do not know the truth, but because you know it.

Believers at Risk of the Temptations of the World

[27]Do not love the world or the things in the world. [28]For all that is in the world is not of the Father but is of the world: [29]the lust of the flesh and the lust of the eyes and the pride of life. [30]And the world passes away, and the lust of it. [31]Let what you heard from the beginning abide in you. [32]If what you heard from the beginning abides in you, then you will abide in the Son and in the Father, [33]and this is what he has promised us, eternal life. [34]As for you, the anointing which you received from him abides in you, as his anointing teaches you about everything, and is true, and is no lie. [35]You have no need that any one should teach you; just as it has taught you, abide in him.

[36]I write this to you about those who would deceive you.

How Believers Can Know Their Status

[37]And by this we may be sure that we know him, if we keep his commandments. [38]Whoever keeps his word, in him truly love for God is perfected. By this we may be sure that we are in him.

[39]He who says "I know him" but disobeys his commandments, is a liar, and the truth is not in him. [40]He who says he abides in him ought to walk in the same way in which he walked. [41]He who says he is in the light and hates his brother is in the darkness still. [42]He who hates his brother is in the darkness and walks in the darkness, and does not know where he is going, because the darkness has blinded his eyes.

[43]He who loves his brother abides in the light, and in it there is no cause for stumbling.

Believe Jesus Christ Is the Son of God

[44]Beloved, I am writing you no new commandment, [45]yet I am writing you a new commandment which is true in him and in you, [46]and the true light is already shining because the darkness is passing away. [47]Yet an old commandment which you had from the beginning, the old commandment is the word which you have heard.

Love One Another
Don't Be Like Cain to Be Born of God

[3:1]For this is the message, which you have heard from the beginning, that we should love one another, [2]and not be like Cain who was of the evil one and murdered his brother, because his own deeds were evil and his brother's righteous. [3]And why did he murder him? [4]Anyone who hates his brother is a murderer, and you know that no murderer has eternal life abiding in him.

[5]If anyone has the world's goods and sees his brother in need, yet closes his heart against him, how does God's love abide in him? [6]By this we know love that we ought to lay down our lives for the brethren, because he laid down his life for us.

The Disciples Knew They Were Born of God

[7]Do not wonder, brethren, that the world hates you. [8]He who does not love abides in death. [9]We know that we have passed out of death into life, because we love the brethren. [10]And by this we know that he abides in us, by the Spirit, which he has given us.

[11]Beloved don't believe every spirit, but test the spirits to see whether they are of God; for many false prophets have gone out into the world. [12]They are of the world, therefore what they say is of the world, and the world listens to them. [13]We are of God. [14]Whoever knows God listens to us, and he who is not of God does not listen to us. [15]By this we know the spirit of truth and the spirit of error.

How Believers Can Know They Are Born of God
Test the Spirits

[16]By this you know the Spirit of God: every spirit which confesses that Jesus Christ has come in the flesh is of God, [17]and every spirit which does not confess Jesus is not of God. [18]This is the spirit of antichrist, of which you heard that it was coming, and now it is in the world already.

[19]Little children, you are of God, and have overcome them; for he who is in you is greater than he who is in the world.

Keep the New Commandment

[20]Little children, let us not love in word or speech but, in deed and in truth. [21]By this we shall know that we are of the truth, because we keep his commandments and do what pleases him. [22]All who keep his commandments abide in him, and he in them. [23]And this is his commandment, that we should believe in the name of his Son Jesus Christ and love one another, just as he has commanded us.

The Gift of Being Born of God: Ask and Receive

[24]Reassure our hearts before him, whenever our hearts condemn us; for God is greater than our hearts, and he knows everything and we receive from him whatever we ask. [25]Beloved, if our hearts do not condemn us, we have

258 · Jesus's Beloved Disciple Calling

confidence before God.

²⁶And this is the confidence, which we have in him; if we ask anything according to his will he hears us. ²⁷If any one sees his brother committing what is not a mortal sin he will ask, and God will give him life for those whose sin is not mortal. ²⁸All wrongdoing is sin, but there is sin, which is not mortal. ²⁹There is sin which is mortal. I do not say that one is to pray for that.

³⁰And if we know that he hears us in whatever we ask, we know that we have obtained the requests made of him.

God's Plan
(1 Jn 4:1–30 RSAV)

The Goal: Love One Another to Be Born of God

⁴·¹Beloved, let us love one another; for love is of God since God is love. He who loves is born of God and knows God. ²He who does not love does not know God. ³Beloved, if God so loved us, we also ought to love one another. ⁴If we love one another, God abides in us and his love is perfected in us.

The Approach
God Sent His Son, Jesus
God's love was made manifest in Jesus, his Son

⁵No man has ever seen God. ⁶In this the love of God was made manifest among us that God sent his only Son into the world. ⁷In this is love, not that we loved God but that he loved us and sent his Son to be the expiation for our sins so that we might live through him.

Obey God's Commands: Love God; Love Your Brother

⁸Whoever confesses that Jesus is the Son of God, God abides in him, and he in God. ⁹God is love, and he who abides in love abides in God, so we know and believe the love God has for us.

¹⁰We love, because he first loved us. ¹¹If any one says, "I love God," and hates his brother, he is a liar; for he who does not love his brother whom he has seen, cannot love God whom he has not seen.

[12]And this commandment we have from him, that he who loves God should love his brother also.[13]By this we know that we love the children of God, when we love God and obey his commandments. For this is the love of God, that we keep his commandments. And his commandments are not burdensome.

Perfected Love

[14]Everyone who believes that Jesus is the Christ is a child of God, and everyone who loves the parent loves the child. [15]In this is love perfected with us. [16]There is no fear in love; for fear has to do with punishment, and he who fears is not perfected in love. [17]Perfect love casts out fear that we may have confidence for the day of judgment, because as he is so are we in this world.

Testimony About Jesus and His Mission
The Disciples Testify

[18]By this we know that we abide in him and he in us, because he has given us of his own Spirit. [19]And we have seen and testify that the Father has sent his Son as the Savior of the world.

The Spirit Testifies

[20]This is he who came by water and blood, not with the water only but with the water and the blood Jesus Christ. [21]There are three witnesses, and these three agree, the Spirit, the water, and the blood. [22]And the Spirit is the witness, because the Spirit is the truth. [23]And this is the testimony, God gave us eternal life, and this life is in his Son. [24]He who has the Son has life; he who has not the Son of God has not life.

True Believers Testify

[25]If we receive the testimony of men, the testimony of God is greater; for this is the testimony of God that he has borne witness to his Son. [26]He who does not believe God has made him a liar, because he has not believed in the testimony that God has borne to his Son.

[27]He who believes in the Son of God has the testimony in himself.

Faith in Their Testimony

[28]I write this to you who believe in the name of the Son of God, that you may know that you have eternal life. [29]For whatever is born of God overcomes the world, and who is it that overcomes the world, but he who believes that Jesus is the Son of God. [30]This is the victory that overcomes the world, our faith.

Choose
(1 Jn 5:1–14 RSAV)

Children of God or of the Devil

[5:1]If you know that he is righteous, you may be sure that everyone who does right is born of him. [2]He who does right is righteous, as he is righteous; whoever does not do right is not of God, nor he who does not love his brother.

[3]He who commits sin is of the devil; for the devil has sinned from the beginning. [4]The reason the Son of God appeared was to destroy the works of the devil. [5]By this it may be seen who are the children of God, and who are the children of the devil.

Children of God Shall See Jesus

[6]No one born of God commits sin, and he cannot sin because he is born of God; for God's nature abides in him. [7]See what love the Father has given us, that we should be called children of God; and so we are. [8]Beloved, we are God's children now; it does not yet appear what we shall be, but we know that when he appears we shall be like him, for we shall see him as he is.

Let No One Deceive You

[9]The reason why the world does not know us is that it did not know him. [10]You know that he appeared to take away sins, and in him there is no sin. [11]No one who abides in him sins; no one who sins has either seen him or known him. [12]And every one who thus hopes in him purifies himself as he is pure. [13]Every one who commits sin is guilty of lawlessness; sin is lawlessness.

[14]Little children, let no one deceive you.

Part V: 2 and 3 John

Reject All False Teaching
2 John 1:1–16 RSAV

Walk in the Truth

¹:¹The elder to the elect lady and her children, whom I love in the truth, and not only I but also all who know the truth, ²because of the truth which abides in us and will be with us forever. ³Grace, mercy, and peace will be with us, from God the Father and from Jesus Christ the Father's Son, in truth and love.

⁴Though I have much to write to you, I would rather not use paper and ink, but I hope to come to see you and talk with you face to face, so that our joy may be complete. ⁵The children of your elect sister greet you.

Beware of the Deceiver Who Is the Antichrist

⁶I rejoiced greatly to find some of your children walking in the truth, just as we have been commanded by the Father. ⁷For many deceivers have gone out into the world; men who will not acknowledge the coming of Jesus Christ in the flesh, such a one is the deceiver and the antichrist.

⁸Anyone who goes ahead and does not abide in the doctrine of Christ does not have God; ⁹he who abides in the doctrine has both the Father and the Son. ¹⁰If any one comes to you and does not bring this doctrine, do not receive him into the house or give him any greeting; for he who greets him shares his wicked work. ¹²He who abides in the doctrine has both the Father and the Son.

Complete Your Journey

¹³Look to yourselves that you may not lose what you have worked for, but may win a full reward.

Walk According to His Commandments

¹⁴And now I beg you, lady, not as though I were writing you a new commandment, but the one we have had from the beginning, that we love one

another. ¹⁵This is the commandment, as you have heard from the beginning, that you follow love. ¹⁶And this is love, that we follow his commandments.

Love All the Brethren
(3 John 1:1–18 RSAV)

Greeting

¹The elder to the beloved Ga'ius, whom I love in the truth, ²I had much to write to you, but I would rather not write with pen and ink; ³I hope to see you soon, and we will talk together face to face. ⁴Peace be to you. The friends greet you. Greet the friends, every one of them by name.

Request for Ga'ius to Render Service to Deme'trius

⁵Beloved, I pray that all may go well with you and that you may be in health. I know that it is well with your soul. ⁶For I greatly rejoiced when some of the brethren arrived and testified to the truth of your life, as indeed you do follow in the truth. ⁷Beloved, it is a loyal thing you do when you render any service to the brethren, ⁸especially to strangers, ⁶ᵃwho have testified to your love before the church. ⁹No greater joy can I have than this, to hear that my children follow in the truth; ¹⁰So we ought to support such men, that we may be fellow workers in the truth.

¹¹You will do well to send them on their journey as befits God's service. ¹²For they have set out for his sake and have accepted nothing from the heathen. ¹³Deme'trius has testimony from everyone, and from the truth itself; I testify to him too, and you know my testimony is true.

Diot'rephes Does Not Admit the Brethren

¹⁴I have written something to the church; but Diot'rephes, who likes to put himself first, does not accept my authority; ¹⁵and not content with that, he refuses himself to welcome the brethren and also stops those that want to welcome them and puts them out of the church. ¹⁶So if I come, I will bring up what he is doing, prating against me with *evil* words. ¹⁷He who does evil has not seen God.

Imitate God

[18]Beloved, do not imitate evil; imitate good; he who does good is of God

Appendix D

Review Questions
and Answers

In the introduction of each chapter, we asked you to consider the following questions. Here are answers.

Chapter 1: Review questions and answers from the _Prologue_

#	Question	Answers
1.	Who is Jesus?	Jesus is the incarnate Word of God. He is the Word who was with God in the beginning. Jesus is the Son of God who was sent to the world to restore eternal life.
2.	What was Jesus's mission?	Jesus came to the world to enlighten everyone in two ways: to restore the opportunity to receive eternal life and provide the means of support for people to receive it. John described this as the grace and truth that came through Jesus: • _The truth_ is Jesus is the Son of God who the Father commanded to give eternal life. • _Grace_ is Jesus's restoration of the gift of eternal life and the blanket of gifts that comprise his ongoing assistance to enable believers to receive eternal life.
3.	Who are the three witnesses of Jesus's identity as the Son of God?	1. God himself bore witness to his Son when he appointed John the Baptist to identify and bear witness to Jesus.

#	Question	Answers
		2. John the Baptist saw and testified to the fact that the Spirit descended and remained on Jesus who was the Son of God.
		3. John the Evangelist who beheld Jesus's glory on the third day when the glorified Jesus came to the disciples and breathed the Holy Spirit onto them.
4.	What does it mean to *know* God?	During the banishment period, no one was able to *know* God intimately and eternally as Adam and Eve did. Jesus restored the opportunity to have a personal and ongoing relationship *knowing* God forever. This kind of *knowing* is to have eternal life.
5.	Why will birthright no longer provide automatic child-of-God status?	The New Covenant expanded who could become a child of God to everyone. Therefore, the basis for its granting had to change from birthright to a person's choice to believe Jesus is God's Son and to live according to God's commands.

Chapter 2: Review questions and answers from the *Testimony of John the Baptist*

#	Question	Answers
1.	Why was John the Baptist's testimony necessary to introduce Jesus as the Son of God?	The Baptist's identification and introduction of Jesus as the Son of God, which came from God to him, was crucial for the launch of God's entire plan because no one could fathom that the Word of God himself would arrive in the form of a human. The Baptist's testimony was so important that God directed him to testify.
2.	How did the Baptist know Jesus was the expected Messiah?	God told the Baptist the Spirit would descend and remain on the "one" who will baptize not with water but with the Holy Spirit (meaning he would

#	Question	Answers
		grant eternal life). When the Baptist saw this event himself, he became qualified to testify.
3.	Why is Jesus considered the Lamb of God?	To say Jesus is the Lamb of God is to consider him like the unblemished lambs in Egypt whose blood protected the Israelites from the bringer of death. This enabled the Israelites to begin their journey to the Promised Land. Jesus's blood (death on the cross and resurrection) will activate God's New Covenant to offer the new children of God the opportunity to receive eternal life, thus saving them from a destiny of permanent death.
4.	What is *the sin* of the world?	*The sin* was Adam and Eve's decision to not love God, which they demonstrated by not keeping his command to *not* eat the forbidden fruit. This led to their and their progeny's banishment from the Garden (eternal life with God). Jesus cannot change the fact that Adam and Eve committed the sin; however, he can reverse the consequence of their choice. So that now, when a person chooses to believe Jesus is the Son of God, he removes the consequence of Adam and Eve's sin—the banishment—so the believer has the opportunity to receive eternal life. This starts the believer's journey to develop a love-based lifestyle, whereby he or she may ask and receive Jesus's forgiveness for future sins they commit.
5.	What is Jesus's baptism with the Holy Spirit?	Jesus's baptism with the Holy Spirit is the granting of eternal life. Only Jesus was authorized by God to grant it, which he does for believers who live love-based lives.

Chapter 3: Review questions and answers from the *First Disciples*

#	Question	Answers
1.	Why did Jesus begin his ministry by gathering his disciples?	Jesus would need witnesses to testify to who he was and what he did after he returned to the Father. To qualify as witnesses in the first century, the disciples had to have been with Jesus from the beginning; hence, his gathering them was the first task of his ministry. *"...and you also are witnesses, because you have been with me from the beginning* (Jn 15:1 RSAV).
2.	Why did Jesus rename Simon to Peter?	In the Old Testament, God renamed people who were designated to play a direct role in his plans. Jesus was doing the same; he renamed Simon to Cephas (Peter), which means rock because Peter would be the foundation stone upon which the new church would be built (Mt 16:18 RSV).
3.	Who did the disciples think Jesus was—human or Divine? Why is it important to get his identity right?	Before his death, resurrection and return to them glorified, the disciples saw Jesus as the following, who are all human: • The Messiah • A prophet like Moses or Elijah • A rabbi • Adopted Son of God, but not the Divine Son of God Jesus had to be God's Son incarnate—a complete human— in order to demonstrate that humans would face their own tribulations, suffer, and die as he did, but if they believe and live a love-based life in obedience to the Father as he did, they will receive eternal life. *Jesus said to him, "I am the way, and the truth,*

#	Question	Answers
		and the life..." (Jn 14:19 RSAV). However, Jesus also had to be the Son of God—for God's plan to work. First, a human cannot grant eternal life—only God can restore what he took away, which is why Jesus his Son had to be restored to his original divine glory to grant it, which he demonstrated when he returned to them and breathed the Holy Spirit on them.
4.	How did Jesus reveal his true identity as the Son of God in this narrative?	Jesus revealed himself as the Son of God by referring to Jacob's dream of angels ascending and descending to and from heaven. In Jesus's paraphrasing of the dream, he laid claim to his being *the gate of heaven,* and by this, he declared he was the Son of God.
5.	What did Jesus indicate by referring to himself as the Son of man?	Jesus's referral to himself as the Son of man ascribes God giving him divine and eternal authority over all people in relation to eternal life, which was what Daniel's prophecy declared. *"I saw in the night visions...came one like the son of man, and he came to the Ancient of Days...and to him was given dominion and glory and kingdom, that all peoples...should serve him; his dominion is an everlasting dominion..."* (Dan 7:13–14 RSV).

Chapter 4: Review questions and answers from the *Last Supper*

#	Question	Answers
1.	What were the two key lessons Jesus taught by his foot washing?	The salvation of the world will depend upon the disciples' testimony, and they had to learn humility and service to be effective. Only by their humble acceptance of their new responsibilities and its associated powers would they be able to offer service to God and not get tripped up by pride.
2.	What is the difference between being clean all over, as the disciples were, and not clean, as Judas was?	The disciples who were *bathed* and *clean* all over, had *no* mortal sin. Even though they had "road dust" (nonmortal sins), they were candidates to receive eternal life. Judas's intent to betray Jesus was a mortal sin that would lead to his permanent death.
3.	Why did Jesus bring up the fact that a disciple would betray him but not tell the disciples who the person was?	Jesus needed to tell the disciples that one of them would betray him before it happened so they would have a basis to continue to believe in him afterward. Had the disciples suspected that Judas was the betrayer, they would have tried to stop him, which would have upset the progression of God's plan.
4.	How is God glorified in Jesus and Jesus glorified by God?	Jesus glorified (honored) God by his willingness to die on the cross, and, in turn, God glorified (praised and honored) Jesus by making his resurrection possible.

Chapter 5: Review questions and answers from *Farewell Discourse*

#	Question	Answers
1.	Why did the disciples fail to comprehend Jesus's remarks at the beginning of the discourse?	The disciples interpreted what Jesus said in worldly terms, but he spoke to them in relation to what they would understand after they saw him glorified. In spite of the fact they didn't completely understand what he was saying, it was important for Jesus to tell them those things to keep them from falling away. He would send the Holy Spirit after he ascended to the Father who would enable them to remember all that he said.
2.	What did Jesus mean when he said that he was *the way*? *"I am the way,...no one comes to the Father, but by me"* (Jn 14:6 RSV).	Jesus is *the way* to eternal life from two standpoints: • He modeled and taught *the way* of living (mode of conduct) that leads to eternal life. • He is *the way* to receive eternal life because the Father has given him the power to decide who may receive it. *Since thou hast given him power (authority) over all flesh so that he can give eternal life...*(Jn 17:2 RSAV).
3.	Can everyone receive eternal life?	Yes! Jesus told the disciples that entrance into God's kingdom (eternal life) is available to all (believers) who love him and keep his word (obey Jesus's commandments). *"If a man loves me, he will keep my word, and my Father will love him, and we will come to him and make our home with him"* (Jn 14:40 RSAV).

#	Question	Answers
		And this is his commandment, that we should believe in the name of his Son Jesus Christ and love one another just as he has commanded us (1 Jn 3:23 RSAV).
4.	What is new about Jesus's commandment to love one another?	Jesus's new commandment to love one another is to love as he loved his disciples. This takes loving one another to a new level—to that of offering sacrificial service to death if necessary.
5.	How do you know that Jesus was really free to lay down his life? Why is this important?	Jesus referred to his freewill choice when he stated that he obeyed the Father's command **of his own accord.** Only by his operating from choice would it be possible for others to know that love, as he stated, was the motivation for his action. *"...I do as the Father has commanded me, so that the world may know that I love the Father"* (Jn 14:28 RSAV). *"...the Father loves me, because I lay down my life ...no one takes it from me, but I lay it down of my own accord; I have the **power** to lay it down...and to take it up again"* (Jn 10:18 RSV).
6.	What is *that day*? Why is it significant?	*That day* is the *third day,* when Jesus came to the disciples in glorified form and breathed the Holy Spirit on them to grant eternal life. This initiated what God sent Jesus to the world to do—to save the world from sin and death. *That day* marks the end of the banishment era and the beginning of the era

#	Question	Answers
		when the world has the opportunity to receive eternal life under the terms of the New Covenant.
7.	How were the disciples able to do greater works than Jesus?	Jesus said he would grant any request made by the disciples for God's glory. This would occur after Jesus granted eternal life to them. *"If you ask anything in my name, I will do it that the Father may be glorified in the Son, and greater works than these will he do because I go to the Father"* (Jn 14:15–16 RSAV). The Greek word for *greater* pertains to quantity as well as quality. Jesus was not necessarily saying the disciples would perform more marvelous works than he, but that they would take his message to a greater quantity of people, and they did. *So those who received his (Peter's) word were baptized, and...added that day about three thousand souls* (Acts 3:41 RSV).
8.	What was the role of the disciples in God's plan?	The disciples were chosen and appointed to testify and bear fruit. They were Jesus's witnesses from the beginning to the end, which included their seeing him in glorified form and being granted eternal life. They would bear witness to Jesus as the Son of God so that people may believe and have the opportunity to receive eternal life.

#	Question	Answers
9.	How would the disciples be assured of success in fulfilling their role?	Jesus would pray to the Father to give the disciples another Counselor after he leaves, who would be with them forever. The Counselor would do the following: 1) Bring to their remembrance all he (Jesus) ever said to them 2) Teach them all things 3) Declare the things that were to come 4) Guide them in all truth In addition, the disciples may ask anything of the Father in Jesus's name, and the Father would grant anything that honors Jesus's mission. *"If you ask anything of the Father, he will give it to you in my name. Ask and you will receive, that your joy may be full* "(Jn15:35–36 RSAV).
10.	Did Jesus put an end to the world's tribulation?	God did **not** send Jesus to save the world from its tribulations of suffering, troubles, and distress. Jesus himself said: *"In the world you have tribulation..."* (Jn15:27 RSAV). God sent Jesus to save the world a more powerful way—to restore access to eternal life. Jesus overcame the power of evil to give people the opportunity to know God's eternal peace. People can have an even stronger reason to have hope now.

Chapter 6: Review questions and answers from the *Farewell Prayer*

#	Question	Answers
1.	Why does most of this prayer focus on the disciples?	Jesus prayed for the disciples' protection, sanctification, and receipt of eternal life so they could be effective bearers of the truth. They would be responsible for the rollout of God's plan after Jesus was glorified. Only through their word would people have the opportunity to believe that Jesus is the Son of God.
2.	Why was Jesus's first request to be glorified?	Jesus could not fulfill his mission of restoring eternal life and preparing his disciples for their continuation of his mission without being glorified.
3.	What are the two types of glory mentioned in this prayer?	1. Jesus gave his disciples the type of glory that enabled them to have a good opinion of another that helped them love one another. 2. Jesus's Divine glory was his perfection and majesty as the Son of God, which enabled him to grant the eternal life.
4.	What is eternal life?	Eternal life is being unified with God and Jesus Christ such that a person is able to personally experience the presence of their ongoing love, peace, and protection. John used the phrase "to *know* God" to indicate this deep and intimate experience. *And this is eternal life, that they **know** thee the only true God, and Jesus Christ whom thou hast sent* (Jn 17:27 RSAV).
5.	Who has the opportunity to receive eternal life?	Everyone who fulfills the following two conditions:

#	Question	Answers
		• Believes in Jesus Christ who is the Son of God • Lives a sufficiently love-based life

Chapter 7: Review questions and answers from *John's Proclamation of Eternal Life*

#	Question	Answers
1.	Who is Jesus?	*This is the true God and eternal life his Son Jesus Christ* (1 Jn1:8 RSAV).
2.	What is *fellowship* as John refers to it?	*Fellowship* is being in an ongoing and intimate relationship with God and his Son, which is eternal life.
3.	What qualified John to write of eternal life?	John was an eyewitness disciple of Jesus from the beginning to the end of his ministry. He and the other disciples heard, saw, and even touched the glorified Jesus and were recipients of eternal life from Jesus's own breath. They knew Jesus defeated death and was the true God who chose and sent them to continue his mission of eternal life.
4.	What is the difference between how Adam and Eve received eternal life and what today's believers must do to receive it?	Adam and Eve were automatically placed in God's Garden without committing to loving him and keeping his commands. Therefore, eternal life was revoked when they sinned. Under the New Covenant, believers must demonstrate their commitment to loving God by keeping his commands up front; then Jesus will grant eternal life to them, and he will not revoke it.
5.	What is the difference between the way the disciples received the Holy Spirit and how believers thereafter receive it?	The disciples were with the glorified Jesus—God himself— who granted them eternal life. They felt his physical breath when he gave them the Holy Spirit. It was a sensate experience that left no doubt that they received it. When believers receive eternal life today,

#	Question	Answers
		the Spirit will not be detectable—it will come like the wind. *"The wind blows where it wills, and you hear the sound of it, but you do not know whence it comes or whither it goes; so it is with everyone who is born of the Spirit"* (Jn 3:8 RSV).
6.	What are the benefits of receiving eternal life while a person is still alive?	Those who receive eternal life while alive will: • abide in eternal union with Jesus Christ and the Father, • be under God's protection from the evil one so they cannot commit mortal sin, as Adam and Eve did, and • not lose eternal life, so they can be confident on Judgment Day.

Chapter 8: Review questions and answers from *The Message*

#	Question	Answer
1.	What are the two parts of the New Commandment?	To receive eternal life, a person must believe in Jesus's name and love one another. *And this is his commandment, that we should believe in the name of his Son Jesus Christ and love one another, just as he has commanded us* (1 Jn 3:23 RSAV).
2.	What are the three categories of sin that Jesus forgives?	Jesus's forgiveness starts when people come to believe in his name. 1. He removes the consequence of the sin of Adam and Eve, which restores the opportunity to receive eternal life.

#	Question	Answer
		2. He forgives all prior sins committed by new believers, giving them a fresh start. 3. Ongoing, he forgives sins that believers confess to him.
3	What is confession?	Confession is the way to ask for Jesus's forgiveness. It is necessary because Jesus honors humanity's freewill; therefore, he only forgives those sins that believers ask him to forgive. Confession entails the following: • Recognizing the sin • Actually admitting it • Being willing to acknowledge its harm • Sincerely intending to not commit the sin again
4.	What does Jesus the Advocate do?	By definition, an advocate does two things: gives aid to another and pleads another's cause. • Jesus comes to the aid of believers. He has the power to forgive sins, which enables believers to become free of guilt and habits of sin in order to develop a love-based lifestyle. • Jesus advocates for qualified believers to be granted eternal life.
5.	What is the pitfall that will keep even sincere believers from receipt of eternal life?	Believers who do not admit their sins fall into the pitfall of self-deception, which leads to failure to deal with their sins. Receipt of eternal life is dependent upon having a loving heart that is not clouded by sin.
6.	Who are the antichrists; what is	Antichrists once believed in Jesus as the Christ, the Son of God, but changed their

#	Question	Answer
	their unforgivable sin?	minds. Their opposition is the unforgivable sin. Jesus cannot forgive this sin because he honors humanity's freewill to choose whether to believe in him or not. Since God gave him sole authority to forgive sin, people who stop believing in Jesus cannot receive his forgiveness and will die a permanent death.
7.	What is the old commandment; how is it now new?	The commandment from the beginning is to love one another. It became new when Jesus restored eternal life, which magnified the benefit of keeping the commandment. Jesus also makes it new by offering powerful support for keeping the commandment, which includes the following: • Ongoing and personalized guidance through the Holy Spirit • Forgiveness of all sins committed prior to coming to belief • Ongoing forgiveness of sins that are confessed
8.	What did Cain fail to do that is a lesson for believers today?	Cain did *not* overcome his emotions as God told him to do. This story identifies where evil initiates its attack and where evil must be mastered. It is always humanity's choice and responsibility to master their anger and other destructive emotions in order to behave lovingly.
9.	How does one identify any of the following: a false prophet, the antichrist, and the spirit of error?	The test is to determine whether they advocate Jesus is the Christ, the Son of God, who was both divine and human when he walked on the earth. Those who do not are not of the truth.

#	Question	Answer
10.	What is the Ask and Receive Prayer?	This prayer is available to born-of-God believers, who themselves are free of sin. If what they ask for is according to God's will, it will be granted (within God's timing).
11.	What is the difference between mortal sin and nonmortal sin?	• **Mortal sin** is the deliberate and severe violation of the love and/or belief components of the New Commandment. Such violation leads to permanent death. For such sin to be released, believers must confess these actions to Jesus, who will provide forgiveness and cleansing. • **Nonmortal sin** is a less severe or unintentional violation of the New Commandment. It does *not* lead to permanent death.

Chapter 9: Review questions and answers from *God's Plan*

#	Question	Answers
1.	What is God's fundamental essence?	God is of love. While God's actions are derived from love, only in John's first letter, in the entire New Testament, is God directly defined as love. *. . . for love is of God, since God is love* (1 Jn 4:1 RSAV)
2.	How is God's love perfected in a person?	God's love becomes perfected (completed) in believers when they love one another as their way of life, such that they no longer commit mortal sin. This is when Jesus grants God's seed that enables believers to become children of God, who are born of God and have eternal life.
3.	How does perfected love cast out fear?	Having perfected love is another way of saying people have eternal life that leads to their

#	Question	Answers
		protection from the evil one. Therefore, they are protected from committing mortal sins and therefore they will nothing to be punished for and although they will die physically, they will not die.
4.	Who testifies to Jesus?	1. **God** gave the first testimony when he told John the Baptist Jesus was his Son, who baptizes with the Holy Spirit. 2. **John the Baptist** saw the Spirit descend and remain on Jesus, and he testified to Israel and to two of his disciples. 3. **The Holy Spirit** saw Jesus's mission from the beginning to the end of Jesus's human life—he descended into Jesus as witnessed by John the Baptist and left upon Jesus's death as witnessed by John the Evangelist. Jesus sends the Holy Spirit to testify to believers when they come to belief. 4. **The disciples** testify—they were with Jesus throughout his earthly mission and received eternal life from the glorified Jesus, who *sent* them to testify. 5. **Believers** who believe in Jesus as God's Son and receive the Holy Spirit testify. They spread the message of Jesus onward to generation after generation.
5.	What is faith?	As John presents it, faith is not simply a belief or feeling of confidence or trust; it is an action—faith is to be lived by what people say and do. The following two truths are what to have faith in because they enable a person to receive

#	Question	Answers
		eternal life. 1. God restored access to eternal life through his Son, Jesus. 2. Because eternal life is only available through Jesus, it is exclusively available to those who believe Jesus is the Son of God and keep his commandment to love one another.

Chapter 10: Review questions and answers from *Choose*

#	Question	Answers
1.	How does a person become righteous?	To be *righteous* is to be acceptable to God. The way to do it is by loving God and demonstrating it by keeping God's commandments: believe Jesus is the Christ, the Son of God, and love one another.
2.	What does it mean that a believer does *not* sin and cannot sin? *No one born of God **commits sin**; and he **cannot sin** because he is born of God for God's nature abides in him* (1 Jn 5:6 RSAV).	John spoke about committing sin in two timeframes. 1. In order to become born of God, believers must choose to refrain from sin of their freewill, by making Jesus's command to love one another their way of life. 2. Since believers who choose not to sin become born of God, they will be continually protected from the evil one, who cannot touch them. Therefore, they cannot be tempted to sin (mortally). *We know anyone born of God does not sin, and the evil one does not touch*

#	Question	Answers
		him (1 Jn 1:5 RSAV).
3.	How did Jesus bring hope to the world?	1. **Jesus unlocked the gate to eternal life:** Jesus's resurrection set his believers free from the destiny of permanent death that Adam and Eve's sin caused. This opportunity to receive eternal life with the loving God brings a magnificent and compelling reason for hope. 2. **Jesus helps believers to keep his commands:** When believers confess their sins to Jesus with the intention to *not* do them again, he forgives their sins, which loosens the devil's hold. This gives believers the hope that they can succeed in living a righteous life.
4.	How does a person become *pure as Jesus is pure?*	Jesus's purity had to do with his making his life sacred by living lovingly. Jesus's purity comes from his love of the Father and demonstrating it by keeping his commands. Believers become pure by doing the same.
5.	What is lawlessness?	John brings up lawlessness as the way to look at sin. To be lawless is about the absence of love, kindness, and compassion behind any behavior.

Chapter 11: Review questions and answers from *2 John*

#	Question	Answers
1.	Who are the elect?	The elect are those who believe in Jesus's name. By their belief, the elect have the opportunity to receive eternal life, which depends upon their living a love-based life style. *Therefore, I endure everything for the sake of the elect, that they also may obtain salvation in Christ Jesus with its eternal glory* (2 Tim 2:10 RSV).
2.	John mentioned the people who *know* the truth; who are they?	People of the truth are those who have received eternal life; they know the truth in their minds and their hearts, because God abides within them forever. They love fellow believers because they live by love. *And this commandment we have from him, that he who loves God should love his brother also* (1 Jn 4:12 RSAV).
3.	Who are the deceivers? What are the ramifications of believing them?	Deceivers outright deny that Jesus is the Christ, the Son of God who came in the flesh. To deny the truth of Jesus is to deny eternal life because God gave Jesus authority over all flesh to grant eternal life. The result of such denial will be permanent death.
4.	What is the work of God?	The work of God is to believe in Jesus. *"This is the work of God, that you believe in him whom he has sent"* (Jn 6:29 RSV). When John says *look to yourselves*, he reminds believers that they made a commitment to Jesus as the Christ, God's Son, when they came to believe in him. This commitment entails abiding by

#	Question	Answers
		Jesus's command to believe and to love one another.
5.	Can denying someone access to your church be a loving act?	John emphatically advises the community to *not* receive any deceiver. However, John is not saying to refrain from interacting with people who have a different belief system in worldly life or insult them in refusing admittance to their church. He is simply saying that the loving act is *not* to allow someone to impose their false beliefs on those who are vulnerable. John advocates protective love for those who are on the journey to eternal life.

Chapter 12: Review questions and answers from *3 John*

#	Question	Answers
1.	What does it mean to follow (walk) in the truth?	A person who follows the truth has received eternal life. Ga'ius walked according to God's will and loves his fellow brothers in the name of Jesus Christ. *...he who loves God should love his brother (fellow Christian) also* (1 Jn 4:12 RSAV)... *"If a man loves me, he will keep my word, and my Father will love him, and we will come to him and make our home with him"* (Jn 14:40 RSAV).
2.	Who are *friends* as John referred to them?	Jesus described *friends* as believers who keep Jesus's commandment to love one another. They are people who would welcome and support missionaries such as Deme'trius. *"You are my **friends** if you do what I command you"* (Jn 16:23 RSAV).

#	Question	Answers
3.	What is the root cause of the evil that John described in this letter?	John described Diot'rephes, as someone who likes to put himself first. This is what Adam and Eve did! It is the opposite of what Jesus modeled. *...but I do as the Father has commanded me, so that the world may know that I love the Father...* (Jn 14:28 RSAV).

Index